SIGMA PHI EPSILON

the
LIFETIME
RESPONSIBILITY
of
BROTHERHOOD

Acknowledgments

Editor: E. Scott Thompson II, Director of Communications
Zollinger House, Sigma Phi Epsilon Headquarters
Design: Design Manifesto, Richmond, Virginia

Special Thanks To:

Douglas D. Scheibe

Charles N. White, Jr.

Kenneth S. Maddox

Gary H. Bonas, Jr.

James C. Nissen

Nonnie Cameron Owens

Jeffrey D. Prouty

Rev. Raymond K. Ackerman

William G. Tragos

Josephson Institute for
the Advancement of Ethics

The North American
Interfraternity Conference

Campus Values — Northeastern
University

Student Success — Tim Walter
& Al Siebert

Library of Congress Catalog Number
90-062707
Printed in the United States of America
by **Banta Book Group**
Visit Sigma Phi Epsilon's web site at: http://www.sigep.org

CONTENTS

RIGHTS & RESPONSIBILITIES OF BROTHERHOOD

Rights of All Members

Welcome! Upon joining Sigma Phi Epsilon, you have made a lifetime commitment. You have chosen to live above the common level of life. Sigma Phi Epsilon is founded on the pursuit of high ideals.

Upon joining Sigma Phi Epsilon, you surrender none of your personal or civil rights. You have, however, taken an obligation, not only to yourself, but also to the Fraternity of which you are a part. This obligation binds you to do your share in its work and assume your share of the responsibilities in Sigma Phi Epsilon. This obligation will in no way interfere with the duty you owe to your God, your country, your fellow man, or yourself.

Upon joining Sigma Phi Epsilon, you have the right to be treated as a chapter member and included in chapter activities and meetings. No hazing or "second-class citizenship" will take place in Sigma Phi Epsilon.

As in any great democracy, all rights have corresponding responsibilities which must be upheld if the organization is to remain strong.

THE BALANCED MAN IDEAL

In ancient Greece, the spirit of competition inspired individuals to live life to the fullest. This spirit clearly differentiated the ancient Greeks from other cultures that came before them—from the Assyrians and the Babylonians, to the Sumerians, the Egyptians, and the Minoans of Crete. Indeed, the emphasis on the individual and the desire for personal perfection of mind and body made the Greeks original, exciting, and truly extraordinary.

"Always to be the best and to excel over others." That is the much-quoted exhortation Peleus gave to his son Achilles as the young hero set off to battle in the Trojan War. The Greeks summed it up in one word: arete—excellence in every part of life—moral, intellectual, and physical—that together contributed to the development of the whole person. In the Hellenic view of things, the mind could not exist without the body. At the same time, the body was meaningless without the mind—"A Sound Mind in a Sound Body" symbolized by the Balanced Man.

In ancient Greece, developing mind and body were two complementary partners of a quality education. The ideal education consisted of philosophy, language, art, music, and exercise. The ancient Greeks exalted the body, and they were great lovers of music. As a result, athletics and music were inextricably linked, joined in education to build the body and stimulate the mind.

These ideals and values were the key elements in the way the Greeks lived life. They inspired timeless concepts like sportsmanship, virtue, honesty, freedom, diligence, and comradeship. They produced some of the world's greatest philosophers and writers—Plato, Aristotle, Socrates, and Homer, and they were the foundation and very essence of the Olympic Games and competitive sports.

At the close of the 1800s, when Cecil Rhodes, a philanthropist, set up the scholarships named after him, he stipulated that men be chosen who exhibited undoubted excellence and also proved themselves to have the balanced qualities of character, intellect, leadership, and physical vigor as shown by fondness for and success in sports. Rhodes wished his scholars to be well-rounded individuals, and he emphatically stated in his will, "No student be qualified or disqualified for election to a scholarship on account of his race or religious opinions." He instructed his committees of selection to choose "a man for the world's fight" with the following traits

SCHOLARSHIP, COURAGE, MANLINESS, DEVOTION TO DUTY, UNSELFISHNESS. A BALANCED MAN HAS ALL THESE QUALITIES.

who would proceed to Oxford University: scholarship, courage, manliness, devotion to duty, unselfishness. A balanced man has all these qualities.

IT IS ALL ABOUT YOU

"Responsibility is a unique concept. It can only reside and inhere in a single individual. You may share it with others, but your portion is not diminished. You may delegate it, but it is still with you. You may disclaim it, but you cannot divest yourself of it."

~ ADMIRAL RICKOVER

Meaning of Brotherhood

Many definitions of brotherhood circulate throughout fraternity chapters each year. Brotherhood is also discussed in Masonic lodges, places of worship, humanitarian shelters, classrooms, and elsewhere. Though the definitions may vary, they usually center on learning, friendship, giving, sharing, love, and family-like relationships.

Brotherhood, for all its meanings, has one common vein—responsibility. Chapters that have "true brotherhood," as judged by themselves and everyone with whom they come in contact, will tell you that each of their members has a burning desire to uphold the principles of their organization, and they each feel personally responsible for both their experience and that of their Brothers. Their chapter is a warm place of learning friendship, giving, sharing, love, and family-like relationships. They feel personally responsible for brotherhood. Conversely, organizations lacking true brotherhood are void of responsibility, filled only with the snow and ice of excuses, back biting, valueless decisions, and members who only take from the Fraternity.

How will you know brotherhood when you have it, or when it is missing? After all, fraternities espouse brotherhood as their main benefit to both their members and to society in general, and what would be the point of being part of a fraternity that did not provide brotherhood? Frankly, these questions are as tough to answer as brotherhood is to define. Fortunately, you can take action to see that brotherhood is real both in your life and the life of your chapter and Sigma Phi Epsilon.

The Fraternity asked you to be a Brother for life, and the Cardinal Principles of Virtue, Diligence, and Brotherly Love were promised through the mystique of ceremony, day-to-day contact with your Brothers, and the verbal and written teachings of the Fraternity. As you have taken an obligation, so, too, has the Fraternity. So, who will be held accountable for upholding these principles, furthering their cause, and ensuring the quality of brotherhood found in your fraternity experience?

You. You are responsible for the brotherhood that you will experience. Sigma Phi Epsilon is designed to provide excellence and balance in your life, and only you know how you need to grow and learn. Obviously, if others forsake their responsibility, that will dramatically affect your experience with Sigma Phi Epsilon, but when all is said and done, you are the only person who can dramatically affect the meaning of brotherhood.

So, how do you become responsible for brotherhood? Members of Sigma Phi Epsilon who are responsible for brotherhood are first responsible for themselves; second, they become responsible for Sigma Phi Epsilon and their community. Brotherhood then becomes a daily part of their lives because of their commitment. Hard to grasp, but brotherhood is not endowed through the Ritual, learned through ceremony, or purchased with membership. Brotherhood is the culmination of taking responsibility for yourself, others, and the Fraternity.

Sigma Phi Epsilon is a lifetime experience, thus your responsibility for brotherhood is not just a four-year commitment or something to strive for at your convenience. Brothers in Sigma Phi Epsilon take a vow for life, and that is what makes our Fraternity special.

Part of the Fraternity's responsibility for brotherhood is to try to give its members a basic understanding of the principles and teachings each man has vowed to uphold. Sigma Phi Epsilon defines brotherhood as the daily practice of Virtue, Diligence, and Brotherly Love, and, toward this end, *The Lifetime Responsibility of Brotherhood* is offered as a major source of education for SigEps. Use this book to have the best experience possible.

This book is a guide to taking responsibility for yourself, those around you, and the Fraternity that has become a part of your life. If you honestly pursue developing yourself, Sigma Phi Epsilon, and the community, you will achieve excellence in your life. Each of these subjects will be explored to make

"THE PRICE OF GREATNESS IS RESPONSIBILITY."
~ Winston Churchill

true brotherhood and balance a reality for each and every Sigma Phi Epsilon.

Self: You must know and love yourself to ever be able to love others and the Fraternity. This part of the book is designed to help you understand yourself and the major issues you will face during and beyond your chapter experience. You cannot grow and mature unless you have a grasp on your attitudes, habits, and ideals.

Sigma Phi Epsilon: Sigma Phi Epsilon is your responsibility. The Fraternity is not a nebulous body where direction and decisions come from "out of the blue." SigEp is an organization with numerous vital parts and functions—with you at the heart of our brotherhood. In a sense, the Fraternity is designed just for you. In another sense, your experience with Sigma Phi Epsilon is that of giving to the Fraternity to further its principles of Virtue, Diligence, and Brotherly Love. However it breaks down, you are responsible for the quality of your Fraternity.

Community: Though you cannot control others, you can dramatically affect them and their experience with you. In this area, *The Lifetime Responsibility of Brotherhood* will give you insight on the dynamics of relationships—skills, you may say, for succeeding in today's complex community, campus and interpersonal environment.

THE CREED OF SIGMA PHI EPSILON

I believe in the American college fraternity. I believe in Sigma Phi Epsilon. I believe in this Fraternity because it would have me strive in every way to live up to the high principles for which it stands. These are **VIRTUE**, **DILIGENCE**, and **BROTHERLY LOVE**.

I believe that the word **VIRTUE** is an inclusive term; that it is not enough that I be merely passively virtuous: I must be positive on virtue's behalf. Therefore, I will stand aggressively for honesty in all walks of life, and I will speak cleanly, play cleanly, and live cleanly. Whenever I can, I will oppose lawlessness and vice.

I believe that unless I succeed in being **DILIGENT**, I cannot be a good fraternity member. Believing that my Fraternity can be no greater than any of its members, I shall strive to make it so high and so worthy that men will consider it an honor and privilege to belong to it, and will strive to be admitted to it. I will not offer concessions to an individual to secure his affiliation, for thus making concessions makes the man more noteworthy than the Fraternity and hence only succeeds in lowering it in his estimation as well as mine.

I believe that **BROTHERLY LOVE** must be given in order to be received, and that it cannot exist without triumph of the principles of **VIRTUE** and **DILIGENCE**, for these are essential parts of it.

I believe that a man will be made better for having been a member of my Fraternity. I know that I cannot expect the Neophyte to be a finished product. Rather I will try to discover whether or not the environment and contact with men of high ideals

Oscar E. Draper, Grand President, 1928-1929

will make of him a good fraternity man.

I believe that as a good fraternity member I must share a rich kinship of spirit with my Brothers. Yet I realize that the members must be men of diversified abilities and talents. Among them are to be found the scholar, the athlete, the builder and craftsman, and the organization leader. But the scholar cannot make a fraternity. Nor can the athlete. Nor the craftsman. The good fraternity member must be par excellent in manhood.

I believe that to be a good member I must be loyal to my Fraternity. In order to be loyal to it I must love it. In order to love it I must strive constantly to make it worthy of my love. To be loyal to my Fraternity I must gain a knowledge of it so that I may understand it. I have an obligation to understand what brotherhood means.

I believe that in any organized society group rights and privileges are based on individual rights and privileges; that in my Fraternity I possess the same rights and privileges and have the same duties as my fellow members. Therefore, I shall at all times respect duly the rights of others.

I believe that obedience to the laws of my community and my country is essential to good citizenship; that the laws and rules of my Fraternity and my chapter are intended to regulate the actions of its members, one with another, and that without fidelity to those laws and rules I cannot be a good citizen and a worthy member of Sigma Phi Epsilon.

I believe I should be generous with the faults of a Brother, as I should wish him to be with mine.

Longtime motivator and football coaching legend Lou Holtz often tells his players there are three universal questions that will be asked of them by everyone they encounter.

1. Can I trust you?

2. Are you committed to excellence?

3. Do you care about me?

To meet these expectations, Coach Holtz lives by three simple rules, and he coaches his players to do the same.

1. Follow the "Do-Right Rule." You know the difference between right and wrong. Do what is right and people will never have a reason not to trust you.

2. Commit to excellence by doing the best you can every time.

3. The Golden Rule. Treat others the same way you want to be treated.

Lou Holtz is not a member of Sigma Phi Epsilon, yet his three rules are identical to our three Cardinal Principles. These rules or principles or values have guided and sustained the civilized world for thousands of years. Do your part—know, accept and live these values. You will have a satisfying life—filled with discovery, passion, and growth.

Dedication

For his tireless contributions to our Fraternity, this book is dedicated to Frank J. Ruck, Jr., Michigan '46.

Brother Ruck exemplified Sigma Phi Epsilon's Cardinal Principles of Virtue, Diligence, and Brotherly Love since joining the Michigan Alpha Chapter at the University of Michigan in 1942. Since that time, Frank served as one of the foremost leaders in Sigma Phi Epsilon's history.

Brother Ruck served on the Fraternity's professional staff from 1946 to 1956. While balancing many professional and family demands, Frank also served on the National Board of Directors from 1965 to 1985 as Grand Treasurer and as Grand President from 1985 to 1987.

Brother Ruck's service to Sigma Phi Epsilon and the Greek community was equally extensive and important in recent years. In 1995, Frank was President of the North American Interfraternity Conference (NIC) after years of service to the interfraternal community and as an NIC board member. He served six years as Chairman of the Balanced Man Development Committee. His activities in these endeavors was indicative of Frank's dedication to the future of Sigma Phi Epsilon and its peers. He served as the leader of the NIC's Select 2000 program and other key initiatives.

For more than 50 years, Brother Ruck gave his time and the best of himself. He created both the past for our great Fraternity and set Sigma Phi Epsilon and its leadership on a course for a purposeful and dynamic future.

RESPONSIBILITY:
SELF

RESPONSIBILITY:
SELF

"Great leaders are not born, they are developed...fired in the crucible of experience and opportunity."

~ ARISTOTLE

Sigma Phi Epsilon's mission is "Building Balanced Leaders for the World's Communities." The first step toward building a balanced man is to have the foundation of self-esteem on which to build. Self-esteem is created through self-appreciation. "Love thy neighbor as thyself."

Your life is shaped by your self-esteem, your ability to grow mentally and physically, your academic success, your career achievement, your individuality, your sexuality, and your spiritual growth. You must know where you stand in these areas and where you need to grow. Without constant attention and self-evaluation, you may never be able to truly love yourself, your neighbors, fraternity brothers, or family.

This section on SELF in *The Lifetime Responsibility of Brotherhood* is designed to give you insight into and understanding of your life, your relationships, and your future. There will probably be issues in this section that require further exploration—by all means, do so. There will probably be issues in this section that require discussion in your chapter—by all means, do so. If Sigma Phi Epsilon is to build balanced leaders in the community, the foundation must be you, the individual man who is a part of the Fraternity. Start by developing yourself.

THE FIRST STEP TOWARD BUILDING A BALANCED MAN IS TO HAVE THE FOUNDATION OF SELF-ESTEEM ON WHICH TO BUILD. SELF-ESTEEM IS CREATED THROUGH SELF-APPRECIATION. "LOVE THY NEIGHBOR AS THYSELF."

SELF-ESTEEM

"You gain strength, courage and confidence by every experience in which you really stop to look fear in the face...You must do the thing you think you cannot do."

~ ELEANOR ROOSEVELT

The Challenge to Yourself

In college, maybe more than any other time in your life, your personal values and beliefs will be challenged, tried, and tested. This is normal. The key to using this as a learning opportunity is to *be in control of the experience.* You will change in some ways in college, and in some ways, you will be more the same than ever. Your personal "balance" relies on your ability to be in control of the ever-present changes you will experience.

After college, you will continue to be tried and tested. If you have learned how to control these experiences in college, you are ahead of the crowd.

Control Your Success

From *Student Success*, Walter and Siebert, Fifth Edition, Copyright 1990

Your self-esteem, self-confidence, self-concept, and self-image control your successes in life.

SELF-ESTEEM is your opinion of yourself. Without strong self-esteem, your actions are controlled by worries about what others might think.

Many people have been programmed never to brag, appear proud, or speak well of themselves.

Unfortunately, this programming causes low self-esteem in many students. The problem is that students with low self-esteem rarely do well in school. When students don't expect to do well, they don't. They can't handle success or praise so they avoid having to deal with it.

Students with low self-esteem put themselves down, constantly repeat how dumb or stupid they are, focus on their mistakes, and engage in self-criticism.

On the other hand, there are students with inflated self-esteem. They constantly brag. They tell everyone how great they are. People with inflated self-esteem cannot engage in the kind of healthy self-criticism that leads to personal improvement.

Strong, healthy self-esteem is like a thick skin. It acts as a buffer to shrug off hurtful criticisms from others. It lets you appreciate compliments. It also determines how much you learn from life's experiences.

> "IF YOU THINK YOU CAN OR THINK YOU CAN'T...YOU ARE RIGHT."
>
> ~ HENRY FORD

SELF-CONFIDENCE is your prediction of how well you will do in a new activity. People lacking self-confidence don't rely on themselves.

People with strong self-confidence know that they can count on themselves more than anyone else. They expect to handle both adversities and opportunities successfully.

SELF-CONCEPT is made up of your ideas about who and what you are. The nouns and adjectives you use to describe yourself during self-talk are like instructions. People with positive self-concepts and people with negative self-concepts all act in ways consistent with their beliefs about themselves.

SELF-TALK is that conversation you are having with yourself right now. Your mind never ceases "talking." The question is, is your self-talk full of words that emphasize your capabilities or do you find your talk to be limiting, hesitant and negative?

SELF-IMAGE determines what you, as a unique individual, strive to achieve, maintain, or avoid in your life. People with a poor self-image won't try to change or leave a bad situation at home or work. They may try to be successful by imitating successful people. Some try to cover up a weak self-image with impressive clothing, titles, high income, important friends, the right address, and other material "proofs" of success. They may try to build themselves up by tearing others down.

"LET HIM THAT WOULD MOVE THE WORLD, FIRST MOVE HIMSELF."

~SOCRATES

People with a strong self-image don't have to prove anything to anyone. They can wear any clothing, be friends with anyone, and live anywhere. They live a unique life that works for them. They have a positive, synergistic effect wherever they are.

They encourage and applaud the successes of others.

A strong, positive self-image is the basis for becoming an excellent professional person. Such people, guided by inner standards and values, are flexible, resilient, and creative. They find a way of working that is unique. Success is measured by results and inner feelings of satisfaction. Prosperity, positions of power, honors, and outstanding success are not goals. They are recognition for being responsible, effective, and needed. People without a strong, positive sense of their unique abilities are destined to be confined to jobs and roles created by other people.

Building a Strong Team of "Selfs"

▶ Self-esteem is the easiest "self" to develop. It is strengthened by positive self-talk. If you have strong self-esteem, it is fairly easy to make a list of all the things you like and appreciate about yourself.

▶ Self-confidence increases as you develop a reputation with yourself for doing things well. Build self-confidence by selecting a challenging goal and then reaching it.

▶ Develop a positive self-concept by spending time writing out positive "I am..." statements. First, notice your self-talk now. Make a list of "I am" phrases and statements you think or say about yourself. Replace negative statements with positive statements.

▶ A positive self-image develops from inner standards, from being helpful to others and from linking imagination with positive expectations. A good place to start is to ask, "What do I expect of myself?" and "What are my reliable strengths?"

When all "self" factors are strong, you believe in yourself, you like yourself, you cope well with new challenges, and you stay healthy.

Self-appreciation & Self-criticism

The ability to be successful in reaching goals, learning from failures, and having good friends usually requires a balance between self-esteem and self-criticism. It takes a blend of self-confidence and self-doubt. It takes a positive self-image open to accept the existence of flaws and weaknesses.

The student who is constantly self-critical without self-appreciation seldom accomplishes much. The person who is constantly self-appreciating without self-criticism seldom admits mistakes, weaknesses, and errors. Balance is the key.

Benefits of Good Self-Esteem, Self-Confidence & Self-Image

▶ Accept praise, recognition, success, and friendship as legitimate.

▶ Examine and learn from mistakes and failures.

▶ Resist being pressured into undesirable situations out of fear.

▶ Resist being manipulated by insincere flattery.

▶ Reject undeserved criticism as something to ignore.

▶ Admit mistakes and apologize to others for them.

▶ Handle new, unexpected developments with self-reliance.

▶ Value yourself as a unique, special human being.

The Hazards & Dangers

You will face problems during college, some of which you will continue to face throughout your life. You, however, must be strong and alert to pitfalls along your path and preserve yourself through self-esteem and self-confidence. A balanced man is diligent in overcoming these hazards.

Going to college is more dangerous than many students realize. Stress, depression, suicide, alcohol abuse, drug use, exposure to AIDS, and poor judgment can ruin your life and health, or could even kill you.

Part of being an effective person is to be alert to these dangers. Effective people look at the negative side of a situation as the first step to taking preventive actions to minimize their risks.

The world is dangerous enough. You can, however, take action to reduce the predictable risks to your life, health, and well-being.

Overwhelming Stress

Feeling overwhelmed by college during the first few weeks is normal. You left familiar places and people behind to enter an unfamiliar world filled with strangers. You changed status from being a seasoned senior in high school to becoming a naive freshman in college.

Life at college is complex, challenging, and fast-paced. Protective adults do not save you from being irresponsible. You now make choices and decisions every day that affect your life.

Part of your growing maturity is the ability to ask for help when you need it.

Many instructors assign more work in the first month of classes than you probably had to do in a year of high school. You may get lower grades than you are used to and feel inadequate. You may feel homesick, but going home is not an option because your younger brother or sister has taken over your room.

The freedom to eat or not eat as you wish and to sleep or not sleep whenever you desire can throw your physical health off balance. Your old friends may not be near you.

Signs of Overwhelming Stress & Depression

▶ Feel sad, discouraged, and helpless.

▶ Feel guilty for letting family and high school teachers down.

▶ Sleep 12 to 16 hours a day or can hardly sleep at all.

▶ Withdrawal from friends, spend most time alone.

▶ Cannot make yourself study, grades drop.

▶ Increased use of medications, drugs, alcohol.

▶ Emotional outbursts — crying, anger, temper, self-criticism.

▶ Overeat or lose appetite.

▶ Feel lonely, unhappy, unlovable, unlikable, unaccepted.

▶ Feel that all chances for a good career are lost.

▶ Consider suicide as a way to escape from the pain and distress.

Did you know that unhappy feelings, loneliness, shyness, and awkwardness are all necessary for growth and development? You need them! Young people who don't experience them remain immature!

Thousands of entering college students have these feelings. Most of them survive this difficult period of adjustment and find ways to turn things around. They seek help from family and friends, and learn to cope with their new responsibilities.

Stress Research & Stress Resistance

1. Talk with family and friends about what you are going through. Do not withdraw from the people who care for you. Be receptive to love and support from people who care.

2. Locate and use resources available. At college this means talking with the counselors in the counseling center, the health service, or at one of the religiously sponsored student centers.

3. Accept that life has painful periods. You will find a way to get through this. Tap into inner resources and problem-solve the situation.

The Counseling Office Can Help

Self-referral is difficult for almost everyone, especially if you are afraid or concerned about giving people a bad impression. Try to remember that it is normal to have "down" or lonely periods and that it is entirely okay to get assistance in overcoming them.

If your car gets stuck someplace with a dead battery, do you ask someone for a jump start? Of course, you'd have to do something. So when you are stuck emotionally, get some assistance. Talk with the counselors. They know ways to handle situations that seem hopeless. You don't have to try to handle these situations by yourself. Masking your feelings with drugs or putting on a front of happiness is not a sign of strength. Emotional strength develops from feeling whatever you feel and letting another human being be close to you when things aren't working perfectly.

Take a few simple, easy steps to decrease your exposure to negative experiences and increase your positive, revitalizing experiences. Give yourself permission to take some selfish actions. The Balanced Man believes in having universal respect, respecting self and others. Do unto others as you would have them do unto you. By having high self-esteem, you will treat others as equals.

WHEN YOU ARE STUCK EMOTIONALLY, GET SOME ASSISTANCE. TALK WITH THE COUNSELORS. THEY KNOW WAYS TO HANDLE SITUATIONS THAT SEEM HOPELESS.

SOUND MIND

"Failure to prepare is preparing to fail."

~ JOHN WOODEN,
Former UCLA Head Basketball Coach

You are reading this book because you chose to pursue a college education and join a fraternity. Sigma Phi Epsilon's goal is to help you fulfill your pursuit of a college education and to do it to the best of your ability.

Sigma Phi Epsilon is a college fraternity. Your entrance into this Fraternity is based on your enrollment in a college or university with a SigEp chapter. The goals of higher education are supported by Sigma Phi Epsilon, and as a member of the Fraternity, you are expected to graduate using all diligence. You are also expected to have a lifelong pursuit of knowledge, developing a Sound Mind.

Sound Mind is more that just academics—it's creativity, critical thought, and knowledge. The Sound Mind is sharp and clever, thoughtful and reflective. It thrives with higher learning and education, conversation, discussion, debate, cultural pursuits.

Academic excellence is a large section of this book because it is your first responsibility in college and as a fraternity member. If academic success is not your first priority in joining Sigma Phi Epsilon, you should resign your membership. Use these resources to be a better student and use your education as a basis for success throughout life. Academic excellence is a hallmark of a "Balanced Man."

Men Must Want

From preface to the *Sigma Phi Epsilon Scholarship Manual*, First Edition, Ulysses Grant Dubach, 1958.

The author of an important book, speaking of the masses of a certain nation said: "The trouble with these people is that they do not know how to want." This should not be true of the members of a great college fraternity. However, since so many college students do seem to flounder and waste time, and themselves as well, it seems pertinent to raise the question, "Why go to college?" The only justification is to develop mind and body. Why associate with a fraternity? To help to attain this objective.

Experience proves that young men associated for great purposes, working together under the stimulus of the idealism of a great fraternity, can better produce an atmosphere that makes accomplishment natural. Good scholarship is one element of such accomplishment. Rules, awards, and penalties can help. Their value is

SOUND MIND IS MORE THAT JUST ACADEMICS— IT'S CREATIVITY, CRITICAL THOUGHT, AND KNOWLEDGE.

largely procedural for the many, and necessarily penalizing for the careless few.

The only real producer of good results is the development of a spirit which motivates. Men will get what they really want. It will mean a price. But men can and will pay the price if there is drive inside them.

All this adds up to the fact that any chapter that develops an understanding of and a love for Sigma Phi Epsilon will have good scholarship as naturally as men breathe. It means an everyday drive to make mind and body better.

Active Students do Better

Success in college is closely related to success in activities outside your academic program. One of the main findings of the 1985 study conducted by the College Board was that the best predictor of success in college is both scholastic achievement and "follow-through" as indicated by "persistent and successful extracurricular accomplishment."

Students in the study agreed. When they were asked to rate each other on success in college, they picked students who got good grades and "who were also hard-working, well-organized achievers in other areas." Your participation in the Fraternity and other activities makes you a potentially successful student.

ANY CHAPTER THAT DEVELOPS AN UNDERSTANDING OF AND A LOVE FOR SIGMA PHI EPSILON WILL HAVE GOOD SCHOLARSHIP AS NATURALLY AS MEN BREATHE.

What this means is that your involvement in varsity athletics, student government, symphony, choir, school newspaper, media productions, church activities, ROTC, special interest groups, clubs, special campus events or "drives," and intramural sports can improve your chances of success in college. The same holds true for working students, non-traditional students, and married students. Active students do better in college.

Why is this so? Why doesn't all this extra activity reduce the chances of success? The answer is that when you have to organize your efforts, avoid wasting time, and do well at the things that really count, you become better at almost everything you do. When the seniors in the College Board study were asked what contributed to a successful and satisfying career in college, 73 percent said the "ability to organize tasks and time effectively."

Time Management is Self-management

"WHAT COUNTS IS NOT THE NUMBER OF HOURS YOU PUT IN, BUT HOW MUCH YOU PUT IN THE HOURS."

To accomplish your purposes for being in college and to succeed in other important activities, you cannot be passive. You must actively control what you do with your time through conscious choices. In other words, you must do well at managing yourself in the time available to you.

Basics of Self-Management

1. Set your priorities and stick to them.

2. Do first things first; do less important things second.

3. Learn to say no to unfair requests for your time.

4. Start and stop specific activities at predetermined times.

When you have major responsibilities in addition to your classes, your "To Do" list can no longer include everything you want to do. Now your list must identify the most important things to do, and you must postpone or not do the less important things. You have to manage yourself well or you will not survive.

Lists, Schedules & Calendars

If you are going to be successful in life, you have to know what you are doing. That statement may seem extraordinarily simple-minded, but it is worth stating. People who do not know what they are doing are rarely successful—at least not consistently.

So the question is, do you know what you are doing? Does what you do each day get you closer to your desired educational goals while you enjoy the action with your friends and fulfill your other commitments? To keep on track, here are some effective ways of organizing your self-management plan:

YOUR DAILY LIST — Get into the habit of making a daily list that combines your scheduled activities and the important tasks you want to accomplish that day. After listing

what you want to do, code the most important items and make sure you give them priority over less important items. Keeping a list will help you put first things first.

YOUR WEEKLY SCHEDULE — To decide what is most important, you need to know your week's schedule. Start each week by making a schedule. Fill in all your class times, meetings, important events, study times, exams, practice hours, support-group meetings, and so forth. Outlining your schedule will help you find time to accomplish the tasks you have.

YOUR TERM CALENDAR — How do you know what to fill in on your weekly schedule? At the start of each term, take the syllabus for each course and fill in your calendar for the term. After your first day of classes, fill in your calendar with every scheduled exam and due dates for papers, projects, and reports. Fill in all the other important events that occur during the term. Keeping a calendar will help you plan and ensure your success.

Self-management is simple. You decide in advance what is important for you to do, and then you do it.

More Time Than You Think

"WHEN YOU PLAY, PLAY HARD; WHEN YOU WORK, DON'T PLAY AT ALL."

THEODORE ROOSEVELT

To prove to yourself that you have more time than you think, for one week, record the time you spend just sitting around, watching television, chatting with friends, and being involved in other activities. After one week, look at your week's record closely. What blocks of time did you waste? What types of activities do you spend your time on that are not really productive?

TIME MANAGEMENT BOILS DOWN TO DECIDING WHAT YOU WANT FROM THE TIME YOU HAVE.

Now, make a weekly schedule, planning your events. Try following your schedule for a week and carry it with you. When you find yourself doing things you want to avoid, look at the schedule and see what you had planned. Then do what you should be doing. Don't make your schedule so rigid you don't have time for any of your old unproductive behavior. Make sure to plan time to spend with your friends. You are going to make changes slowly, don't expect too much too fast.

No one follows a schedule to the letter.

Each night take some time to go over your schedule to see whether you did the main activities you had set out to accomplish. By the end of the week, you'll see the changes that are beginning to take place in your life. You'll be able to scan your chart and know whether you are eliminating some of the time-wasters and saving time for the naps, movies, and other activities you have been missing.

Decide what you are willing to spend less time doing, whether it is reducing your television time or video game action, or the nap after class. Next, figure out what it is you would rather be doing. Would you be better off going to the library between classes to complete your studying so you'll have time for a concert this weekend?

Time management boils down to deciding what you want from the time you have. Decide what you are going to eliminate and what you are going to add. Then practice substituting things from which you derive greater pleasure or payoffs for things that are less important to you.

Thinking Positively to take Action

Before getting started with your time management plan, it is important to consider the types of voices (*self-talk*) that may guide your behavior. As Larry Smith has noted, successful time management is enhanced by becoming aware of two types of voices that often guide our actions. These voices are the "Take Action Now Voices" and the "Do It Later Voices."

The Voices that Guide you

Take Action Now Voices

- ▶ Let me get it over with.
- ▶ It is already late.
- ▶ You know it, just do it.
- ▶ They'll be pleased.
- ▶ It is a challenge.
- ▶ It will be fun when I get into it.
- ▶ Once I get started, it will go quickly.
- ▶ I will have to do it later anyway.

Do It Later Voices

- ▶ I do not feel like it now.
- ▶ There is still time.
- ▶ I will do it later.
- ▶ This other thing is more important.
- ▶ It may solve itself if I wait.
- ▶ If I wait, someone else may do it.
- ▶ I need more information.
- ▶ I will be better prepared later.

As you listen to the voices that guide your behavior, you'll discover that a major step to becoming a successful student and person is to recognize and cope with "Do It Later Voices." "Do It Later Voices" hinder your time management. You'll want to consider replacing those voices with "Take Action Now Voices."

When you have more to do, you can be more effective by being more efficient. Skipping classes, depending on friends' notes, and buying term papers are not ways to increase your efficiency. You really don't need risky shortcuts to succeed. By working to acquire efficient and effective time management, learning, and reading skills, you are using the challenges of college to become a competent, well balanced person. These skills will help you in your personal and professional life.

Becoming a "Take Action Now" person may be hard work. Once you have developed the habit of letting "Take Action Now Voices" guide your behavior, you'll be in a better mental framework to achieve your goals. You will find that life is more enjoyable, you will accomplish more, and you will finish tasks on time, and you will not worry about what you have been putting off.

Setting your Academic Goals

Begin with the end in mind. With what GPA do you want to graduate? To get started in a good career, you need to have a 3.0 or better. Do you want to graduate with academic honors such as Summa Cum Laude, Magna Cum Laude, or Cum Laude?

What do you need to achieve each term to reach your goal? What do you need to earn in each class to hit that mark? How is each class graded, and what do you need to achieve in the course?

You need goals to know where you're going in the process of your education. When you know what you want to achieve, you can set your mind to it, create a plan, and do it. Setting

specific measurable goals is one of the strongest ways to motivate you to study efficiently and effectively.

Goal Setting

A good goal is a written statement defining a specific, desired result, in measurable/objective terms. Goals must be:

▶ Written.

▶ Dated.

▶ Measurable/objective.

▶ Realistic/achievable.

▶ Simple (keep them easy to remember).

In 1953, a study was done at Yale University. At that time, three percent of the undergraduate students had written goals, the other 97 percent did not. When these same individuals were polled 30 years later, the net worth of the three percent with the written goals was greater than that of the other 97 percent.

Students who do not set specific, measurable academic goals are usually uncertain about when they are going to do what they have to do in order to succeed in their courses. If you can determine what you should study to ace a course and set up a schedule to achieve those goals, you'll be in good shape. First, you need to know how to set study goals to design an action plan.

On a sheet of paper list all your courses. For each one, put down the grade you hope to earn in the course. After looking more closely at what lies ahead, you may want to modify this intended grade. That is all part of the process.

Next, analyze the challenges you face in each course and identify resources that can help you. From that analysis, set up specific study goals for each course. To determine your goals, you first have to determine what you have to do to get the desired grade in the course. The best sources of information are all available to you; you just have to ask.

Best Sources for Course Information

▶ Your instructor.

▶ Assigned course material.

▶ Course outlines or syllabi.

▶ Course schedules.

▶ Other students.

▶ Class discussions.

▶ Student manuals and programs.

From these sources you will usually be able to tell what important tasks you have to accomplish to achieve your desired grade.

Dr. Richard "Chip" Voorneveld, former Dean of Students at the College of Charleston, has some interesting things to say about improving GPA. He identifies six behaviors of successful students. If you adhere to these habits, your GPA will improve.

1. Never, ever miss a class.

Education is one thing many of us pay for but do not demand that we receive. Students are happy when class is canceled. They should treat class like a job. You simply have to go, no matter what is happening or how you feel. If you are way ahead or totally lost in a class, I guarantee that you will pick up valuable information at class that you would have otherwise missed. That can make the difference on a test.

2. Sit in the first row.

Studies show that sitting up front has fewer distractions and it is easier to hear, see and ask questions. The professor will also notice you more, which cannot hurt.

3. Read your notes from the last class before the next class.

Where does the professor always start? He or she often says, "Now where did I leave off last time?" If you know, you will be "in sync" with what comes next.

4. Do the assigned reading, but DO NOT highlight the book.

If something is important, write it on a note card. Then, study the note cards. Writing it down will help you remember it and studying the note cards is a good study aid. Flip through the note cards as you study, adding new ones as you go and setting aside ones you "have cold" for studying for tests.

5. Visit your professor once a week during office hours.

Getting to know your teacher personally has many benefits. They will know you are serious about their class, you can get clarification on certain ideas in the course material, and it will make it that much more difficult for them to give a low grade when they know of the effort you are putting forth (and they see you in every class). *Your chapter should have a relationship with a member of the faculty. Some SigEp chapters have their Faculty Advisor or Faculty Fellow meet in the chapter house. This interaction does not exist anywhere else on campus, and helps improve a SigEp's college experience.*

6. Do any extra credit that is offered.

Extra credit affects the bottom line. If you get a C on a test and the teacher offers extra credit, you can often turn that C into a B. You simply must take advantage of that. If the members of your chapter are able to buy into each of these, and they do them religiously, I can guarantee that their grades will go up by the equivalent of one full letter grade. It is that easy.

Progress Records, Checklists & Rewards

Okay. You'll give the study schedule and progress records a try. Are there any special rules you should follow in using them? Yes. First, you should always *post* your schedules, checklists, and progress records where they will be highly visible.

SCHEDULE YOUR WORK SO THAT ALL THE WORK FOR A PARTICULAR COURSE IS NOT CRAMMED INTO A SHORT PERIOD OF TIME BY SPREADING YOUR WORK OUT.

Your checklists and progress records will serve as constant reminders of what you should be doing and how well you are doing it.

Second, ask yourself what you should really be able to do in the amount of time you have to accomplish your goal. *Schedule* your work so that all the work for a particular course is not crammed into a short period of time by spreading your work out. Give yourself time to relax before the test or the date your paper is due.

Third, list the rewards that you will receive for accomplishing your goals.

Always reward yourself as you accomplish your goals.

Fourth, show your friends and study partners how well you are doing. The response from students throughout the years to checklists, schedules, and progress records has been exceedingly favorable. Students have enjoyed the benefits of having more predictable study schedules. Needless to say, students also enjoyed their rewards. Equally important, students have seen improvements in their grades. If you would like the same results, give these tactics a try.

Study Regularly

Most people act as though being a successful student is different from being a successful musician with the New York Symphony Orchestra or a quarterback with the Oakland Raiders. To be a successful musician or athlete, you need to practice regularly if you want to achieve your learning goals with the greatest amount of pleasure and the least pain. Accept the fact that in college you will have to study almost every day and do more studying than you did in high school.

The orchestra conductor would never say to the members of the orchestra, "Our next concert is three weeks away. Let's get together the night before the concert, and we'll practice for seven hours." Can you imagine the football coach saying to the team, "Guys, to prepare for next Saturday's game, we'll practice 14 hours on Friday. Until then, have fun and get ready for a real workout!"

The conductor and football coach know that to perform well, you have to practice frequently for reasonable periods of time. Too much practice too late will be ineffective.

One of Parkinson's Laws is that "work expands to fill available time." You may have experienced this phenomenon in regard to a project such as washing and waxing your car. If you have three hours available, it will probably take you three hours to get the job done. If, before you can finish the job, you receive a telephone call informing you that some very special people want you to drive over and pick them up, you would probably, in that circumstance, be able to wash and wax your car to your satisfaction in less than an hour. You decide what has to be done, do it, and then stop.

Guide to Studying

There are some specific skills vital to survival and success in college. Taking notes, writing papers and taking tests are the staples of your educational diet.

Taking Lecture Notes

I. Instructors often give clues as to what is important to note. Some of the common clues are:

A. Materials written on the blackboard.

B. Repetition.

C. Emphasis.

1. Emphasis can be judged by the tone of voice and gesture.

2. Emphasis can be judged by the amount of time the instructor spends on points and the number of examples he uses.

D. Word signals (e.g., "There are two points of view on...," "The third reason is...," "In conclusion...").

E. Summaries given at the end of class.

F. Reviews given at the beginning of class.

G. The course syllabus.

II. Each student should develop his own method of taking notes, but most students find the following suggestions helpful:

A. Make your notes brief.

1. Never use a sentence where you can use a phrase. Never use a phrase where you can use a word.

2. Use abbreviations and symbols; invent your own shorthand when necessary.

B. Put notes in your own words. However, the following should be noted exactly:

1. Formulas.

2. Definitions.

3. Specific facts.

C. Use outline form and/or a numbering system. Indentation helps distinguish major from minor points.

D. If you miss a statement, write key words, skip a few spaces, and get the information later.

E. Do not try to use every space on the page. Leave room for coordinating your notes with the text after the lecture. (You may want to list key terms in the margin or make a summary of the contents of the page.)

F. Date your notes. Perhaps number the pages.

III. Three rules for reviewing lecture notes.

A. Review lecture notes IMMEDIATELY after class! Make changes or enhancements while it is "fresh."

B. Cross-reference lecture notes and reading assignments which reinforce learning and identify material not understood.

C. Recite major points covered in lecture. This assists your memory and checks understanding.

Preparing for Tests

1. Keep up with your reading assignments so that studying for a test will involve reviewing of familiar material. Frantic last-minute cramming of new material usually results in faulty remembering and little learning.

2. To avoid re-reading textbook assignments, prepare them for review by underlining key words and phrases in pencil or highlighting.

3. Do not be afraid to ask questions about material you do not understand. You cannot remember something unless you understand it!

4. Review each course at least once a week during the semester. Re-read class notes, workbook exercises, outside reading notes, textbook underlinings, etc.

5. Prepare a list of likely test questions and make certain that you can give the correct answers to each in your own words.

6. Keep, correct, and review returned quizzes and exams. Check with your instructor if you are uncertain about the correct answer to a question that you missed—those questions are likely to pop up again in some form on the final exam.

7. Study your instructor's "test technique" so you will know what type of objective questions he or she favors and what kind of essay answer he or she expects.

8. Concentrate on remembering specific details (who, when, where) when studying for an objective test. Concentrate on understanding broad concepts (what, why, how) when studying for an essay exam. Memorize important facts for fill-in-the-blanks and essay tests; simply review and be able to recognize the correct information for multiple-choice and true-false tests. Review for problem-solving tests by memorizing necessary formulas, equations, and working examples of each type of problem likely to appear on the test.

9. Study and practice on questions from your textbook, workbook, and previous exams.

10. Ask the instructor what material will be covered on an exam—textbook assignments, class lectures, outside readings, movies and filmstrips, laboratory experiments, etc.

11. Complete long-term projects well in advance of scheduled exams so that your time will be free for intensive reviewing.

12. To minimize study fatigue, break intensive study sessions with five-minute rest periods every hour.

13. Review likely test questions with other students in small study groups of two to four members after each has first studied independently.

14. Do not endanger your health and test grade by using pep pills to stay up all night "cramming" for an exam. You will be able to think more logically if you get a reasonable amount of sleep on the night before a major test.

Taking Tests

General hints:

1. Read the test directions twice, making sure you fully understand what is expected, and follow instructions exactly.

2. Read each test question carefully and completely before marking or writing your answer.

3. Ask your instructor for help in interpreting a test question that is unclear or ambiguous to you.

4. Do not be disturbed about other students finishing before you do; take your time, think carefully, do not panic.

5. Be sure to make arrangements with your instructor about making up any test that you have missed or will have to miss.

Hints for objective tests:

1. Answer all questions in order without skipping or jumping around.

2. Do not linger too long on any one question; mark your best answer and return later. Identify doubtful answers by marks in the margin.

3. Be cautious about changing answers on multiple-choice and true-false questions without a good reason. Your first answer is more likely to be correct than are subsequent guesses.

4. On true-false questions, be alert for qualifying words such as "all," "none," "always," and "never," which generally make a statement false, or "most," "some," "usually," and "seldom," which tend to make a statement true.

5. On true-false questions, be alert for modifying or limiting phrases inserted into the sentence.

6. On true-false questions, be alert for multiple ideas or concepts within the same statement. All parts of a statement must be true, or the entire statement is false.

7. On matching exercises, first match out those choices about which you are sure, then match out the rest about which you are uncertain.

Hints for essay tests:

1. Read all the questions through first so that your answers will not overlap each other and you can judge a proper rate at which to work.

2. Concentrate on answering one question at a time.

3. Keep track of time so that you do not get carried away answering one question. Give the major points and leave space for later elaboration if time permits.

4. Make a brief outline before you start writing your answer to ensure good organization and prevent careless omissions. Include your outline with your essay answer.

5. Include as many specific facts as you can to support your answer. These give evidence that you know what you are talking about.

6. Decide what kind of answer the question requires before you begin writing. A different style of answer is required for: "illustrate," "list," "define," "trace," and "compare" questions.

7. Write legibly and make your corrections as neatly as possible.

8. Proofread all answers for content accuracy, careless omissions, and mistakes in grammar, spelling, and punctuation.

Hints for problem-solving tests:

1. Write down hard-to-remember formulas, equations, rules, etc., before you actually begin working on the test problems.

2. If you are unable to work a problem, go on to the next one, and come back later.

3. Even if you know that your answer is wrong, turn in your work because you may get partial credit for using the right process.

4. Show all the steps in your work and clearly identify or label your answer so that it can be quickly found.

5. To minimize careless errors, recheck all computations and check for misplaced decimal points before turning in your paper. Do not be in a hurry to leave.

Academic All-Americans

Some of the best athletes in football, basketball, baseball, soccer, track, volleyball, swimming, and other sports are able to compete while also doing very well academically. At a national level many of these athletes are recognized as "Academic All-Americans." Sigma Phi Epsilon should recruit and support brothers who are "Academic All-Americans" because these men are the Balanced Men we seek. They are responsible.

It is true that a few colleges with highly competitive sports programs let a few marginal student athletes slip by to keep them eligible to play. The average athlete, however, does as well in college as his or her classmates. Their ability to manage academic and

Andy Lane, Tennessee '06

extra-curricular activities makes them excellent examples of responsibility.

A study of the academic effects of freshman participation in varsity athletics, conducted by the Educational Testing Service and the American College Testing Program, shows that "on measures of persistence and grade-point averages, the athletes did as well or better than a matched group of non-athletes at the end of the freshman year. This finding held true across the 57 participating institutions, despite their diversity in size, selectivity, and athletic prowess."

Be A Jock

Why do student athletes do so well, considering the extra demands on them? There are many reasons:

▶ They work closely with their academic advisors.

▶ More than other students, they use academic support services.

▶ Athletes know they have little time to waste, so they apply themselves well.

▶ They receive attention from the coaches, who encourage their studies.

▶ They respond to failure and defeat by trying harder, not giving up.

SIGEPS OF ALL ACADEMIC BACKGROUNDS CAN LEARN FROM THE BALANCE OF "ACADEMIC ALL-AMERICANS."

Courtney Wright, Florida State '06

SOUND BODY

"The difference between a successful person and others is not a lack of strength, nor a lack of knowledge, but rather a lack of will."

John F. Kennedy said, "The Greeks sought excellence not only in philosophy and drama, art and architecture but in athletics. The same people who produced the poetry of Homer and the wisdom of Plato and Aristotle—they also produced the Olympic Games. The Greeks understood that mind and body must develop in harmony to produce a creative intelligence. And, so did Thomas Jefferson, when he said, 'Not less than two hours a day should be devoted to exercise.' If a man who wrote the Declaration of Independence, was Secretary of State, and twice President could give it two hours, we certainly must be able to fit it into our schedules for the good of our minds as well as our bodies."

Sound Body is more than just athletics—it's total wellness, conditioning, and endurance. The Sound Body is ready and able, robust and nourished. It is fostered with regular exercise, relaxation, healthy limits, medical screenings, and proper nutrition.

Continuous Improvement

You have two things you can do to make your body a solid vessel for a full life—do not do things that are harmful to you and do work to improve yourself physically. It seems almost ridiculous to point out that harming yourself is damaging. Yet, despite many warnings, some people continue self-destructive behavior. Smoking, alcohol abuse, unsafe sex, and unhealthy diets are all things students are warned to avoid, but, year after year, members and chapters suffer great losses because these warnings are unheeded.

Unfortunately, self-destructive behavior begins in college. Members who were among the healthiest students suddenly find they do not have time to exercise or eat a healthy meal as they did in high school. Organized sports may not be available to them. Added stress combined with new temptations of alcohol and drugs can seriously harm a person's health.

Many times, those who abuse their bodies in college take their bad habits with them through life. Stress, smoking, alcohol can all lead to more serious problems such as heart and lung disease. These health problems have the potential to kill, ending what should have been a long, productive life prematurely.

SOUND BODY IS MORE THAN JUST ATHLETICS—IT'S TOTAL WELLNESS, CONDITIONING, AND ENDURANCE.

Chapters must provide programs to educate men to make smart decisions, and SigEps must make those smart decisions at every turn. The consequences are too great to do otherwise.

Eating healthy foods, avoiding fast foods high in fat and sodium, regular exercise, and adequate sleep will all help ensure that you are healthy and fit. The benefits of involving yourself in positive, healthy activities are numerous—lower stress, better self-esteem, a longer life. Whether you are physically challenged or an Olympic athlete, you can do what it takes to make yourself better...eat right, manage stress, and exercise.

Part of being diligent is the steady work and practice to better yourself.

A Sound Body, as the ancient Greeks believed, is part of a balance that rounds out a man's life. A Sound Body, as great men of our time believe, is what separates great from good and life from death. Take time to create a healthy lifestyle to develop your healthiest body.

Building a Body for Life

From *Health Manager* magazine

Weight training strengthens bone and connective tissue as well as builds muscle mass. The result is an increase in what researchers call *functionality*, the ability to perform the tasks of everyday life. Pollock notes, for instance, that 85 percent of lower-back problems are associated with muscle weakness.

Kerry Steward, Assistant Professor of medicine at Johns Hopkins University, has shown that specific types of strength training may even help individuals with heart disease and mild high blood pressure resume their normal activities. "Our research over the last 10 to 15 years has shown that, taking into consideration a person's physical limitations, moderate weight training builds muscles and bolsters cardiovascular endurance," he says.

Retaining Your Vigor

The message is clear. People who push themselves physically, who combine weight training with aerobic activity, have a much better chance of retaining their vigor, stamina, and overall health as the years go by. A comprehensive fitness program will not only improve the quality of your life but also increase the probability of your enjoying a self-reliant old age.

Prevent Burnout

Who wouldn't want to reap the benefits that come from being fit? A healthier heart, toned muscles, weight control, better sleep, even improved handling of stress can be the rewards of as little as 15 to 30 minutes of exercise three times a week.

Here are some strategies for sticking with an exercise program:

1. DON'T OVERDO IT IN THE BEGINNING. Sure, experts recommend 15 to 30 minutes of exercise at a time. But if you can't handle that, start with what you can do. As you build up your stamina, you'll enjoy doing more.

2. PUT VARIETY INTO YOUR WORKOUT. Any activity that engages the large muscle groups in a rhythmic and continuous manner can be considered exercise. That means you can walk, hike, run, swim, skate, bicycle, row, cross-country ski, jump rope, or climb stairs. It all counts!

3. SET YOURSELF UP TO WIN BY KNOWING YOURSELF. Some people thrive on routine; others feel confined by it. Plan a routine that calls for walking on Monday, swimming on Wednesday, and tennis Friday. Or, if you're the spontaneous type, set aside only the time and leave the activity open.

4. STAY CLOSE TO HOME. If you have to go somewhere to exercise, make sure getting there is easy. If possible, choose an activity close to home and use the extra time for your workout.

5. STEAL THE TIME. Getting away from your studies for a vigorous half-hour walk at lunch time will help your psyche as much as your body.

6. MAKE EXERCISE A PART OF YOUR DAILY LIFE. You don't need to climb into your sweats for a workout. Take the stairs instead of the elevator.

7. BUY YOURSELF A WORKOUT WARDROBE. Ever wonder why so many people like the tight new knits of today's exercise outfits? Not only are they attractive, their fit is flattering. And when you suit up, you'll remind yourself that you're ready for business.

8. WALK...TO THE LIBRARY. Fitness magazines are full of ideas and personalities to inspire you to keep going. At the very least, you may find an engrossing book to make time fly while pumping away on your stationary bicycle.

9. ACCENTUATE THE POSITIVE. Be sure to remember the energy charge you felt during an early evening bike ride or the sense of calm that can come with a brisk walk before class.

Finally, if you feel your resolve flagging, remind yourself of how important your workout is and focus on your goal at hand. Re-check your cholesterol and blood pressure. Tack a "before" picture on the mirror while you wait for the "after" to take shape. All it takes to win at the fitness game is to stick with it.

Playing it Safe

A pulled or sprained muscle can take you out of the game. A few principles of prevention and recovery can minimize the downtime. All it takes is one wrong move during your aerobics class or pushing yourself a little too far on the morning jog. Sports injuries are a common phenomenon.

Most of the time, the discomfort is minor—some muscle aches or stiffness on the morning after. Slightly more serious are pulls and sprains, a result of overstretching, overusing, or actually tearing muscles and ligaments. They can put a crimp in your exercise routine for a week or longer. Symptoms range from extreme tenderness, in the case of a muscle pull (strain), to the shooting pain, severe swelling, and bruising of a sprain. Back pain from over-twisting (common in tennis and basketball) and shin splints (sharp shin pain caused by running, jumping, or walking on too hard a surface) also make routine movements difficult and can take a while to heal.

Fortunately, most symptoms fade quickly if the injury is treated with rest, ice, compression, and elevation. Pain diminishes within a few days, and you can expect to regain your full range of motion within a week or two. Even better, however, is avoiding injury altogether.

Most sports injuries can be traced to a group of common causes: poor conditioning, inferior equipment, bad technique, or overuse. Following the basic principles of playing it safe may keep you up and running, injury-free.

GET INTO SHAPE GRADUALLY. If you're just starting an exercise program, your muscles are probably not up to the rigors of intense exertion. Moderate, daily exercise is safer than wearing yourself out in a spurt of weekend activity.

FIRST AND LAST. Spend five minutes at the beginning (warm up) and end (cool down) of each routine to ease your muscles into and out of activity. This increases flexibility and regulates muscle temperature, which help keep muscles from pulling or tearing.

GET INTO THE RIGHT GEAR. Many ankle, foot, and knee injuries can be blamed on worn-out athletic shoes that have lost their support.

CHOOSE YOUR SURFACE WITH CARE. Keep in mind that jogging on the springier surface of a running track will be easier on your body than the jarring impact that comes from pounding hard asphalt or concrete. Whenever possible, opt for wood floors rather than concrete for your basketball or aerobics workouts.

REVIEW YOUR TECHNIQUE. If you find that you're consistently sore after tennis or golf, don't assume it's an

> MOST SPORTS INJURIES CAN BE TRACED TO A GROUP OF COMMON CAUSES: POOR CONDITIONING, INFERIOR EQUIPMENT, BAD TECHNIQUE, OR OVERUSE.

inevitable cost of playing the game. Something may be wrong with your backhand or swing that taking a few lessons can sort out.

KNOW YOUR LIMITS. You may be having the time of your life, but if you play tired or push your muscles harder than usual, you're setting yourself up for injury. Any pain you experience during a workout is your body's way of telling you that you're overdoing it.

Eating Better

You don't have to be "on a diet" to recognize the importance of improving your diet. Though each month seems to yield a new crop of fad foods, nutritionists have been consistently championing the goodness to be found in vegetables and fruits. Don't use the word "diet" because a "diet" has a starting and ending point. Living and eating properly are components to a healthy lifestyle. Consume smaller, more frequent meals that contain portion sizes around the size of your clenched fist of healthy, whole foods.

Examples of healthy, clean foods:

▶ PROTEINS: chicken breast, lean red meats, turkey breast, fresh fish (salmon, tuna, etc.), wild game, low fat cottage cheese, and lean ham.

▶ COMPLEX CARBOHYDRATES: yams, brown/wild rice, oatmeal, beans, barley, fruit, fat free and low sugar yogurt, and squash.

▶ VEGETABLES: broccoli, asparagus, spinach, cucumber, tomato, mushrooms, green beans, carrots, celery, dark green lettuce, and bell peppers.

▶ FATS: flax seed oil, sunflower oil, grape seed oil, natural peanut butter, avocado, sunflower seeds, pumpkin seeds, low-sodium/raw nuts, olives.

▶ FOODS TO AVOID: butter, margarine, mayonnaise, whole fat dairy, fried foods, sweets, fatty meats, poultry skin, processed pork products.

Most of us have only a vague idea of what we really eat. We grab our meals on the run, eat what gets put on our tray at the cafeteria, or unthinkingly satisfy our cravings. Keeping a food diary for a single week can be a remarkable eye-opener. The only requirement is to jot down every single thing you eat or drink, along with the approximate size of the portion. If you put ketchup on your sandwich, jot it down. If you have a breath mint after a meal, jot it down. At the end of the week, add everything up. Referring to a book of nutritional values, total up the number of calories and how many grams of fat, protein, and carbohydrate really make up your diet. You may be surprised by the results.

STAY HEALTHY: EAT WELL, DRINK LOTS OF FLUIDS, AND GET PLENTY OF SLEEP AND EXERCISE TO KEEP UP YOUR RESISTANCE. AND STAY CALM.

Resting Up

If you think your daytime fatigue is caused by too little night-time slumber, try these tips from the sleep experts:

▶ Make your room an inviting place to sleep. Minimize light and noise, and keep the room comfortably cool.

▶ Take the television out of your room.

▶ Reduce your intake of caffeine, nicotine, and alcohol, all of which can disrupt sleep patterns.

▶ Get exposure to sunlight each day. This helps reset your internal clock, restoring your natural sleep cycle.

▶ Get relaxed. Relaxation exercises such as progressive muscle relaxation, meditation, and biofeedback help counteract the daily buildup of anxiety that interferes with proper sleep. A late afternoon or early evening workout can also soothe your stressed nerves.

▶ Limit eating before going to bed. This eases digestion and helps induce sleep.

▶ Try going to bed earlier to reset your body clock. However, if you can't sleep, get out of bed, and do something relaxing until you feel sleepy.

▶ Get up at the same time each morning, even if you fell asleep late. You'll eventually start going to sleep earlier as your natural cycle is set.

Fewer Sniffles

Aunt Irene's chicken soup recipe may be your family's cure for a cold, but with a little less stress, you might avoid those sniffles in the first place.

One recent study points out the clear connection between stress and how low a cold can bring you down.

Researchers isolated 17 college students in a hotel and exposed them to a cold virus. When they were satisfied that all the students were infected, they recorded the symptoms the students reported. Nearly one-third of them claimed they never felt as if they had a cold.

At the start of the experiment, the student subjects had filled out a questionnaire that revealed information about the amount of stress in their lives. It turned out that those who suffered no symptoms reported about a third as many stressful events as those who felt sick. The researchers concluded that stress influences the severity of our bodies' response to colds.

In today's stress-filled world, what can you do to avoid catching the common cold and suffering unduly? Wash your hands frequently with soap and warm water, especially if you're in contact with a cold sufferer. Eat well, drink lots of fluids, and get plenty of sleep and exercise to keep up your resistance. And stay calm.

Alcohol & Other Drugs

Here are some brief facts about alcohol and other drugs. Visit the following sites for more information:

Center for Substance Abuse Prevention

www.prevention.samhsa.gov

Drug Enforcement Administration

www.dea.gov

National Institute on Drug Abuse

www.nida.nih.gov

White House Office of National Control Policy

www.whitehousedrugpolicy.gov

Facts:

1. Alcohol is the #1 drug of choice on college campuses. Use it responsibly if you are of age or abstain.

2. Marijuana is not the same as alcohol:

   ▶ It is the #2 drug of choice after alcohol.

   ▶ The law doesn't treat it the same as alcohol.

   ▶ Marijuana use impacts motivation, health, and eating habits.

3. Cocaine is not glamorous. The U.S. population is 5 percent of the world's population, yet it uses over 50 percent of the world's cocaine.

A freshman wanting to be accepted and liked by other students is easily led into frequent bouts of drinking and drug use. According to Eugene Hakansen, director of a college counseling service, "The greatest instigator of alcohol and drug use in college is a friend. Roommates get roommates to try drugs; older students influence freshmen to drink and use drugs."

Bob Meehan, a recovered addict agrees. According to Meehan, Founder of the Palmer Drug Abuse program that has helped over 300,000 people, "Teenagers do drugs to gain acceptance." He says, "Peer pressure to take drugs is so strong that one teenager in two will say he gets high before he actually does."

The National Institute on Drug Abuse conducted a nationwide research project into the use of alcohol and other drugs by high school and college students. The researchers found that the reason given most often for using any substance is "to have a good time with my friends."

What are some of the consequences of alcohol abuse by college students, both of legal age and underage?

The consequences of excessive and underage drinking affect virtually all college campuses, college communities, and college students, whether they choose to drink or not. The following figures were taken from the National Institute on Alcohol Abuse and Alcoholism web site on college drinking, *www.collegedrinkingprevention.gov.*

▶ DEATH: 1,400 college students (ages18 to 24) die each year from alcohol-related unintentional injuries, including motor vehicle crashes.

▶ INJURY: 500,000 students are unintentionally injured under the influence of alcohol.

▶ ASSAULT: More than 600,000 students are assaulted by another student who has been drinking.

▶ SEXUAL ABUSE: More than 70,000 students are victims of alcohol-related sexual assault or date rape.

▶ UNSAFE SEX: 400,000 students had unprotected sex and more than 100,000 students report having been too intoxicated to know if they consented to sex.

▶ ACADEMIC PROBLEMS: About 25 percent of college students report academic consequences of their drinking including missing class, falling behind, doing poorly on exams or papers, and receiving lower grades overall.

▶ HEALTH PROBLEMS/SUICIDE ATTEMPTS: More than 150,000 students develop an alcohol-related health problem, and between 1.2 and 1.5 percent of students indicate that they tried to commit suicide within the past year due to drinking or drug use.

▶ DRUNK DRIVING: 2.1 million students drove under the influence of alcohol in 2001.

▶ VANDALISM: About 11 percent of college student drinkers report that they have damaged property while under the influence of alcohol.

▶ POLICE INVOLVEMENT: About 5 percent of college students are involved with the police or campus security as a result of their drinking and an estimated 110,000 students are arrested for an alcohol-related violation, such as public drunkenness or driving under the influence.

▶ ALCOHOL ABUSE AND DEPENDENCE: 31 percent of college students met criteria for a diagnosis of alcohol abuse and 6 percent for a diagnosis of alcohol dependence in 2001, according to questionnaire-based self-reports about their drinking.

How does alcohol affect you physically?

▶ Alcohol is absorbed slowly into the bloodstream. The majority of alcohol enters the bloodstream through the small intestine, though it is also absorbed through the lining of the stomach.

▶ Alcohol in the bloodstream is carried to the brain. There it slows down the thought process.

▶ Alcohol is a depressant. It effects the central nervous system which controls breathing, body temperature, and heart rate, among other vital processes. Alcohol abuse can slow breathing, cause irregular heartbeats, or stop both breathing and heartbeat.

▶ Alcohol poisoning can cause choking on vomit (asphyxia) and irreversible brain damage.

▶ Because alcohol disrupts the regulation of body temperature, it can cause hypothermia (low body temperature) which can lead to cardiac arrest.

▶ Alcohol is eliminated slowly through the body. The liver can process about 1 ounce of alcohol in one hour. One drink (one beer, 1.5 ounces of 80 proof liquor, or five ounces of wine) is eliminated in one hour.

▶ Coffee or a shower not will sober a person up. Only time can sober someone up.

What are some consequences of marijuana use?

▶ May cause frequent respiratory infections, impaired memory and learning, increased heart rate, anxiety, panic attacks, tolerance, and physical dependence.

▶ Use of marijuana during the first month of breast-feeding can impair infant motor development.

▶ Chronic smokers may have many of the same respiratory problems as tobacco smokers including daily cough and phlegm, chronic bronchitis symptoms, frequent chest colds; chronic abuse can also lead to abnormal functioning of lung tissues.

▶ A study of college students has shown that skills related to attention, memory, and learning are impaired among people who use marijuana heavily, even after discontinuing its use for at least 24 hours.

What are some of the consequences of using Ecstasy?

▶ In addition to chemical stimulation, the drug reportedly suppresses the need to eat, drink, or sleep.

▶ When taken at raves, where all-night dancing usually occurs, the drug often leads to severe dehydration and heat stroke in the user since it has the effect of "short-circuiting" the body's temperature signals to the brain.

▶ An Ecstasy overdose is characterized by a rapid heartbeat, high blood pressure, faintness, muscle cramping, panic attacks, and, in more severe cases, loss of consciousness or seizures. One of the side effects of the drug is jaw muscle tension and teeth grinding. As a consequence, Ecstasy users will often suck on pacifiers to help relieve the tension.

Ecstasy may cause hyperthermia, muscle breakdown, seizures, stroke, kidney and cardiovascular system failure, possible permanent damage to sections of the brain critical to thought and memory, and death.

Hotline Numbers

▶ National Drug & Alcohol Treatment Hotline 800-662-HELP

▶ National Domestic Violence Hotline 800-799-7233

▶ National Adolescent Suicide Hotline 800-621-4000

▶ National Runaway Hotline 800-621-4000

▶ Panic Disorder Information Hotline 800- 64-PANIC

▶ Project Inform HIV/AIDS Treatment Hotline 800-822-7422

CAREER ACHIEVEMENT

"Don't measure yourself by what you have accomplished, but what by what you should have accomplished with your ability."

~ JOHN WOODEN

"Each week there's a new encounter, each year a new challenge. But all of the rings and all of the money and all of the color and all of the display, they linger only in the memory. The spirit, the will to win and excel, these are the things that endure. These are the qualities that are so much more important than any of the events that occasion them. I'd like to say that the quality of a man's life has got to be a full measure of that man's personal commitment to excellence and to victory, regardless of what field he may be in."

~ VINCE LOMBARDI,
Legendary Coach of the Green Bay Packers

Based on Sigma Phi Epsilon's Cardinal Principle of Diligence, it is important that all SigEps take on the goal of outstanding achievement in the career of their choice. The first step toward outstanding achievement is the attainment of the diploma. Applying diligence, the diploma should be pursued with all one's determination and interest. Nothing less than the highest academic marks and honors should be sought, because this is the first step to career achievement.

Your Career Starts Now

Those who say "grades don't matter" are not seeing the full picture. Leaders in their careers, and especially those responsible for hiring the leaders of tomorrow say that a man's performance in the classroom is the best indicator of his potential in his career. A man's work habits, his ability to complete assignments, and his enthusiasm for learning are clearly apparent in his grades. So, as is asked of all SigEps in our Ritual, it is vital to make your college education the highest priority.

NOTHING LESS THAN THE HIGHEST ACADEMIC MARKS AND HONORS SHOULD BE SOUGHT, BECAUSE THIS IS THE FIRST STEP TO CAREER ACHIEVEMENT.

Foundation Trustee James L. Clayton, Tennessee '57, provides internship opportunities for undergraduates in the Tennessee Alpha Chapter at the University of Tennessee.

Upon graduation and entering the ranks of Sigma Phi Epsilon's alumni, you must remember your vow of diligence that you took as an undergraduate. The Cardinal Principles of the Fraternity are guides throughout life. Everyone becomes discouraged with his progress at one time or another. However, a diligent person will work through these rough times and come out ahead for it. Your job may be changed, or you may even start an entirely new career. A diligent person will find new opportunities for success in his path.

THE BROTHER WHO IS COMPLACENT WILL SOON FIND HIMSELF NO LONGER IN CONTROL AND FAILING TO MEET HIS POTENTIAL AND THE NEEDS OF THOSE AROUND HIM.

Conversely, some may become complacent with early success and disregard diligence. Success is a journey, not a destination. Sigma Phi Epsilon emphasizes the need to be diligent and constantly look for further challenges. The brother who is complacent will soon find himself no longer in control and failing to meet his potential and the needs of those around him. Prepare yourself now for the career you will begin when you graduate. In addition to good grades, you can follow a few simple steps that will help ensure your success in the future.

Your Career Search

By Jeff Prouty, Iowa State '79, past Head of College Recruitment for Coopers & Lybrand, founder of The Prouty Project, Member Sigma Phi Epsilon National Board of Directors.

I was invited to speak to the University of Minnesota second-year MBAs. The topic: how to market yourself in the job search. With all the recent corporate layoffs and competition for jobs in all fields, perhaps you can benefit from the key points of this presentation:

1. Remember the Boy Scout Motto — PREPARATION includes a résumé, a high-quality printer, a box of thank-you cards, an answering machine, and a tickle file.

2. It's a Numbers Game — 100 letters and 100 follow-up calls will lead to 20 meetings and five opportunities.

3. Identify the Bulls-Eye — Effective niche marketing means targeted industries, companies, and decision-makers.

4. Stand by the Hors D'oeuvres — Go to association meetings and remember that 10 percent of any group influences the other 90 percent.

5. T-Minus 210 Seconds — When telemarketing, "close the deal" (i.e., achieve your objective) in three-and-a-half minutes or less.

6. Short Notes Yield Long Results — Every meeting deserves a thank-you note.

7. Greasing the Skids — Ask for referrals and remember quid pro quo (i.e., how can I help you?).

8. Stay the Course — As you begin to get more leads than you can handle, keep the bulls-eye in focus.

9. The Personal Touch — Differentiate yourself by taking the time to say thanks, write a note, or send an article.

10. The Ruth of the Matter — Remember, Babe Ruth struck out 1,330 times. If you bat .300, or even .150, you will have more opportunities than you can handle. Good luck!

Career Achievement

Sigma Phi Epsilon recognizes those who succeed in their chosen careers with the Sigma Phi Epsilon Citation. Citations are given at each Conclave to men who live diligence through outstanding career achievement— scientists, artists, businessmen, athletes, are all a credit to the Fraternity, their families and their chosen field. Many men have received the Sigma Phi Epsilon Citation. See Appendix D for a listing of Citation recipients.

ETIQUETTE

> "Class is being honest—both with yourself and with others. Class is treating others as you would like them to treat you."
>
> ~ JACK NICKLAUS

To all you meet, you are the Sigma Phi Epsilon Fraternity. Regardless of what more than 258,000 members have built with love and integrity for nearly a century, the man or woman who meets you in any circumstance will say of you, "That is Sigma Phi Epsilon." With good manners and social conduct, people will appreciate that you are the quality Balanced Man. You never get a second chance to make a first impression.

Good manners are important in every walk of life. Politeness, courtesy, and proper behavior make relationships enjoyable and pleasant. Sigma Phi Epsilon expects that your conduct and bearing shall be that which becomes a gentleman and a fraternity man. Your standards will bring credit to you, your Fraternity, and your alma mater. Sigma Phi Epsilon will not settle for anything short of your best effort. Courtesy and good manners are not things to be put on like a coat and tie for special occasions and tossed away when the event has passed.

These goals can be realized by practicing proper social conduct, good etiquette, and the development of character. Being able to show the world that you possess a "touch of class" depends on your attitude toward these attributes. Learning what to do and when to do it separates you from the crowd. Developing good character marks you as a Balanced Man.

The Ideal SigEp Brother

Any man can wear a SigEp pin, but without character he will never be a true SigEp Brother. A true SigEp is a mover, thinker, and achiever. He is a disciplined person with a clear sense of values, who tackles difficult tasks with vigor, works to reach his potential, and pushes others to meet theirs. He is an optimist. With character, other traits can develop. Traits of a strong SigEp brother include:

SIGMA PHI EPSILON EXPECTS THAT YOUR CONDUCT AND BEARING SHALL BE THAT WHICH BECOMES A GENTLEMAN AND A FRATERNITY MAN.

ACCOUNTABILITY: Keeping commitments, including paying your bills on time, is essential. Be responsible for your own actions.

ATTITUDE: You should always keep and exude a positive mental attitude, for it has an effect on others and usually leads to positive achievements.

APPEARANCE: The way you look affects the way you feel, and the way others feel about you. Looking sharp reflects pride; looking unkempt reflects a lack of pride. Personal grooming and cleanliness are very important.

PERSONALITY: Be cheerful, pleasant, courteous, friendly, enthusiastic, and have a sense of humor. Be honest and tactful. Show appreciation and give thanks for any favor or courtesy. Apologize when you fall short of your obligations, and do favors when there is an opportunity to do so.

PUNCTUALITY: To be on time is to keep a promise; to be late is to break one. Punctuality is part of integrity. If conditions prevent you from being on time, call the waiting party and explain the reason.

SPORTSMANSHIP: Follow the rules of sportsmanship graciously. Do not be impolite, crude, or impatient. Win without boasting, lose without excuses.

Good Introductions

First impressions are often made through formal introductions, and you will have an opportunity to shine by knowing a few simple rules. You will have many opportunities to make formal introductions in the coming years. Introductions are often made improperly but are very simple if you know what to do. Remember: the male is always presented to the female, and the younger person is always presented to the older person. The person being presented is mentioned second. For example, "Carol Downs, I would like you to meet my fraternity brother, Billy Phillips." (Female first...male second.)

THE MOST BASIC PUBLIC RELATIONS STRATEGY FOR A FRATERNITY IS TO TREAT GUESTS WITH RESPECT AND COURTESY.

"Uncle Billy, I would like you to meet my roommate, Jim Olson." (Older male first...younger male second.)

As with most rules, there are exceptions, and you must use good judgment. For example, "Senator Thompson, I would like you to meet my sister, Janet Young." (Older male of distinction first...younger female second.) "Grandmother Armstrong, I would like you to meet Senator Thompson." (Older female first... younger male, even though distinguished, second!)

Relax and take your time. If you are at ease, the people you are introducing will be also.

First Impressions & A Firm Handshake

A good, firm handshake can be the difference between a successful first impression and a weak one. A limp handshake is a turn-off, while a firm handshake carries with it sincerity, solidarity, and warmth. Do not crush

A good, firm handshake can be the difference between a successful first impression and a weak one.

the bones in anyone's hand, especially a woman, but do not extend a weak hand or shake hands at an uncomfortable angle—at least uncomfortable for the other person. ALWAYS stand up, unless you are handicapped, too old, or too weak. Standing is a sign of honor. Practice with your brothers until you have developed a strong, natural handshake. This simple technique will be invaluable to all of your relationships, especially so in your career. It is important to teach new members this skill.

Entertaining Alumni & Guests

The most basic public relations strategy for a fraternity is to treat guests with respect and courtesy. Not long ago, an alumnus returned to visit his chapter after being away almost 20 years. He entered the house and was greeted by silence. Everyone went his own way, not stopping to say hello. Some were watching television and continued to do so, ignoring the alumnus. He finally cornered someone and introduced himself, asking for the chapter president. When the president arrived, the alumnus showed him a $1,000 check he was going to give the chapter, but he changed his mind because he felt his gift would not be put to good use in a chapter with this type of atmosphere.

This true story is not about receiving money by being friendly and hospitable, but rather that your chapter's atmosphere of hospitality reflects upon the overall quality of your chapter, of Sigma Phi Epsilon, and of each member. You attract new members and demonstrate that you have a successful brotherhood with an atmosphere of honest hospitality and friendliness. Every successful chapter has learned this lesson, and diligently passes it on from year to year.

MAKE GUESTS FEEL WELCOME AND IMPORTANT. TREAT YOUR GUESTS AS YOU WOULD WANT TO BE TREATED.

A variety of individuals will be guests of your chapter at one time or another—parents, campus officials, alumni, recent graduates from outside the chapter, and potential new members. All are impressionable, and all should be treated with respect. Make guests feel welcome and important. Treat your guests as you would want to be treated.

Points to Remember

▶ When greeting a new member to the Fraternity, WELCOME him to the Fraternity.

▶ Let others outside of Sigma Phi Epsilon CONGRATULATE him on joining.

▶ Never remain seated while an older guest or woman stands.

▶ When a guest, faculty member, or alumnus enters the room stand up.

▶ Remain standing until the guest asks you to be seated.

▶ Promptly and pleasantly welcome guests and introduce yourself.

▶ If you are among the first to greet a guest, ask if you can be of assistance.

▶ If the guest arrives near mealtime, ask him or her to join you.

▶ Keep guest areas clean, including hallways, restrooms, living room, etc.

▶ Have toilet paper and towels in the restrooms.

▶ Invite local alumni, faculty, or school administrators to meet your guest.

▶ Introduce guests at the beginning of a meeting and thank them for attending.

▶ Make your guest feel important by showing a genuine interest in him or her.

▶ Give the guest an appropriate farewell when leaving.

Everyday Conduct in the House

Living together in the fraternity house, sometimes in rather close quarters, can present problems which may be new to you. These points also apply to roommates who do not live in a fraternity house.

▶ Remember to respect other members, that includes their feelings and property.

▶ Return things to their proper places.

▶ Maintain the appearance of the commons area.

▶ Do not use other's property without permission.

▶ If you borrow something, leave a clear note.

▶ Respect other people's privacy. Remember to knock.

▶ Respect others' studying or sleeping.

▶ Keep television, music at a low volume during quiet hours.

▶ Ask guests to respect quiet, and instruct them in chapter rules.

Measuring Your Chapter's Manners

Phone Courtesy

▶ Does someone answer the phone promptly? ...or does everyone in the house play "guess who is going to give in and answer the phone?"

▶ Is the phone answered with a simple phrase? ...or does someone just say "yeah?" ...or mutter nonsense? (There are few things more annoying than having people answer the phone with an oration. Parents, college administrators, potential employers, and long-distance callers are not impressed.)

▶ Is the caller put on hold? ...or is the phone dropped while the person called is paged at full volume? Is the caller ignored while hunting for the person being called?

▶ If the person being called is not home, is the caller told properly and asked to leave a message? ...or is the caller left on hold indefinitely?

▶ Are messages actually delivered accurately? ...or do they get misplaced, if ever taken?

▶ Is a message pad and pen next to the phone?

Guest Courtesy

▶ Is the visitor invited in and made to feel welcome? ...or is he/she just left standing while someone is called?

▶ Do chapter members introduce themselves and initiate conversation? ...or is the visitor made to feel as if he/she has something contagious and thus is to be avoided?

"Mom Nonnie" is the national authority on etiquette for Sigma Phi Epsilon Fraternity. She has been a housemother for SigEp at Southern Methodist University and at Purdue University. As a certified business etiquette consultant, Nonnie travels across the country to facilitate etiquette and interpersonal skills programs for corporations and colleges. She is seen here facilitating at the Ruck Leadership Institute.

▶ Is the visitor told what the chapter's customs are at mealtime...or does he/she have to play "Simon Says" in an attempt to follow the action?

▶ Is the visitor introduced to the housemother? ...or does the housemother have to find out for herself that there is a visitor present?

▶ Do chapter members get up from their seats when the housemother or visitor enters the room? ...or do members ignore the housemother or visitor so that they will not have to talk to them? (All gentlemen are expected to stand up immediately whenever a woman enters a room or is excused from the table.)

▶ When there is an after-dinner speaker, does the entire chapter move into the living room? ...or does half the chapter disappear immediately after the meal?

▶ Do members respect the privacy of others? ...or does everyone assume that a closed door is to be opened without a knock?

▶ If someone requests help with a project, do others respond? ...or does everyone suddenly become very busy?

▶ Do chapter officers hold a weekly meeting with the housemother and cook so they are informed about upcoming events? ...or do they rely on ESP and minor miracles to make 40 pork chops feed 50 people?

▶ Do quiet hours mean quiet prevails? ...or do quiet hours mean study if you can't find anything else to do?

▶ Do members take time to thank each other for jobs well done? ...or is vocal communication limited to complaining?

Interacting with Women

Women are impressed with a man who knows how to properly handle himself in "mixed" company and in a dating situation. Knowing when and how to apply social graces and when to be more casual is a personal judgment call you will have to make. You will find, however, you can rarely overdo good manners. The problem comes when one does not know what to do and blunders ahead. A simple "rule" to follow is—treat every woman as you would your mother, sister, or girlfriend.

Tips with Women

▶ Offer to open the door for a woman.

▶ When walking up stairs, the woman leads.

▶ When walking down stairs, the man leads.

▶ When escorting a woman, she should always be on the right side, or on the "inside" when walking along a street.

▶ In any type of transportation, the woman enters first and exits last.

▶ Never use profanity or "off color" remarks in front of a woman.

▶ Always stand when a woman enters a room.

▶ Never sit until the woman has done so or asks you to sit.

▶ The gentleman should always be on the side of greatest "danger."

▶ Remember proper manners when you meet your dates' parents.

Although many of the traditional rules of etiquette have changed over the years regarding how men deal with women, particularly in business, there are still several important ways for a gentleman to show respect for women. When a woman enters a room for the first time, all men should rise to greet her. At the dinner table, a woman should be shown to her chair before any men take their seats. Men should also rise any time she leaves or returns to the table. It is still fashionable to open and close the door when a woman is entering or leaving a room or a car. However, when entering a taxi or a revolving door, the man should enter first because it is easier for him to slide across the seat of a taxi or to push the door and start its rotation.

When buying a corsage, always ask your date about the color and the style of her dress. She may prefer a wrist corsage to a pinned one.

You may come upon a situation where a woman needs help, such as having car trouble. Whenever possible, offer every assistance, or offer to call for assistance and then stand by to see that no harm befalls her before it arrives.

Delicate situations call for tact, diplomacy, intuition and a friendly but firm manner. If a fellow SigEp is not conducting himself as a gentleman, call him aside and address his behavior. He may be angry at the moment; but both he and the woman will be grateful later.

Above all, NEVER speak about your intimate relationships with a woman to another man. It always causes more grief for both of you than it was worth to boost your ego.

Table Manners

People who have good table manners are able to keep the mechanics of eating an incidental part of the dinner, giving their chief efforts to free and natural conversation. Men who do not know how to eat properly find eating in public an embarrassing, painful process for not only themselves but also for the other diners.

The business of eating should be handled quietly. Attract as little attention as possible when eating; relax and do not appear too stiff or too formal. Eat slowly and pause frequently to talk; take care to finish at the same time as others.

Recognize the three utensils that we eat with today—the knife, fork, and spoon. Each has a specific use, purpose, and a proper way to be handled. Normally, they are placed on the table in order of use, starting from the outside and working to the plate. A good guideline is to use a fork on a flat plate and a spoon with a bowl. It is also important to hold a knife, fork, and spoon properly.

Tips at the Table

▶ Enter your seat from the left. Exit your seat to the right.

▶ Sit straight up with both feet on the floor. Never slouch.

▶ If you leave the table during a meal, place the napkin on your seat.

▶ If you leave the table after a meal, place the napkin left of your plate.

▶ Keep your napkin folded in half on your lap during a meal.

▶ If needed, blot your mouth then replace your napkin in your lap.

▶ Never put used silverware back on the table. Place it on the plate.

▶ Place the knife on your plate with the blade facing inward.

▶ Place the knife and fork in the center of the plate parallel together when finished.

▶ Once a utensil is lifted from the table, always put it on the plate.

▶ Chew your food slowly and thoroughly.

▶ Pass food to your right; receive food from the left. Food is passed counterclockwise.

▶ When you are first to pass the bread basket, offer right then pass left.

▶ Always pass the salt and pepper shakers together.

▶ Take soup from side of spoon, scooping thitherwardly.

▶ Take small mouthfuls. After three bites, rest your utensil.

▶ Eat fruit, vegetables, and pie, with a fork...not a spoon.

▶ Keep the salad and bread plates to your left—do not move them around.

▶ Beverages are on the right, even if you are left-handed.

▶ Be natural and at ease.

Dining Out

This is where your social graces are really on display. Women, the restaurant staff, others in your party, the people around you in the restaurant, and interviewers will plainly see if you know what you are doing. Your tasks are simple but extremely important in making those around you feel at ease. It starts with you opening and holding the door.

YOUR TASKS ARE SIMPLE BUT EXTREMELY IMPORTANT IN MAKING THOSE AROUND YOU FEEL AT EASE. IT STARTS WITH YOU OPENING AND HOLDING THE DOOR.

Then continues with knowing who leads to the table, how to seat women properly and then yourself, ordering the meal for the woman (if she prefers) and ultimately paying the check and leaving a tip.

You must know in advance if reservations will be required and about dress requirements. Then remember the following:

▶ Upon entering a restaurant, you will probably be met by someone—host, hostess or maitre d'. When the table is ready, proceed with the host/hostess leading the way, followed by the woman and then you. If there is more than one woman, the older woman goes first and is followed by the younger one. The men bring up the rear, oldest to youngest again.

▶ Everyone is seated from the left side of his/her chair unless something prevents it.

▶ Ordering for the woman is courteous. It is even expected procedure in some "traditional" restaurants; place her order before yours.

▶ Tipping is expected unless there is a service charge on the bill. Expect to tip at least 15 percent unless you have had poor service; tell the head waiter of your poor service and of your reduced tip. Do not leave a small or no tip and leave without explaining. Do not, however, make a scene or appear rude. This will make others around you uncomfortable and really will not accomplish anything.

Personal Correspondence

When done correctly, personal notes are an excellent way to make a lasting and positive impression.

▶ A note should be legible and in your own handwriting, not typewritten. The note should be conversational and should not sound like a form letter. For "thank-you" notes, you should describe the name of the gift (if it is money, do not mention the amount), express your pleasure and appreciation in receiving the gift, and thank the person for his or her generosity and consideration.

Always look your best!

▶ Notes should promptly follow the occasion.

▶ Use plain note paper or stationery—perhaps with your name or monogram. Do not use a page from a spiral notebook.

▶ Check a good reference manual for the proper placement of date, etc.

▶ Email is popular and easy. It is better than no mail. Handwritten thank-you notes are best. Ask business people for permission to correspond by email.

Looking Sharp Every Day

The standards of dress and personal grooming vary from campus to campus, and according to the occasion, the way you wear your clothes is much more important than what clothes you wear.

Keep your eyes open...talk with those you trust...read the "Dress for Success" book. Your clothes should always be kept clean and neat. Properly cleaned and pressed clothes wear longer as well as look better. It's better to be over-dressed than under-dressed.

Regardless of how expensive or inexpensive your clothing is, you can keep it clean and you can wear it appropriately. You can also keep yourself clean and neat. This means more than frequent trips to the shower. Your fingernails and hair deserve careful attention. Fingernails should be kept short and clean. Hairstyles are a personal matter, but regardless of the style, the way you have it cut should look good on you. Avoid the excessive use of cologne and aftershave lotion—a very slight fragrance is OK, but the overwhelming smell of cologne can be offensive. Be well showered and clean.

Through observation, you will soon learn how you are expected to dress on campus. Remember that some on-campus styles are not appropriate off campus. Keep this in mind when you are in town to visit the office of an alumnus. A suit and tie or sport coat and slacks are much more appropriate.

Business casual is not "cargo pants and Birkenstock-type shoes." If you attend a "business casual" event, wear nice slacks, open collar shirt, and a jacket.

A good wardrobe is adaptable. Lean toward the traditional styles and rely on men's fashion classics, and you will end up with a selection of clothes that can survive shifting trends.

SEXUALITY

"A man of quality is not threatened by a woman of equality."

One of the most significant areas of personal development during the collegiate years is that of a person's sexuality. The fraternity experience offers you many opportunities to grow in social skills and awareness. This is equally true with the often puzzling and frequently misunderstood dimension of human sexuality. Just as there are many opportunities for growth, there are equally as many experiences which could hurt a man now and for years to come.

Personal Choices

The Balanced Man ought to be knowledgeable about the issues regarding sexual activity and, more importantly, prepared to make some serious decisions.

The choice to become sexually involved with someone should not be taken lightly. Every man knows that the physical part of sex is pleasurable; not every man understands that the psychological component is often more important and potentially damaging. During your college years, you should be earnestly involved in developing your personal identity. Part of this identity is defined by your sexuality. Sexuality is a complex array of feelings, emotions, and attractions—only one of which is the physical. Consider your values, morals,

and religious beliefs. They will shape and influence the decisions you make.

Sexual Health

In the 1980s, the issue of sexual health usually concentrated on such topics as conception, prevention of unwanted pregnancies, and sexually transmitted diseases. The 1990s opened a new era. While issues are still present, there are

SEXUALITY IS A COMPLEX ARRAY OF FEELINGS, EMOTIONS, AND ATTRACTIONS— ONLY ONE OF WHICH IS THE PHYSICAL.

new and perhaps more overriding concerns. There are now strains of sexually transmitted diseases that are relatively immune to normal treatment. Some, such as herpes, cannot be cured and must continually be treated. Others, such as hepatitis, are extremely contagious and life-threatening. And, there is AIDS, a disease which has captured the attention of the nation.

Acquired Immune Deficiency Syndrome (AIDS) is a deadly disease with no known cure. It is spread primarily through unsafe or unprotected sexual activities or through the sharing of unsterilized drug apparatus (needles, nasal sniffers, etc.). Once thought to be confined to the male homosexual population of large cities, this disease is now quite prevalent within the heterosexual community and knows no geographic or socio-economic boundaries.

With an incubation period from six months to 10 years, many seemingly healthy young men and women are unknowingly infected with the AIDS virus (labeled HIV) and are potentially infecting others with whom they are having risky contact. Perhaps as much as one to two percent of the population affected with the virus is asymptomatic (carriers infected with HIV but who display none of the symptoms of AIDS).

SIGMA PHI EPSILON POLICY STATES, "IF A BROTHER OF SIGMA PHI EPSILON IS STRICKEN WITH AIDS, THEN HE SHOULD BE TREATED LIKE ANY OTHER BROTHER AFFLICTED WITH A LIFE-THREATENING ILLNESS—WITH UTMOST DIGNITY AND BROTHERLY LOVE."

Understanding how this disease affects and infects people is important. Equally important is the knowledge that AIDS is *not* transmitted through casual contact (shaking hands, sharing eating utensils, etc.). To be transmitted, the infected body fluids (blood, semen, or vaginal secretions) of the infected person must come into contact with the blood (through an open cut or wound or through a porous membrane) of the non-infected person. While AIDS testing is helpful (for example, in screening the blood supply), it is not always accurate.

Sigma Phi Epsilon policy states, "If a brother of Sigma Phi Epsilon is stricken with AIDS, then he should be treated like any other brother afflicted with a life-threatening illness—with utmost dignity and Brotherly Love."

Encourage your chapter to have frank discussions about AIDS, date rape and issues of tolerance.

At the 2005 Conclave in Nashville, SigEp extended its strategic partnership with YouthAIDS. YouthAIDS is working in more than 60 countries to educate and protect young people from HIV/AIDS. Ashley Judd is the Global Ambassador for YouthAIDS and is seen here with SigEps from the University of Kentucky. For more information visit www.youthaids.org.

Group Behavior

The synergy that can develop within a fraternity is astounding. It can empower a group to accomplish many things that far exceed our normal expectations. The group becomes greater than the sum of its parts. This synergistic effect often results in very positive behavior. Occasionally, however, it can lead to very negative outcomes in men participating in activities that, individually, they would never consider. Such is especially the case regarding actions that are abusive or insulting to women or to people with a different sexual orientation. Sexually abusive behavior on the part of a chapter or its members has been the death knell to all too many groups. Such behavior is not tolerated in Sigma Phi Epsilon.

Rape &
Sexual Assault

Date or acquaintance rape is a continuing problem on college campuses today. Those who would

SEXUALLY ABUSIVE AND INTOLERANT BEHAVIOR ON THE PART OF A CHAPTER OR ITS MEMBERS HAS BEEN THE DEATH KNELL TO ALL TOO MANY GROUPS.

discount date rape as an excuse or a problem of perception are tragically mistaken. Date rape is a real problem, a real crime, with real and tragic consequences for all involved.

Men serve prison terms for date rape, and the women these men abuse are physically and psychologically scarred for life. Many times, date rape can be prevented by thinking, talking, listening and sobriety. Here are some facts about date rape.

▶ Rape is a crime of violence, motivated primarily by the desire to control and dominate, rather than by sexual desire. Rape is illegal.

▶ Forcing yourself on a woman is never okay, even if:

> ▶ She teases you.
> ▶ She dresses provocatively or leads you on.
> ▶ She says "no," and you think she means "yes."
> ▶ You've had sex with her before.
> ▶ You've paid for her dinner or given her expensive gifts.
> ▶ You think women enjoy being forced to have sex or want to be persuaded.
> ▶ The woman is under the influence of alcohol or drugs.

▶ No one ASKS to be raped. No matter how a woman behaves, she does not deserve to have her body used in ways she does not want.

▶ "No" means NO. If you do not accept a woman's "no," you might risk raping someone whom you THOUGHT meant "yes."

▶ The fact that you were intoxicated is not a legal defense to rape. You are responsible for your actions, whether you are sober or not.

▶ Be aware that a man's size and physical presence can be intimidating to a woman. Many victims report that the fear they felt based on the man's size and presence was the reason why they did not fight back or struggle.

Points to Consider

▶ Do not assume you know what your partner wants.

▶ Confirm your assumptions; communicate with your partner.

▶ Be sensitive to whether the woman wants to have sex.

▶ If you put pressure on the woman, you may be forcing her.

▶ Do not assume you both want the same degree of intimacy.

▶ A woman may not be interested in sexual contact.

▶ Ask yourself if you are really HEARING what she wants.

▶ Do not let your desires control your actions.

▶ If you have ANY doubts, STOP. ASK. CLARIFY.

▶ Not having sex is okay. You do not have to "score."

▶ A woman who turns you down for sex is not necessarily rejecting you.

Questions for Personal Consideration

1. How would you define the terms: sexism, sexual abuse, rape, and date rape?

2. Have you ever been involved in an event in which you succumbed to peer pressure, doing something you would never have done alone? Was it positive or negative? How do you feel about that event now?

3. What programs or events in your chapter might be considered by outsiders as "sexist"?

4. What could be done to eliminate such programs?

5. In what ways is date rape different from rape by a stranger? Are the criminal penalties any different?

6. Where could you go for additional information or help on this matter?

INDIVIDUALITY

"As we let our own light shine, we unconsciously give other people permission to do the same."

~ NELSON MANDELA

A Fraternity of Individuals

In Sigma Phi Epsilon, not only do members have to be conscious of themselves, but they must be conscious of the principles and standards of the group. Unlike some organizations, the Fraternity has values that need to be "lived" to preserve the integrity of the organization.

Each member of the Fraternity binds himself to its values and ideals through his Oath of Obligation. This oath also requires a member to actively maintain the good name of Sigma Phi Epsilon. Sometimes, when a member's "individuality" is overriding the group's integrity, the group must remind the individual of his obligations.

The Fraternity values individuality and rewards individual accomplishments. Sigma Phi Epsilon is driven by individual contributions and that is always recognized. However, each individual must evaluate his needs and the needs of Sigma Phi Epsilon to keep them in balance.

Rights & Responsibilities

The following section is from *Campus Values*, Northeastern University.

Once secured, the right of individual expression, like any other right, can be used responsibly or irresponsibly. If individual expression is to be exercised wisely, it must be applied with judgment and not blindly as an automatic response in all situations. Like muscular power, its effectiveness is diminished when no considerations or principles other than strength are used to guide its application. To the degree that today's collegians continue to enjoy success in their fight for expression, they will find that winning the war to express themselves was easier than maintaining the peace of appropriate application of this right.

Each individual who is capable of doing so has an obligation to speak out in order to help creatively reform society. Without individual expression, this essential function cannot be accomplished. This obligation applies to youth as well as to the more mature. When one recognizes that youth can make a constructive contribution to society,

EACH INDIVIDUAL MUST EVALUATE HIS NEEDS AND THE NEEDS OF SIGMA PHI EPSILON TO KEEP THEM IN BALANCE.

the critical question becomes how youth can learn to apply this right constructively, effectively, and in ways which will serve to maintain and enhance it.

Constructive and artful exercise of the right of individual expression involves many considerations. Examination of a few of these considerations will point up the complex learning and judgment-making which are involved in an individual's exercising this right constructively.

Balancing Individual & Group Concerns

One of the first considerations about which an individual must make judgments when expressing himself is how to strike a balance between individual and group concerns. On many campuses today, such an inquiry elicits a response that the rights of individual expression are inviolable. The argument for this position is supported by the idea that, short of barbaric violations of another's rights, an individual is accountable only to himself for his actions. This appears to provide a simple and sensible rationale for resolving all complexities involved in individual and group relations.

However, research accumulated in the field

of group dynamics indicates that the individual's behavior has a variety of influence on a group. The individual's behavior should, to a degree, be governed by the needs of the group because what he does has consequences for the group as a group and for the other individuals in the group *as individuals.*

Benefits the Group Provides

Another finding from research suggests that groups can provide unique benefits for individuals in helping their development. However, to carry on its work and provide these benefits for its individual members, each group or organization must provide for certain group needs, functions, structure, and so forth.

Opting only for individual expression when one is a member of a group or of an organization may mean the forfeiture of individual expression for some

other members of the group. This is not simply the problem that when several people express themselves often and at length, there is no time left for others to express themselves. There is, in addition, a more subtle problem. To obtain the constructive contributions (individual expressions) of all its members, a group must establish a climate

Meaningful Individuality

By Charles W. Havice

Some argue that individual expression must be nurtured and championed as a means of resisting the depersonalizing forces in modern American life. And so it must. But rigid, rote adherence to individual expression is only a means of depersonalizing independent expression. To be most human, most a person, necessarily involves thought, judgment, and the ability to discern when to submerge one's precious individuality, or right to express it, to the need of others. One can never have meaningful individuality or the right of expression until he has learned when and where to give it up and when not to use it. The right of individual expression becomes a personalizing force only as each individual makes thoughtful decisions which constructively shape its application and limitations.

which is conducive to reasonable expressions of opinion and concern and a climate which ensures that all will feel reasonably comfortable in speaking. This climate requires such things as a reasonable degree of order and some form of structure. It requires further that group members take it upon themselves to protect the less forward members from the more outspoken and to guarantee the opportunity for everyone's view to be given a fair hearing.

If loud, aggressive, irrelevant, or self-indulgent expressions dominate a group's functioning, the climate will be such that many individuals will not feel free to express themselves. Group members, as well as the leader, have to contribute to the development of a climate in which all members are given an opportunity to make constructive contributions. Individual judgments about the relevance of each remark are necessary if the group is to move toward its goals, maintain the attention and interest of its members, and have the benefit of its quieter, more reflective members.

Questions for Personal Consideration

1. Where do you draw the line between individuality and group standards? ...for inappropriate behavior that reflects on Sigma Phi Epsilon? ...academic achievement? ...self-destructive behavior? ...financial obligations?

2. What standards has your chapter set regarding behavior? Are they enforced? How could they be improved?

3. What concerns do you have regarding the behavior of your brothers?

A SigEp bows his head during the Necrology at the 48th Grand Chapter Conclave in San Antonio.

SPIRITUALITY & RELIGION

"No one could tell me where my soul might be;
I searched for God but he eluded me; I sought my
brother out and found all three."

~ ERNEST HOWARD CROSBY

The teachings and principles of Sigma Phi Epsilon embody the teachings and principles of the great religious philosophies of the world—each conveying the affirmation that life has meaning and purpose. Although no allegiance to a particular creed or religion is required, each member must hold high values and principles, namely Virtue, Diligence, and Brotherly Love.

Sigma Phi Epsilon is not a religion or sect. However, the root of the word religion refers to realignment, and Sigma Phi Epsilon's Cardinal Principles of Virtue, Diligence, and Brotherly Love give members a guide for daily realignment in their lives.

In 1901, Sigma Phi Epsilon's Founders set out to establish Virtue, Diligence, and Brotherly Love as viable principles to guide a man's life. The Fraternity should only add to the values, teachings and principles you bring with you, either from your family, church, synagogue, or mosque. The Fraternity's teachings are meant to *enhance* one's life and should in no way interfere with your personal beliefs.

A man's spirituality should grow in the fraternity experience. A chapter is a spiritual entity in and of itself. The chapter and each member must work to discover the principles that fulfill men spiritually. Whether the chapter attends a different place of worship each week, holds study groups, or simply encourages spiritual and "religious" growth, the chapter must be a place of reverence for higher principles and a source of strength for each member.

The Fraternity calls us into something greater than ourselves, with the realization that we are a part of a larger process, a greater meaning, and a higher purpose. The experience of the spiritual tends to "grasp us," touching us in ways we could never make happen on our own. The experience of brotherhood is spiritual because it draws us into intimate relationships based on shared commitments to high ideals and a belief that life has purpose and meaning. The Oath of Obligation of Sigma Phi Epsilon is sacred and, when embraced as such, draws us into the world of the sacred...something greater than ourselves.

A belief in God or a power greater than ourselves places demands on our being. We are asked to measure ourselves in accord with those beliefs, and this ideal of brotherhood also places demands on us to live in response to higher principles and values.

RESPONSIBILITY:
SIGMA PHI EPSILON

RESPONSIBILITY:
SIGMA PHI EPSILON

"Some men see things as they are and ask why. I dream things that never were and ask why not."

~ JOHN F. KENNEDY

Part I of this book gave insight into the responsibility you have for yourself and an understanding of key areas that affect your self-esteem, self-respect, self-confidence and self-talk. Part III of this book will help you in your relationships with the community, following the principle, "Love thy neighbor as thyself."

Part II of *The Lifetime Responsibility of Brotherhood* is designed to help you ensure the best possible fraternity experience for you and your Brothers. Make the most of it. You control the quality of your chapter. Seek excellence in all areas and an experience that fosters balance in its members. Sigma Phi Epsilon deserves nothing less. You deserve nothing less.

By joining Sigma Phi Epsilon, you have made a decision that will affect the rest of your life. In the coming months, years and decades, through your involvement in Sigma Phi Epsilon, you will develop your skills and talents through leadership, service, time management, academics, meaningful relationships, and more.

You were invited into membership in Sigma Phi Epsilon because the men in your chapter identified traits in you that are becoming of a SigEp Brother. You are now a part of one of the greatest college fraternities in America. You should be proud and honored.

This also means that you have certain expectations to uphold for as long as you are a member. You now represent Sigma Phi Epsilon in everything you do. Your conduct should be above that of the "rest of the crowd." Your academic performance should be above that of others—after all, that *is* what you came to school for in the first place. You are not common; you are expected to strive for excellence in all areas to become a Balanced Man.

We expect you to be a good member—an integral part of the chapter "team." Your membership development program should be designed to include all members of the chapter and emphasize building a Sound Mind and a Sound Body. The intent of any good development program is to create *Balanced Men*. Remember, all members of Sigma Phi Epsilon are on a journey of brotherhood. There is no finish line. Likewise, there is no point at which your chapter's development program should end.

You should expect a fraternity experience that is positive in every way. You will be a much greater person when you receive your diploma because you are a SigEp, and SigEp will be a much greater Fraternity because of you.

**YOU ARE NOT COMMON;
YOU ARE EXPECTED TO STRIVE
FOR EXCELLENCE IN
ALL AREAS TO BECOME
A BALANCED MAN.**

Purdue Brothers, 1906

THE AMERICAN COLLEGE FRATERNITY

"I like the dreams of the future better than the history of the past."

~ THOMAS JEFFERSON

TO UNDERSTAND SIGMA PHI EPSILON, YOU MUST UNDERSTAND THE AMERICAN COLLEGE FRATERNITY.

The year 1776 holds special significance because it marks the birth of the United States of America and the beginning of the American Revolutionary War.

That year is of importance for another, less-known reason.

The "revolutionary spirit" in the American colonies also found its way into the realm of higher education and aided in the beginning of the American college fraternity.

College students in this period had a limited and strict curriculum. Studies centered around Greek and Latin, and electives were virtually non-existent. Higher education emphasized strict discipline and was primarily limited to book learning; little time was allowed for fun and relaxation.

This is not to say, however, that extra-curricular activities did not exist. Students had to make an extra effort to find relaxation and to learn about life and reality outside of the classroom.

In 1750, students at the College of William & Mary in Williamsburg, Virginia, would gather at Raleigh Tavern and talk over a bowl of punch.

Some regulars to this punch-bowl discussion formed an official group, calling themselves the Flat Hat Club. The nature of this society is uncertain, but these men, unknowingly, had organized the first general college fraternity.

Other groups at William & Mary followed their example, but they were socially limited. They concerned themselves with becoming literary societies in hopes of meeting with faculty approval. They met to discuss or critique compositions or to stage oratorical contests. The names they called their groups denoted their purpose: Ciceronian, Calliopian, and Philopeuthion, to name three.

One of these groups determined that a student, John Heath, a superior Greek scholar, was unworthy of membership. Heath, rejected but undaunted, took three Greek letters and four friends and held the first meeting of what was to become the first secret Greek-letter society or fraternity—

DECEMBER 5, 1776: WILLIAM & MARY STUDENT JOHN HEATH ESTABLISHED THE PHI BETA KAPPA SOCIETY

Phi Beta Kappa. The Apollo Room of the Raleigh Tavern, where Phi Beta Kappa was born, was also the place where men such as Thomas Jefferson, George Washington, and Patrick Henry met to discuss the ideas that led to the birth of another great society in that same year—the United States of America.

Phi Beta Kappa developed a secret grip, mottos, a ritual, a code of laws, and a distinctive badge. Those five elements remain today as the trademark elements to fraternities. The most important legacies of Phi Beta Kappa, however, are their commitment to *moral ideals, scholastic achievement,* and *friendship between men.* Phi Beta Kappa believed the college experience should prepare the student for future responsibilities by preparing him socially. They shared this belief with other campuses and founded new chapters at Harvard and Yale in 1779 with more to follow. As time progressed, Phi Beta Kappa turned its attention toward purely intellectual matters and became a scholastic honorary, revealing that its name meant "Philosophy, the Guide of Life." Today, Phi Beta Kappa recognizes undergraduate men and women who show superior achievements in academics and extra-curricular activities on more than 270 college campuses.

PHI BETA KAPPA TOOK ITS PRINCIPLES OF "LITERATURE, MORALITY, AND FRIENDSHIP" TO OTHER CAMPUSES AND BECAME THE CORNERSTONE OF OTHER GREEK-LETTER ORGANIZATIONS.

Phi Beta Kappa took its principles of "literature, morality, and friendship" to other campuses and became the cornerstone of other Greek-letter organizations. Four Phi Beta Kappa men at the University of North Carolina took the lead in 1812 and organized Kappa Alpha, which then expanded to 20 campuses throughout the South. Unfortunately, it would not survive the Civil War.

Other local fraternities arose after Kappa Alpha. Pi Beta Phi was founded in 1813, followed by Chi Delta Theta in 1821, and Chi Phi in 1824. Only Chi Phi survived, becoming the basis for Chi Phi Society at Princeton in 1854. This society has had continuous existence since that date.

The Union Triad

While Phi Beta Kappa became national in character with its expansion to Harvard and Yale in 1779, the social roots of fraternities did not come to seed until a chapter of Phi Beta Kappa was established at Union College in Schenectady, New York. Inspired by this founding, John Hunter and other members of the class of 1826 formed the Kappa Alpha Society (not to be confused with Kappa Alpha of 1812 or the modern Kappa Alpha Order) which was to become the first national organization to endure as a men's general national social fraternity to this day. Due to its secrecy, this society was opposed by the Union faculty and some students. Other students, admiring the Kappa Alpha Society concept, founded Sigma Phi and Delta Phi in 1827. These three, known as the Union Triad, put the American college fraternity on the map.

Orville Dow, Colorado '28

The Beta Alpha Chapter of Theta Upsilon Omega (TUO) in 1931. When TUO merged with SigEp this chapter became the Massachusetts Beta Chapter at Worchester Polytechnic Institute.

Eventually, Union students founded six fraternities which has earned Union College the honored epithet of "Mother of Fraternities."

Fraternities continued to expand with Sigma Phi founding a second chapter at Hamilton College in Clinton, New York. Hamilton students, inspired by this founding and seeking an alternative to two rival literary societies, founded Alpha Delta Phi, another Greek-letter society, in 1832. Alpha Delta Phi expanded to a second chapter, this time west of the Allegheny Mountains at Miami University in Oxford, Ohio.

The Miami Triad

A prominent student of Miami University, John Reilly Knox, envisioned a society similar in organization and spirit of Alpha Delta Phi but based on "good without the ingredient of evil." With this in mind,

Knox formed the first fraternity founded west of the Alleghenies in Beta Theta Pi in 1839.

Beta Theta Pi and Alpha Delta Phi both had to exist in secret due to the disapproval of the Miami faculty. In 1847, members of the organizations were expelled after they were found to have taken part in a student revolt against the Miami University administration. This left the campus virtually without fraternities. To fill this void, Phi Delta Theta was founded in 1848 and Sigma Chi in 1855. Thus, Beta Theta Pi, Phi Delta Theta, and Sigma Chi became known as the Miami Triad.

Founding of Sororities

The decade of the 1850s also marked the beginning of women's fraternities and sororities with the founding of the Adelphian Society at Wesleyan Female College in Macon, Georgia, in 1851, and the Philoniathean Society in 1852. For 50 years, these remained local in nature until expanding with the Greek names Alpha Delta Pi and Phi Mu, respectively. Sororities were on the move.

By the beginning of the 1860s, 22 of the present-day national fraternities had been founded. However, in 1861, fraternities, as well as the nation, were threatened by the outbreak of a great conflict pitting brother against brother—the Civil War. The war forced many colleges and fraternities to be closed and halted expansion and development of new ones. Only one fraternity was founded during the war, Theta Xi at Rensselaer Polytechnic Institute in Troy, New York, in 1865. Theta Xi was formed as the first professional fraternity and later became a general college fraternity.

During the war, whole chapters enlisted in the South to fight for the Confederacy. Men from fraternities, North and South, fought each other for four bloody years. What fraternities had sought to achieve— friendship among brothers—was almost destroyed by the war, leaving the country with deep wounds to heal at its end.

Because of their beliefs and commitments, fraternities were well suited to the task of healing those wounds. Alpha Tau Omega was the first to answer the call, becoming the first fraternity founded after the Civil War. Close behind was Kappa Alpha Order

MIT Brothers in the '80s. Today, Sigma Phi Epsilon has chapters on over 255 campuses across the United States.

in 1865, Pi Kappa Alpha in 1868, and Sigma Nu and Kappa Sigma in 1869. All of these were founded in Virginia, and all are in existence today.

Following the war, many changes occurred in the fraternity world. The most significant of these was the increased enrollment of women in colleges across the nation. Some women noticed the advantages and admired the qualities of the fraternal experience and began forming their own groups. I. C. Sororsis, now Pi Beta Phi (not to be confused with Pi Beta Phi of 1813), was founded at Monmouth College in Monmouth, Illinois, in 1867, becoming the first

> WHAT FRATERNITIES HAD SOUGHT TO ACHIEVE— FRIENDSHIP AMONG BROTHERS—WAS ALMOST DESTROYED BY THE WAR, LEAVING THE COUNTRY WITH DEEP WOUNDS TO HEAL AT ITS END.

national sorority. I. C. Sororsis was followed by Kappa Alpha Theta in 1870 at DePauw University in Greencastle, Indiana. Kappa Alpha Theta is known as the first women's Greek-letter society. Sororities were now established on American college campuses.

Fraternities experienced hard times near the end of the 1890s as anti-fraternity legislation threatened their existence. However, the strong fraternities survived, as people again realized the importance of fraternities and what they endeavored to achieve. Several fraternities were founded at the beginning of the new century, and others continued expanding. A few

ambitious men were working hard to found fraternities based on high moral ideals, scholastic achievement, and lifelong friendship between brothers. In the year 1901, one such farsighted individual was attending Richmond College in Richmond, Virginia. He formed a bond of fellowship with five other men and sought to create a new fraternity, based on the love of God and the principle of peace through brotherhood. These six men were to be the first Founders of our great Fraternity, Sigma Phi Epsilon.

Now, Sigma Phi Epsilon has a chapter at Miami University (Ohio) and on over 255 others campuses across the United States.

Famed politician and orator William Jennings Bryan and Ohio Northern University President Smith at the dedication of the Ohio Northern chapter house in 1916.

Ryland Hall, 1901, the birthplace of Sigma Phi Epsilon. Members originally met in the dormitory room of Founders Gaw and Wallace. After the group was recognized as an official student organization, the group was granted the Tower Room in the center of Ryland Hall for official fraternity functions.

THE HISTORY OF SIGMA PHI EPSILON

This Fraternity will be different; it will be based on the love of God and the principle of peace through brotherhood...its purpose shall be to intensify and perpetuate friendship and promote happiness among its members, to encourage literature and education, and to create such sentiments, mold such opinions, and perform such deeds as shall conduce to the building of a noble and pure manhood.

~ SIGEP CHARTER,
OCTOBER 20, 1902

The Place of our Origin

Richmond College, where Sigma Phi Epsilon was founded in the early 20th Century, was, at the time, attended by a mere 200 students, and perhaps between a third and a half of this number belonged to five fraternities. Kappa Alpha Order had come there in 1870, Phi Kappa Sigma in 1873, Phi Gamma Delta in 1890, Pi Kappa Alpha in 1891, and Kappa Sigma in 1898. Phi Delta Theta, Sigma Chi, and Sigma Alpha Epsilon also had established chapters there which had expired. The little Baptist college was founded in 1830, and many of its graduates became Baptist ministers.

Most of the national fraternities, as their histories show, have been established simply because they were needed. The hunger for brotherhood was at the bottom of an unrest in young men's souls. Sigma Phi Epsilon was founded because 12 young collegians hungered for a campus fellowship based on ideals that neither the college community nor the fraternity system at the time could offer. Sigma Phi Epsilon was needed. It was founded, moreover, because the leadership which is required for such a project asserted itself in fortunate ways.

Sigma Phi Epsilon Founded

THERE SHALL BE ONLY ONE DEGREE CONFERRED BY ANY SUB-CHAPTER AND ANY PERSON TAKING SAID DEGREE SHALL BE TERMED A SIGMA PHI EPSILON AND SHALL BE CALLED "BROTHER," THOUGH HE MAY BE REFERRED TO AS A "MEMBER."

SIGMA PHI EPSILON *Constitution & Laws*, 1908, ONE OF THE EARLIEST KNOWN EDITIONS OF FRATERNITY BY-LAWS, DEFINING MEMBERSHIP IN THE FRATERNITY. UPON ACCEPTING AN INVITATION TO JOIN SIGMA PHI EPSILON, A MAN WAS CONSIDERED A BROTHER.

Carter Ashton Jenkens, the 18-year-old son of a minister, had been a student at Rutgers University, New Jersey, where he had joined Chi Phi Fraternity. When he transferred to Richmond College in the Fall of 1900, he sought companions to take the place of the Chi Phi brothers he had left behind at Rutgers. During the course of the term, he found five men who had already been drawn into a bond of an informal fellowship, and he urged them to join him in applying for a charter of Chi Phi at Richmond College. They agreed, and the request for charter was forwarded to Chi Phi only to meet with refusal because Chi Phi felt that Richmond College, as any college with less than 300 students, was too small for the establishment of a Chi Phi chapter.

Wanting to maintain their fellowship, the six men, Jenkens, William Carter, Thomas Wright, William Phillips, Benjamin Gaw, and William Wallace, decided to form their own local fraternity.

Of the six, Jenkens was the only one who really knew what a fraternity was, so the task of drawing the plans for the new fraternity fell to him.

The Jenkens Lesson

As he so often told the story of the founding, the following passage became known as "The Jenkens Lesson." Brother Jenkens was sitting at his desk one evening, studying a passage of Greek for the next day, and he fell asleep and dreamed.

"I dreamed that I saw a great black cloud over this University," he said, "and I saw lightning, and heard the reverberations of the thunder. I saw nations at war, I saw homes destroyed; I saw ten hundred thousand monuments to the newly dead soldiers of the earth. And I asked the Recording Angel, who stood by my side, what meant such a scene in the University of God. And he answered me quietly, saying, 'Men have failed to understand the simple teachings of the Prince of the Earth.'

"I woke, and I bowed my head and when I slept the Angel returned and he showed me a world in which the cloud had broken. I saw children, neatly clad, wending their way to school. I saw workmen singing for joy at their work. I saw the churches filled, institutions of learning crowded, and the nations of the earth were at peace, every nation with its brother nation.

"And I asked the Angel of God what had brought about this change in the old universe. And he pointed me to a passage of Scripture, in Matthew 22:37 to 40— 'Thou shalt love the Lord thy God with all thy heart, and with all thy soul, and with all thy mind. This is the first and great commandment. And the second is like unto it, 'Thou shalt love thy neighbor as thyself.'

"Thus the name of Sigma Phi Epsilon was born in the philosophy of love—the only foundation on which the world can have peace. This is the principle on which our Fraternity was founded."

Early records described young Jenkens' thorough search for a philosophy upon which a new college fraternity could be built. He discovered in the Bible what he called "the greatest truth the world has ever known."

The First Meeting

While in the formative stages, the six original found six others who were also searching for a campus fellowship that neither the college campus nor the existing fraternity system could offer. The six new members were Lucian Cox, Richard Owens, Edgar Allen, Robert McFarland, Franklin Kerfoot, and Thomas McCaul.

The 12 met one day in October, 1901, in Gaw and Wallace's room on the third floor of Ryland Hall to discuss organization of the Fraternity they would call "Sigma Phi." The exact date of this meeting is not known, and if any minutes were kept, they have been lost. However, the meeting was probably held before the middle of the month, because the 12 founders are named as members on November 1, 1901, in the first printed roster of the Fraternity. Jenkens is listed as the first member.

Fraternity Recognized

A committee of Jenkens, Gaw, and Phillips was appointed to discuss plans with the administration of the college. These men met with a faculty committee, where they requested to present their case. The fraternity committee requested that the new group explain:

1. The need for a new fraternity since chapters of five national fraternities were on the campus and the total enrollment at Richmond College was less than 300.

Fifteen of Sigma Phi Epsilon's first 21 members. This photograph was taken in 1901-1902 when Sigma Phi Epsilon was a local fraternity at Richmond College. Front row, left to right: W. H. Carter, C. H. Howell, C. A. Jenkens, R. A. McFarland, T. V. McCaul, L. B. Cox, W. A. Wallace. Back row, left to right: W. L. Phillips, C. W. Dickinson, Jr., R. L. Hudgins, J. E. Oliver, T. T. Wright, E. M. Gathright, E. W. Hudgins, R. R. Oliver. Not pictured: B. D. Gaw, R. S. Owens, E. L. Allen, F. W. Kerfoot, W. D. Wildman, A. M. Kerfoot.

2. The wisdom of this attempt to organize a new fraternity with 12 members, of whom seven were seniors.

3. The right to name the new fraternity Sigma Phi, the name of an already established national fraternity.

The fraternity committee answered: "This fraternity will be different, it will be based on the love of God and the principle of peace through brotherhood. The number of members will be increased from the undergraduate classes. We will change the name to Sigma Phi Epsilon." Though the discussion lasted some time, the faculty committee was friendly, and permission was granted for the organization of the new fraternity to proceed, provided full responsibility for the consequences would rest on the group of 12 students.

> **"AS A MEMBER OF AN IDEAL FRATERNITY, THE RESOURCES OF EVERY MEMBER OF THAT BODY ARE MY RESOURCES..."**
>
> ~ FOUNDER LUCIAN COX

Immediately at the close of the conference with the faculty committee, the fraternity committee rushed to Jenkens' room to borrow Hugh Carter's Greek-English Lexicon; convinced themselves that Epsilon had a desirable meaning, and then telegraphed jeweler Eaton in Goldsboro, North Carolina, to add an E at the point of each of the 12 badges which were manufactured and ready for

shipment. Before the job of adding an E on the badges was complete, eight other students were invited to join SigEp. The purchase order was then increased to 20 badges at $8 each, with the initials of each man engraved on the back of his badge.

These 20 original heart-shaped badges were of yellow gold, with alternating rubies and garnets around the edge of the heart, with the Greek characters ΣΦ and the skull and crossbones in gold and black enamel in the center and a black E in gold at the point. (William Hugh Carter's and Thomas V. "Uncle Tom" McCaul's original badges are on display at Zollinger House.)

Founder Lucian Cox reflected on the "brotherhood that had inspired him and his Brothers" when he wrote in the Sigma Phi Epsilon *Journal*, Vol. 1 No. 1, March, 1904: "As a member of an ideal fraternity, the resources of every member of that body are my resources, the product of their lives is my daily life. The Fraternity is a common storehouse for experience, moral rectitude, and spirituality; the larger and purer the contribution of the individual the greater the resources of each member."

Five men were invited to join before Christmas and became members in January, 1902. The last three of the first group of 20 joined on February 1, 1902, and another in March.

Meeting in the Tower Room

In November or December, 1901, an unheated, unfurnished single room, about 10 by 12 feet, in the tower of Ryland Hall, was assigned to the new fraternity by the college. Before January 1, 1902, SigEps had lined all open wall space with wide board benches. The wall was papered—purple and red. A rostrum, shaped like a horseshoe, was built in a corner. The small oil stove would not heat the room, so secret meetings continued to be held in SigEp dormitory rooms until March, 1902.

Virginia Alpha's Second Year

By March 4, 1902, the number of SigEps stood at 21 out of the total of 209 students enrolled. Seven of these 21 SigEps graduated in June, 1902, and six others did not return to college the following September. Of the remaining eight who did return to Richmond College the next session, only two were Founders—Gaw and Wright. College records show that of the eight who returned, four were sophomores, three juniors, and one a senior.

After recruiting many students, only one new man joined in the fall, and another in the spring. The small college enrollment of 223 students in the session of 1902-1903, no hope for a large increase of enrollment in the next few years, and increasing competition for new members from the chapters of five national fraternities on the campus made the members of Sigma Phi Epsilon realize the crucial position of their local fraternity.

Founder Carter Remembers

Before his death in 1971, in an interview with the Sigma Phi Epsilon Headquarters staff, Founder William Hugh Carter remembered these months.

"…*It was in the tower of the middle section of the main building. Yes, and Billy Phillips papered it himself. He had some experience in paper hanging. We didn't have any money; there wasn't a man in the crowd that had any money. We paid 25 cents a month dues, and I think we paid a two dollar membership fee, a dollar the first month and a dollar later. We bought paper and material for the benches we made. Billy hung the paper—a purple background with red flowers in it—then we made the benches and padded the tops of them with excelsior and covered them with cretonne.*

"*We had big ideas—even discussed buying a home there on Grace Street as our fraternity home. We were going to take out an insurance policy on one man's life, the Fraternity pay for the premium, and borrow money on that policy to buy the house. Oh, we had big ideas.*"

After discussing the situation at several meetings, a momentous decision was reached. Sigma Phi Epsilon must either convert the local into a national fraternity immediately or watch the local die. The secretary was instructed to request Founder Lucian B. Cox, an attorney in Norfolk, Virginia, to write an application for a state charter for Sigma Phi Epsilon Fraternity and return it to him at the earliest possible moment.

This charter was signed by all eight SigEps enrolled at Richmond College on October 18, filed in the Circuit Court of Richmond City on October 20, and recorded by the Secretary of the Commonwealth of Virginia on October 22, 1902. (The original charter is on display at Sigma Phi Epsilon Headquarters.) Under that state charter, Virginia Alpha established chapters at five other colleges that session; one of these, at West Virginia University, is active today.

Sigma Phi Epsilon's Growth

Sigma Phi Epsilon ended its fifth year of operation with 14 chapters in nine states. Nineteen chapters had been chartered, despite the little money that the group had to work with. But the will of our first Brothers to expand and develop our Fraternity prevailed, and chapters spread west to Colorado,

A MOMENTOUS DECISION WAS REACHED IN THE SPRING OF 1903. SIGMA PHI EPSILON MUST EITHER CONVERT THE LOCAL INTO A NATIONAL FRATERNITY IMMEDIATELY OR WATCH THE LOCAL CHAPTER DIE.

north to Illinois, Indiana, Ohio, and New York, and south to North and South Carolina.

The next five years brought forth 17 new chapters and representation in a total of eighteen states. In addition to those mentioned, Sigma Phi Epsilon was chartered in Alabama, Arkansas, California, Delaware, Georgia, Kansas, Nebraska, New Hampshire, Vermont, and the District of Columbia. And this momentum continued with the appointment of the first Grand Secretary of Sigma Phi Epsilon.

Our First Grand Secretary

William L. Phillips, Sigma Phi Epsilon's first Grand Secretary, in 1938

The fifth Grand Chapter Conclave, held in 1908, is particularly significant because it was at this Conclave that the laws were changed to provide for a central office and the employment of a full-time chief executive officer to bear the title of Grand Secretary. Founder William L. Phillips ("Uncle Billy") was employed as Grand Secretary and, according to the minutes, was to receive a salary of $900 in the first year.

An article by Francis W. Shepardson, first published in the 1927 edition of *Baird's Manual of American College Fraternities*, refers to the "latest development in fraternity administration...the establishment of a central office (headquarters) with a full-time secretary in charge." It is apparent from this that the Grand Chapter of Sigma Phi Epsilon, in taking this step, was showing remarkable forethought as a pioneer in fraternity administration, as it was to be later, in being one of the first two fraternities to own a headquarters building.

In slightly less than 10 years, Sigma Phi Epsilon had grown from a single chapter to a fraternity with chapters in 21 states and the District of Columbia.

War, Depression & Recovery

World War I took its toll on college attendance, and had an adverse effect on fraternities, both in membership and expansion.

The *Journal* editor reported: "Already men are leaving in large numbers, while a great many institutions...devote their athletic fields to drilling..." Congress passed a draft bill with age limits from 21 to 30 years. The editor advised all chapters that, "while fulfilling every duty to our country, let us also strive to maintain every chapter."

The cover of the October, 1917, *Journal* featured two SigEps in army uniforms. Grand President Knauss wrote of his pride in the Brothers' response to the call of duty. He warned, however, "The ranks of active fraternity men have been depleted all over the country...these are trying times, and for some chapters, they will be crucial ones." He also recommended that each chapter buy a Liberty Bond to help fund the war effort.

As an institution, Sigma Phi Epsilon survived World War I well. While three chapters were in danger of closing, only one—Rhode Island Alpha at Brown University—failed to survive the war.

IN 1924, 24 OF OUR 50 ACTIVE CHAPTERS WERE RATED BY THEIR PEERS IN THE TOP HALF OF ALL FRATERNITIES IN QUALITY ON THEIR CAMPUSES.

It was during our third decade that the quality of our chapters was first measured annually by the independent College Survey Bureau. In 1924, 24 of our 50 active chapters were rated by their peers in the top half of all fraternities in quality on their campuses.

Expansion during this period was slowed as the Great Depression descended upon the nation; only 15 new chapters had been installed by 1930.

In 1938, a major development took place...a merger between Sigma Phi Epsilon and the Theta Upsilon Omega (TUO) national fraternity. Four chapters of TUO merged with four of our existing chapters, and seven others became Sigma Phi Epsilon chapters. With the merger, scores of dedicated TUO alumni became members in our Fraternity, and many became important leaders in Sigma Phi Epsilon.

February 1943 Journal

In 1940, there were 69 active chapters. The 1940s saw the Fraternity's expansion increase, with 27 new charters granted by 1949.

Cincinnati SigEps head to Conclave, from the May 1955 Journal.

The 1950s

After 34 years as the Fraternity's first Grand Secretary, Uncle Billy retired in 1942. The National Board of Directors appointed Herb Heilig, Lawrence '23, to take Brother Phillips' place as Grand Secretary. Serving for two difficult years during World War II, Brother Heilig, laid the groundwork for the Fraternity's post-war rebuilding program and resigned in 1944.

The Board then appointed William W. Hindman, Jr., Pennsylvania '39, to the position of Grand Secretary. Brother Hindman had served as Traveling Secretary and later Assistant to the Grand Secretary under Uncle

Billy, and held the position of Grand Secretary for 13 years. Brother Hindman was instrumental in establishing 51 new chapters during the 1950s.

By 1959, Sigma Phi Epsilon had 148 active chapters. With the Fraternity's rapid expansion, the leadership at Headquarters once again changed with Bedford W. Black, Wake Forest '41, taking over after the retirement of Bill Hindman. Bedford Black's charge was to determine how the Headquarters should best be organized to operate Sigma Phi Epsilon as an emerging "large fraternity."

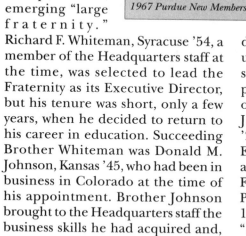

1967 Purdue New Members

Richard F. Whiteman, Syracuse '54, a member of the Headquarters staff at the time, was selected to lead the Fraternity as its Executive Director, but his tenure was short, only a few years, when he decided to return to his career in education. Succeeding Brother Whiteman was Donald M. Johnson, Kansas '45, who had been in business in Colorado at the time of his appointment. Brother Johnson brought to the Headquarters staff the business skills he had acquired and, during his tenure from 1961 to 1971, implemented many organizational changes at Headquarters and enlarged the professional staff.

The 1960s

Sigma Phi Epsilon chartered 33 new chapters between 1960 and 1969, and memberships reached their highest levels. In 1968, the College Survey Bureau reported that 59 percent of our 173 chapters were among the top chapters on their campuses.

The 1960s began with Sigma Phi Epsilon making a transition to a more business-like operation, necessitated by its dramatic growth during the 1950s. During this time, the professional staff located in Richmond, Virginia, grew and became more specialized in developing an array of services for undergraduate chapters. The most significant event of the 1960s, and perhaps the most important event in our history, was the emergence of J. Edward Zollinger, William & Mary '27, as the leader of the Sigma Phi Epsilon Educational Foundation and the Fraternity. He served the Fraternity as Grand President from 1967 to 1971. "Zolly" came from the successful I.B.M. Corporation, serving as assistant to the founder of I.B.M., and was very involved in developing I.B.M.'s corporate culture.

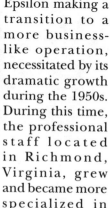

IN 1968, THE COLLEGE SURVEY BUREAU REPORTED THAT 59 PERCENT OF OUR 173 CHAPTERS WERE AMONG THE TOP CHAPTERS ON THEIR CAMPUSES.

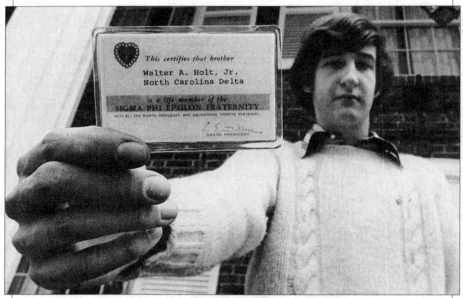

Walter A Holt, Jr., North Carolina '77, SigEp's 100,000th member, from the April 1973 Journal.

The successful experience of Ed Zollinger in the business world and the stability of a long-term professional staff in Richmond brought together ingredients necessary for Sigma Phi Epsilon's emergence as a leader among all national fraternities in the 1970s. It was the vision of excellence, and the personal dedication to that vision, which made Ed Zollinger unique and which gave Sigma Phi Epsilon its commitment to the future.

The 1970s

In 1971, the National Board of Directors divided Headquarters responsibilities between the area of alumni operations and undergraduate and financial operations, appointing Charles N. White, Jr., of Western Michigan '62, to the undergraduate and financial area as Executive Vice President. Donald M. Johnson assumed responsibility for the alumni and Foundation area, also as an Executive Vice President.

This organization structure continued until 1976 upon the retirement of Brother Johnson, at which time Brother White was named Executive Director responsible for the entire Headquarters operation. During Brother White's tenure, the Regional Leadership Academy program was created and instituted, the professional Headquarters staff was expanded, and its responsibilities enlarged.

The late 1960s and early 1970s were difficult times. Fraternities began losing their popularity. A generation mistrustful of established institutions was arriving on campus in greater numbers, and many of them scorned the Greek system as elitist, outdated, and immature. Unfortunately, enough chapters behaved in just that way so that the charge stuck.

The "student movement," centered on the war in Vietnam, alienated fraternity chapters still further. Faced squarely with a breakdown of campus and chapter values, many chapters of Sigma Phi Epsilon and other fraternities lost direction. Men were no longer attracted to membership with ease. None of the old recruitment formulas seemed to work. Some of SigEp's oldest and strongest chapters died during this era because they refused to change and adapt.

By 1972, Sigma Phi Epsilon chapters were suffering. The number of members significantly decreased, and alumni support was weakening—college students of the time were bucking traditions and the ways of "anyone over 30." The Fraternity's Headquarters went into deficit financial operation, but the National Board of Directors and Executive Director refused to cut back on the service to undergraduate chapters at this time when the chapters needed it the most. The strength of SigEp over the years

has been largely a function of alumni guidance and Headquarters services to the undergraduate chapters. It was that devotion to service that pulled SigEp through the early 1970s with fewer scars than most other strong fraternities.

THE STRENGTH OF SIGEP OVER THE YEARS HAS BEEN LARGELY A FUNCTION OF ALUMNI GUIDANCE AND HEADQUARTERS SERVICES TO THE UNDERGRADUATE CHAPTERS.

The investment in the belief that the hard times would come to an end paid off. In the late 1970s, students began to change again—demanding a return to the ideals that had lapsed earlier in the decade. Fraternities were again in prime position to meet those desires, and because of continued efforts during tough times, SigEp was ready.

The 1980s

The growth of the late 1970s continued into the first half of the 1980s and did not show any signs of slowing. Sigma Phi Epsilon held its strongest position ever, with 250 chapters in 45 states. With 16,000 undergraduates on college campuses, 170,000 members, and more men joining SigEp than any other fraternity, we became the strongest and most popular fraternity in history.

Chapter house at the University of Colorado. The chapter celebrated its 100th anniversary in 2005.

During the 1970s and 1980s, a commitment to undergraduates and undergraduate housing emerged as a central theme with special emphasis on long-term financial stability. Also, at this time, Sigma Phi Epsilon's leadership in the interfraternity world was acknowledged as it led all fraternities in innovative approaches to programming and undergraduate development.

At the close of the 1980s, a commitment to alumni began to emerge from the Headquarters operation through a focused plan to develop the Sigma Phi Epsilon Educational Foundation as a primary resource for the Fraternity's future. In 1987, Kenneth S. Maddox, Oregon State '75, was named Executive Director, and Brother White began full-time management of the Educational Foundation as its President. The Fraternity has benefited greatly from the increased strength of the Foundation.

A number of important initiatives began at the close of the decade. In 1987 the Self-Esteem Committee met under the leadership of Past Grand President Donald C. McCleary, Texas '71, to discuss the issues facing and threatening the Fraternity. From the Self-Esteem Committee developed some of the concepts for the Balanced Man Program, a membership development

DURING THE 1970S AND 1980S, A COMMITMENT TO UNDERGRADUATES AND UNDERGRADUATE HOUSING EMERGED AS A CENTRAL THEME WITH SPECIAL EMPHASIS ON LONG-TERM FINANCIAL STABILITY.

program aimed at preserving Sigma Phi Epsilon's values while providing for the needs of future members. Also, in 1989 the Fraternity developed the first formalized strategic plan—a detailed blueprint designed to take the Fraternity into the next millennium as the premier Greek-letter organization.

The 1990s

The 1990s marked a major shift in the Greek world. The negative perceptions of Greek life earned by fraternities during the 1970s and 1980s have resulted in declining membership and dramatically increasing insurance costs for all organizations. Yet through this time of turmoil in the interfraternity world, Sigma Phi Epsilon has remained the largest and fastest growing fraternity in history. As the founding member of the Fraternity Insurance Purchasing Group (FIPG) in the 1980s, Sigma Phi Epsilon has been instrumental in leading the Greek community to better risk management.

The Fraternity's Educational Foundation also continues to support undergraduates and innovative programs. It took a giant step by completing the $5 million Campaign for the Heart in 1993. This was SigEp's largest fund-raising effort to date, and it enabled SigEp students to enhance leadership and scholarship skills for the 1990s and beyond. Through a leadership gift from Curtis L. Carlson, Minnesota '37, the Regional Leadership Academies were renamed in his honor.

The Balanced Man Program was introduced in 1991, the first no-pledging, no-hazing program in American college fraternities.

A membership program unique among college fraternities was established with Grand Chapter legislation in 1991—the Balanced Man Program. This program is a no-pledging, no-hazing, four-year, continuous development program centered on the Balanced Man Ideal. The program seeks to build positive habits and key life skills through mentoring and experiential learning, and it matures and builds upon itself as the student's needs change and progress throughout college. Using self-reflection, discussion, evaluation, and personal written goals, SigEp created the Balanced Man Program to bolster the self-esteem and overall quality of life of its members.

In March of 1996, Brother Maddox announced his intentions to return to his home state of Oregon where he and his wife wanted their children to spend their formative years. The National Board of Directors selected Jacques L. Vauclain, III, Davidson '91, to succeed Brother Maddox. After four years as the Fraternity's Executive Director, Brother Vauclain and his wife left Richmond to return to Philadelphia. Craig D. Templeton, Kansas '81, was appointed Vauclain's successor in October of 2000.

The Second Century

At the 47th Grand Chapter Conclave, held in Washington, D.C., over 1,600 attendees helped to celebrate the Centennial of our great Fraternity. Sigma Phi Epsilon entered its second century as the largest fraternity and continues to break new ground. In 2001, the National Board of Directors adopted the Strategic Plan, which provides the vision of what the Fraternity will look like in 2011. The plan focuses the efforts of

THE STRATEGIC PLAN PROVIDES A VISION FOR SIGMA PHI EPSILON IN 2011, AND FOCUSES THE EFFORTS OF ALUMNI, VOLUNTEERS, UNDERGRADUATES AND THE HEADQUARTERS STAFF

our alumni, volunteers, undergraduates and Headquarters staff.

The Leadership Continuum, developed throughout the late 1990s and 2000, is recognized for its innovation in program development. It is comprised of four different programs—EDGE, Carlson Leadership Academies, Ruck Leadership Institute, and the *Tragos Quest to Greece*—that develop a young SigEp from his first days in the chapter throughout his college days and beyond.

Members of the Ruck Leadership Institute 2005 class comprised of 120 undergraduates from 109 chapters around the country. The Ruck Leadership Institute takes place each year at the University of Richmond campus.

▶ EDGE is a 24-hour, high intensity retreat where new members from local chapters learn about the history of the Fraternity, set personal goals and learn about the pitfalls of college life and how SigEp helps them achieve the Balanced Man Ideal. EDGE takes place in the fall and spring of each academic year. As the program evolves, it aims to reach every new member recruited.

▶ The Carlson Leadership Academies (CLAs) are a three-day conference held in February of each year, designed to help new chapter officers learn how to improve their operations. In 2005 a little over 1,900 SigEp undergraduates and volunteers attended nine CLAs.

▶ The Ruck Leadership Institute is held every year at the University of Richmond. Selected undergraduates from across the country learn advanced leadership skills and learn to promote the Balanced Man Ideal. In 2005 120 undergraduates from 109 chapters attended two separate sessions. As the program evolves, it aims to have every chapter send one member.

▶ The *Tragos Quest to Greece* is a scholarship program of the Sigma Phi Epsilon Educational Foundation. It is the pinnacle of the undergraduate experience—a pilgrimage to the ruins of Ancient Greece. The *Tragos Quest* is an exploration of all aspects of the Balanced Man Ideal and of the relationship to the roots of Greek-letter fraternities. Only a handful of SigEp's best and brightest are selected to journey to Greece.

Using student-faculty interaction, leadership development, a sense of belonging and tradition, and an academic focus, SigEp has set about to convert chapter houses and living facilities into Residential Learning Communities (RLCs). The RLC provides undergraduates with the positive mentoring of recognized university faculty members to help members achieve personally, academically, and professionally. Residential Learning Communities create a supplement for today's college student by providing a home away from home with responsible peers and university faculty who are committed to helping him succeed in a positive living-learning environment. Your Fraternity is committing the resources to providing the best fraternity experience possible.

SigEp is proud of its heritage as a pioneer, with its members, chapters, and with the Greek community. Our pride will continue to lead the way.

Strength from Innovation

Brothers of Sigma Phi Epsilon have always taken strength from this history, a history of change and innovation. Our Founders were young men of high moral character who took great pride in their accomplishments. The splendid example set by these early planners and builders served to inspire high standards of leadership through the years. At many SigEp gatherings, Founder Jenkens declared that the principle on which Sigma Phi Epsilon was founded is the principle of peace among men through brotherhood. Other Founders have similarly exhorted the Brothers of Sigma Phi Epsilon to face tough challenges: "Be men! Unless you be men, you cannot be Brothers."

The Founders

SigEp's Founders went on to be great men in their own fields. They acted on their ideals and goals and set high standards for all Brothers to follow. And remember, they were no older than you when they started Sigma Phi Epsilon.

SIGMA PHI EPSILON WAS FOUNDED ON THE PRINCIPLE OF PEACE AMONG MEN THROUGH BROTHERHOOD.

CARTER ASHTON JENKENS was born in Oxford, North Carolina, on April 9, 1882, and received his early education in New Jersey. He graduated from Richmond College in June, 1902, and then taught for two years at Chase City, Virginia, Military Academy and Richmond Preparatory. He received a baccalaureate degree in the ministry at Crozer Seminary, Chester, Pennsylvania, and served for more than 20 years as pastor in churches in Hampton, Norfolk, and Richmond, finally to become an evangelist

Founder Jenkens

and conduct revivals throughout the United States. His gift for inspiring oratory was so outstanding that the famed evangelist Billy Sunday is reported on one occasion to have exclaimed, "If only the Almighty had blest me with the voice of Carter Jenkens!" His twilight years were spent in Louisville, Kentucky, where he died on July 23, 1952.

BENJAMIN DONALD GAW came to Richmond College, where he worked his way through school, acting as pastor of the East End Baptist Church of Richmond, to graduate in 1906. He had come from Stuart's Draft, Virginia, where he was born on August 20, 1870. He married and later received the bachelor of divinity degree at Colgate. For six years thereafter, he was pastor at the West Washington Baptist Church, Washington, D.C., and in 1917 was called to the First Baptist Church in Durham, North Carolina. He died in Washington, D.C., on January 10, 1919, from pneumonia. He is buried in Montgomery, Maryland.

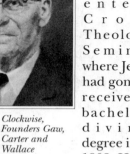

Clockwise, Founders Gaw, Carter and Wallace

WILLIAM HUGH CARTER was born near Danville in Pittsylvania County, Virginia, February 2, 1878. The family moved to Salem, where he attended the public schools. For one year, he taught in a public school in Roanoke County, Virginia, and in September, 1897, entered Richmond College to prepare for the Baptist ministry. After being out of college for one year, he received the B.A. degree from Richmond College, June, 1902.

Founder Carter's campus activities included debate, YMCA, and varsity basketball. He became a teacher in Southside Academy, Chase City,

Virginia, in 1902-1903 and was principal of the Chase City Graded School for the next two years. During this three-year period, he served as the editor of the *Chase City Progress*. In September, 1905, he entered Crozer Theological Seminary, where Jenkens had gone, and received the bachelor of divinity degree in May, 1908. He then became pastor of the First Baptist Church, Winchester, Virginia, for six-and-a-half years. Subsequent pastorates were at Hertford, North Carolina, three-and-a-half years; Crewe, Virginia, ten-and-a-half years; and Marion, Virginia, 18 years.

Retiring from active pastorates, he served as field worker for the Sunday School Department of the Varina Baptist Board of Missions and Education. Brother Carter died in Salem, Virginia, on January 5, 1971, at the age of 92.

WILLIAM ANDREW WALLACE, the second of the roommates at Ryland Hall, was invited to join that group by Gaw, his roommate. He came from Gaw's home town, Stuart's Draft, where he was born on May 7, 1882. He did not graduate but transferred to the Medical College of Virginia for his M.D., on which campus he launched the Beta Chapter (now Virginia Commonwealth University), becoming its first member. By this act, Sigma Phi Epsilon's expansion began.

He left the Medical College for an internship in the Boston Floating Hospital, which he left for another internship in a hospital in Richmond. Later, in 1908, he located in Spartanburg, South Carolina, continuing in practice to become one of the best-known practitioners in the state, and a devoted SigEp until his death in 1929.

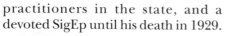

Clockwise, Founders Phillips and Wright

THOMAS TEMPLE WRIGHT was born at Locust Grove, Caroline County, Virginia, May 21, 1883. He was tutored at home, entered Richmond College in 1900, received the B.A. in 1904, and was graduated from the Engineering College, Cornell University, in 1907.

Wright roomed with Jenkens at the "Cottage." His intimate friends knew him as "Those," after the abbreviated form of his name. The fifth member of the Fraternity, he was one of the two Founders who returned to college in September, 1902, and as treasurer of the group signed the corporate charter secured from the Commonwealth of Virginia October 22, 1902.

Wright started his professional career as a United States surveyor with

the Mississippi River Commission in Vicksburg, Mississippi. He later became a railroad civil engineer, first with the Canadian Pacific Railroad at Ottawa, Canada, then with the Canadian Northern Railroad on construction in Ontario, and finally with the Baltimore and Ohio. In 1917, "Those," on leave from the B & O, was construction engineer for the United States Army Camp Taylor at Louisville, Kentucky. The following year, he became head of the Warsaw and Fredericksburg offices of the Henrico Lumber Company, making his home in Warsaw, Virginia. In 1933, he and his brothers formed Wright Brothers, Inc., with offices in Richmond, West Point, Tappahannock, and Philadelphia. He continued to be active with this firm for many years. He died on February 15, 1958.

WILLIAM LAZELL PHILLIPS devoted virtually all the mature years of his life to Sigma Phi Epsilon. A study of the leadership pattern of the founding group reveals that he is the one titan after Jenkens. The latter said to his brothers, "This is how we must build our Fraternity." Phillips built it. Born in Normal, Illinois, in 1873, William L. Phillips came to Richmond College in September, 1901, to study law and the Bible. He attended one year, dropped out for a year, and then returned, but his pursuit of legal studies gave way to his devotion to Sigma Phi Epsilon and he never graduated.

The first Conclave at Richmond College in December, 1903, authorized the establishment of the *Journal* and appointed Uncle Billy as its first editor. The first issue, March, 1904, "Published by the Grand Council in the interest of the Fraternity," reveals that Uncle Billy was determined to make the *Journal* carry news from all chapters and thus add dignity and strength to his young Fraternity.

Phillips was the first editor of The Journal.

In addition to his work as the first editor, he played some baseball and football (not on the college team), attended the Philologian Literary Society and classes in law. He was the first secretary of Virginia Alpha in 1901-1902.

A complete record of his professional career tells the story of his work for Sigma Phi Epsilon: Editor of the *Journal*, 1904-1912, 1919-1921; business manager of the *Journal*, 1904-1911, 1919-1942; member, Ritual Committee, 1907; editor of membership directories, 1915 and 1921; trustee of the Endowment Fund, 1925-1939, 1944-1949; trustee of the national Headquarters, 1927-1942; trustee of the Student Loan Fund, 1930-1940; Grand Secretary, 1908-1942; Grand Secretary Emeritus, 1942-

1956; Grand Vice President, 1943; Grand President, 1944; North American Interfraternity Conference, founder, 1909; vice chairman, 1929-1930; member, War Committee, 1942; a founder of College Fraternity Secretaries Association; chairman, 1939-1940.

Uncle Billy passed away at his home on June 20, 1956, and left his personal estate to the Fraternity, which founded the Phillips Fund within the Sigma Phi Epsilon Educational Foundation. That fund provides scholarships for members of the University of Richmond chapter.

He loved his Fraternity intensely and had attended every one of the 24 Conclaves from the first one at Richmond College, 1903, to Cincinnati, 1955. William L. Phillips must be numbered among the first handful of the truly great builders of the American college fraternity system. No one has achieved a greater record.

LUCIAN BAUM COX was born November 13, 1879, in Princess Anne County, Virginia. He attended a one-room public school, and worked at his father's farm and sawmill. In September, 1898, he entered Richmond

Founder Cox

College, first as an academic student and later as a law student, where he received a bachelor of law degree in June, 1902.

As an under-graduate, he taught Bible class in Calvary Baptist Church on Sunday mornings and to a group of inmates at the Virginia Penitentiary in the afternoons. In July, 1902, he began the practice of law in Norfolk, Virginia.

Clockwise, Founders Owens, Allen, and McFarland

Founder Cox wrote the application for the corporate charter for Sigma Phi Epsilon. In 1939, he published his first edition of *Titles to Land in Virginia*, and a second edition was published in 1947. This book was followed in 1951 by his work on *Principles and Procedure in Equity*. Brother Cox died in Norfolk, Virginia, on June 10, 1971, at the age of 91.

RICHARD SPURGEON OWENS was a minister's son, and was born October 28, 1880, in Hempstead, King George County, Virginia. When he graduated from Richmond in 1904, he spent four years at Colgate Theological Seminary, to become a minister, graduating in 1907. His career in the ministry called him to Baptist churches in Washington, D.C., Roanoke, Virginia, and for four years, 1917-1921, as instructor in Fishburn Military Academy in Waynesboro. Before his death on July 6, 1950, he was a trustee of the University of Richmond,

Bluefield College, and also of the Baptist Orphanage in Salem, Virginia.

EDGAR LEE ALLEN was born on January 6, 1880. His career: lawyer. Born in Virginia, attending private schools in King and Queen County, he was not a consistent Virginian, moving to Birmingham, Alabama, in October, 1902. After three liberal arts years at Richmond, he completed graduate work in law in 1902. After taking up residence in Birmingham, Founder Allen practiced law in that city steadily, serving as judge in various courts until his death on March 21, 1945.

ROBERT ALFRED McFARLAND was born on a farm near Oxford, North Carolina, on January 31, 1876. He attended Granville County public schools; three years at Bethel Hill Institute, North Carolina; four years at Richmond College—received a B.S. in 1902; received a bachelors of theology degree from the Southern Baptist Theological Seminary at Louisville in 1908 and an honorary doctor of divinity degree from the University of Richmond in 1921.

McFarland made the motion to found Sigma Phi Epsilon; and he was chairman of the Committee on the Constitution.

McFarland held important pastorates in three states. In North Carolina, he was a member of the Baptist State Board, a trustee of the Baptist Orphanage and Wake Forest College, and was vice president of the Baptist State Convention. In Virginia, he served as a member of the Baptist State Board, a trustee of the Baptist Hospital, the Fork Union Military Academy, and the Southern Baptist State Convention.

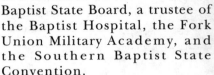

Founders Kertoot and McCaul

McFarland was once written up in a London journal as a "representative" minister of the United States. He died on March 14, 1960.

FRANK WEBB KERFOOT, who died in an accident on August 29, 1918, was another Baptist preacher. A native Virginian, he was born October 2, 1876, in Buckland, Prince William County, and at Richmond was a member of the Class of 1902. At the time of his death, he was a chaplain in the Army. He had been pastor of parishes in Buckingham and Middlesex Counties, and Chatham, Virginia; Nowata, Oklahoma, and Fort Smith, Arkansas.

THOMAS VADEN MCCAUL was born in Charles City County, Virginia, on November 25, 1878. He attended Richmond public schools, graduated from Richmond High School, and entered Richmond College as a pre-law student in February, 1898. In September of that year, Uncle Tom returned to Richmond College as a ministerial student, being convinced of a call to preach. He received his B.A. from Richmond College in June, 1902; the masters of theology from the Southern Baptist Theological Seminary in 1905, and the M.A. from the University of Virginia in 1908. The honorary degree of doctor of divinity was conferred upon him by the University of Richmond and Stetson University.

While at Richmond College, Uncle Tom was active in debates and oratorical contests. He won the writer's medal offered by his literary society his senior year. He won the orator's medal at the University of Virginia in 1907. Uncle Tom served as the first president of Virginia Alpha in 1901-1902 and wrote the Fraternity's first song, "Our Fraternity," in 1902. In the Fall of 1902, he visited Bethany College, West Virginia; Washington and Jefferson College, Pennsylvania; and West Virginia University and

The sixth Grand Conclave in Washington D.C., 1910

formed a nucleus for chapters in all three. He helped to establish Virginia Eta at the University of Virginia in 1907 and Florida Alpha at the University of Florida in 1925. He was appointed National Chaplain in 1947 and served until 1959.

Uncle Tom served as pastor of Baptist churches in Kentucky, Virginia, South Carolina, and Florida. After more than 26 years as pastor of the First Baptist Church of Gainesville, Florida, he retired on January 1, 1949. He remained in Gainesville, frequently looking in on his young Florida Alpha Brothers. He continued to attend Conclaves, his last being the 32nd Grand Chapter in Atlanta in 1971. On November 18, 1972, he died peacefully in Gainesville at the age

of 93. He was the Fraternity's last remaining founder.

These are 12 names inscribed in Sigma Phi Epsilon's Hall of Fame, but these were also 12 young men who formed a chapter of Sigma Phi Epsilon—a chapter far different from those of today and yet one noteworthy for its similarities. The first, Jenkens, was pre-eminent for his vision, his ability to dream grand dreams, and to spellbind with noble words, and the sixth—Phillips—built for the Fraternity even while he slept. There were no drones among the 12.

During their first year, they took every honor and prize given on the campus except one—a mathematics prize.

Signing the guest book in the lobby of Zollinger House, Sigma Phi Epsilon Fraternity Headquarters.

YOUR NATIONAL FRATERNITY

"Change is the law of life. And those who look only to the past and the present are certain to miss the future."

~ JOHN F. KENNEDY

When you joined your chapter, the determining factors undoubtedly were the men in the chapter and the opportunities you saw in Sigma Phi Epsilon on your campus. To any great extent, the national Fraternity may not have influenced your decision to join. But, now that you are associated with Sigma Phi Epsilon, you will become more familiar with your Brothers nationwide, and you will find that in addition to joining the Sigma Phi Epsilon chapter on your campus, you are a member of the leading national fraternity. You will meet SigEps across the nation and throughout the world, and your resources have greatly increased because you are a member of Sigma Phi Epsilon.

The national Fraternity is all of the chapters, the undergraduates, the alumni of Sigma Phi Epsilon, and you.

You will invest time, effort and money in Sigma Phi Epsilon during your undergraduate years and as an alumnus. This investment will be important as you gain experience while you are an undergraduate. Equally important will be your interest in the future of your chapter. Being a member of a strong national fraternity is important to you and your chapter because it protects your investment. As an alumnus, your ongoing support of the Fraternity is a component of your responsibility as a member of Sigma Phi Epsilon. Sigma Phi Epsilon is deeply committed to its undergraduate chapters.

The Fraternity with a Plan

Between 1988 and 1990, the Fraternity, through alumni and undergraduate discussions, undertook an exhaustive examination of the business of "fraternity." At issue: "Just exactly what is the future plan or vision of Sigma Phi Epsilon?"

The result of that study was the creation of a strategic plan or direction for the future of Sigma Phi Epsilon. Revisions were made, and the Fraternity had a vision statement—something to measure each effort by. Sigma Phi Epsilon's vision is: "Building Balanced Leaders for the World's Communities."

"WE ARE WHAT WE REPEATEDLY DO. EXCELLENCE, THEN, IS NOT AN ACT, BUT A HABIT."

~ ARISTOTLE

The Fraternity's vision statement, strategic plan, and the process from which it was determined are but representations of the innovative management practices of the National Board of Directors and the Fraternity.

The 23rd Grand Chapter Conclave, Portland, Oregon, 1953

The Fraternity Operations

You, and other undergraduate Brothers, run Sigma Phi Epsilon. Every two years, each chapter elects a delegate and alternate to attend the Grand Chapter Conclave, our national convention. These Brothers become part of the governing and legislative body of our Fraternity. District Governors, National Directors, and chartered alumni chapters also vote at Conclaves. Approximately 85 percent of the voting delegates are from the undergraduate chapters.

The delegates elect our volunteer leaders: Grand President, Grand Treasurer, and nine other members of the National Board of Directors. The Grand Chapter also adopts legislation at Conclave, which the Board of Directors carries out until the next Grand Chapter Conclave.

The National Board of Directors appoints District Governors, as well as chairmen and members of various national committees. The Board also relies heavily on more than 1,000 Alumni and Volunteer Corporation members nationwide. None of these volunteers receive any salary for the thousands of hours they devote to our Fraternity. Many of them also contribute their travel and meeting expenses. Without the guidance and support of volunteers, the Fraternity would not be as strong as it is today.

The Grand Chapter

The Grand Chapter is the legislative body of the Fraternity. Its membership is: National Board of Directors, District Governors, and the official representatives (regularly elected delegates) of the undergraduate chapters. The Grand Chapter is the original source of all power and authority in the Fraternity, subject to such limitations as set forth in the

Bylaws and Administrative Policies and Procedures (APP). The Grand Chapter ordinarily meets in biennial conventions (Conclaves). The meeting of the Grand Chapter may be likened to congress or a state legislature, the legislative branch of government. The purpose of the Grand Chapter is to set the direction for the Fraternity.

Each undergraduate chapter and alumni chapter selects a delegate and alternate delegate to serve as its official representative, but a member need not be a delegate or alternate delegate to attend the session. Members present at more than one Conclave receive the title of "Loyal Legionnaire."

Grand Chapter Voting Breakdown

▶ Undergraduate
   Delegates   (85 percent)

▶ National Board of Directors

▶ District Governors   (15 percent)

The National Board of Directors

The National Board of Directors is given the authority of the Grand Chapter between Conclaves and is responsible to that body for the satisfactory operation of the national Fraternity, individual chapters, and all activities of the Fraternity.

The members of the National Board of Directors are all volunteers. Composed of nine Directors, plus the Grand President and the Grand Treasurer, the members are elected by the Grand Chapter. Three of the nine Directors are Student Directors who serve two-year terms, the other six Directors serve staggered six-year terms, and the Grand President and Grand Treasurer serve two-year terms. National Directors are prominent in the business and professional world or, in the case of the Student Directors, are exceptional student leaders. They are selected because of their noticeable devotion to their Fraternity and they receive no compensation for this position except for necessary expenses. It is the practice of the Board of Directors to meet twice a year, with the laws providing for continuous action on fraternity business through contact with the executive officers of the Fraternity.

THE NATIONAL BOARD OF DIRECTORS ARE ALL VOLUNTEERS. COMPOSED OF NINE DIRECTORS, PLUS THE GRAND PRESIDENT AND THE GRAND TREASURER, THE MEMBERS ARE ELECTED BY THE GRAND CHAPTER.

The National Board of Directors provides experience and expertise in leading the Fraternity.

Volunteers—Our Continuity & Strength

The success of your chapter, and of Sigma Phi Epsilon nationwide, depends on our volunteer alumni. Your Chapter Counselor and Alumni and Volunteer Corporation provide the wisdom and guidance that continue to build a strong chapter. Nationally, our volunteers provide the guidance, direction, and energy needed for a strong, innovative Fraternity.

The Chapter Counselor

The Chapter Counselor provides alumni guidance and continuity. While the chapter officers change each year, and the entire chapter membership turns over every four years, the Chapter Counselor remains.

The Chapter Counselor is responsible for the overall excellence of the chapter they serve and may not necessarily be an alumnus from your chapter or a SigEp at all. These volunteers bring a unique viewpoint. You can help your Counselor's performance—be sure the chapter recognizes their efforts, and includes their significant other in chapter plans. Remember, they volunteer their time for the benefit of your chapter.

The Chapter Counselor is a "communicator." Their work with the undergraduate chapter in all areas will allow them to speak from a more informed perspective. The Chapter Counselor is the member of the Alumni and Volunteer Corporation who understands the chapter's perspective on issues. Their position requires

YOU CAN HELP YOUR COUNSELOR'S PERFORMANCE—BE SURE THE CHAPTER RECOGNIZES HIS EFFORTS, AND INCLUDES HIS SIGNIFICANT OTHER, IN CHAPTER PLANS.

them to speak with *both* the AVC and the undergraduate chapter. This communication link is essential to sound operations and cooperation.

The Headquarters staff looks to the Counselor for a successful chapter; the Alumni and Volunteer Corporation looks to the Counselor for a well-managed chapter, and the chapter looks to the Counselor for guidance and counseling.

The Alumni and Volunteer Corporation

The Alumni and Volunteer Corporation (AVC) has the responsibility of providing continuity and financial stability to the undergraduate chapter. Acting as a "board of directors," the Alumni and Volunteer Corporation remains a constant presence, having a long-term perspective of the Fraternity.

Purpose of the Alumni and Volunteer Corporation

The Grand Chapter Bylaws outline the purpose of the Alumni and Volunteer Corporation. The Bylaws list these responsibilities of an AVC:

▶ Approve undergraduate chapter budget.

▶ Budget and control receipts and disbursements of the undergraduate chapter.

▶ Install and monitor systems of financing and accounting.

▶ Hold legal title to any land, buildings, and any furnishings acquired and/or occupied by the chapter.

▶ Ensure the proper financial statements are completed, reviewed, and sent to Sigma Phi Epsilon Headquarters.

Each Alumni and Volunteer Corporation is made up of important alumni volunteers who work closely with the undergraduate chapter. These volunteers provide knowledge and advice in the areas of housing, finance, law, academic programming, and alumni contact.

Arizona State Alumni visit during a recent reunion. The AVC is an important resource for your chapter.

The Alumni and Volunteer Corporation is typically directed by four officers: President, Vice President, Treasurer, and Secretary, and usually between three and five other members round out the corporation. Each corporation's own bylaws dictate the election and voting process, the exact term of office and responsibilities of each elected officer and member.

The Alumni and Volunteer Corporation President and Alumni and Volunteer Corporation Treasurer work closely with the undergraduate chapter, District Governor, Headquarters, and other key volunteers throughout their term of office. Other volunteers on the AVC, including the Chapter Counselor, bring valuable insight, direction, and support to help

better the Sigma Phi Epsilon chapter on that campus.

The Alumni and Volunteer Corporation President is responsible for the general supervision, direction, and well-being of the corporation. They preside at all meetings and see that the duties of other board members are properly performed. The President also represents and speaks for the corporation as assigned them by the AVC. The AVC should meet at least monthly at the chapter facility, if applicable.

The Treasurer is responsible for all financial transactions and records of the corporation. They closely monitor the undergraduate chapter's financial operations by working with the Vice President of Finance. Their supervision of the chapter finances ensures that proper financial paperwork is promptly filed with Headquarters, the chapter is collecting dues, the Grand Chapter account is at a zero balance at the end of the year, and the proper income tax forms are filed with the IRS. The Alumni and Volunteer Corporation plans for future financial needs of the chapter and its facility through savings and investments. The corporation should have a working plan for the current and/or future facility.

The District Governor

The District Governor position is one of high esteem in the Fraternity. He is a distinguished alumnus who represents the Fraternity in one of the 28 SigEp districts.

THE DISTRICT GOVERNOR IDENTIFIES AND RECRUITS NEW ALUMNI AND VOLUNTEERS TO WORK WITH THE LOCAL CHAPTER(S) IN HIS DISTRICT.

The District Governor identifies and recruits new alumni and volunteers to work with the local chapter(s) in his district. He also works with the Chapter Counselor and Alumni and Volunteer Corporation to see that both are educated on their respective responsibilities as well as fraternity policies. The District Governor attends ceremonial occasions when invited, undertakes special assignments and is a resource for the chapters and volunteers in his district.

The position is designed to encourage outstanding Brothers to become involved in fraternity affairs, serving as a resource to your Chapter Counselor and Alumni and Volunteer Corporation.

National Committees

Since the beginning, Sigma Phi Epsilon has employed a variety of committees to help in the planning and execution of important Fraternity responsibilities. A committee structure composed of dedicated volunteers is appointed by the Grand President. These committees serve the Fraternity in a variety of ways.

Sigma Phi Epsilon Headquarters

Located in Richmond, Virginia, home of the Fraternity's founding, Zollinger House, the Fraternity's Headquarters, is the administrative office for the Fraternity where all support activities and services are developed and coordinated.

The Grand Chapter determines the scope of the Headquarters operation through its decisions on fees and funding. Today, Sigma Phi Epsilon Headquarters is providing a high level of service to campus chapters, alumni and volunteers. Your Headquarters is recognized nationally as an innovative, energetic, highly professional operation which serves the needs of the Fraternity well.

The Headquarters staff is a team. You will see the Regional Director most often during your undergraduate experience. These young alumni travel throughout the year visiting chapters to consult on fraternity operations, assist volunteers, and work with university administrators.

To assure continuity for the Fraternity's operations, there is a team of senior staff members; all are Fraternity alumni based in Richmond, Virginia.

EXECUTIVE DIRECTOR: The Executive Director is responsible for the Fraternity's financial operations, strategic planning process, and success of the Headquarters staff. He develops and implements programs of service and leadership activities to assure that Fraternity needs are met. The Executive Director also works closely with the National Housing Corporation, Educational Foundation, and National Board of Directors.

HEADQUARTERS STAFF: Working with the Executive Director are other senior staff members, including the Director of the Balanced Man Initiative, Director of Volunteers, Directors of New Chapter Development, Director of Chapter Services, Director of Health and Wellness, Director of Residential Life, Director of Resource Development, Director of Operations, Director of Communications, Director of Real Estate, Director of Recruitment, and the Director of Technology. Key programs such as the Carlson Leadership Academies, Grand Chapter Conclaves, Balanced Man Program, chapter housing support, volunteer recruitment and education, new chapter development, the Balanced Man Scholarship, Residential Learning Community, Resident Scholar Program, EDGE, Ruck Leadership Institute, *Tragos Quest to Greece* and *The Journal of Sigma Phi Epsilon,* are all executed through this team of senior staff members.

SigEp National Headquarters is located at 310 S. Boulevard in Richmond, Virginia.

An integral part of the Fraternity's Headquarters staff is the administrative staff who coordinate communications, help plan events and services, manage fraternity merchandise and bookkeeping, record membership information, administer the Fraternity's database, and work with the senior staff to support the Fraternity's programs. The administrative staff of the Fraternity forms a vital link between undergraduates, volunteers, and university officials by providing services and information.

REGIONAL DIRECTORS: Regional Directors conduct chapter visitations, provide chapter evaluations, lead strategic goal-setting retreats, conduct recruitment seminars, work with District Governors to recruit and educate volunteers, communicate with Chapter Counselors, advise Alumni and Volunteer Corporations regarding fraternity policy and financial management, assist with district activities, and manage the Carlson Leadership Academies and EDGE. These select staff people provide a wealth of services and knowledge to the chapters with whom they work.

SIGMA PHI EPSILON HAS THE LARGEST TRAVELING STAFF IN THE FRATERNITY WORLD, AND SIGEP REGIONAL DIRECTORS ARE RECOGNIZED NATIONALLY AS LEADING FRATERNITY PROFESSIONALS.

Undergraduate fees provide the major funding for Headquarters services, so when a staff member visits your chapter, particularly a Regional Director, you should take full advantage of his expertise.

Regional Directors Can Help You

❱ Facilitate strategic planning for all areas of chapter operations.

❱ Conduct chapter recruitment seminars and programs.

❱ Provide guidance for academic programming.

❱ Assist with education of chapter leadership.

❱ Advise on effective membership development.

❱ Provide guidance for financial operations.

❱ Facilitate goal-setting retreats and program evaluation.

❱ Work with volunteers in providing guidance to the chapter.

Your Regional Director is your chapter's most important fraternity resource. Regional Directors undergo a comprehensive summer development program in Richmond in preparation for their chapter visits during their year of service. They travel full-time and return to Richmond for three staff meetings during the year. Sigma Phi Epsilon has the largest traveling staff in the fraternity world, and SigEp "RDs" are recognized nationally as leading fraternity professionals.

The personal growth and development that you can achieve as a Regional Director are unmatched anywhere. Interviews for the Regional Director positions are held each fall, and any Brother may apply. Early application is encouraged. For more information, please contact Headquarters or talk to your current Regional Director.

Zollinger House

The national Headquarters has had 10 locations. The first, from 1903 to 1905, was housed in Richmond in office space rented in the Fowler Extract Manufacturing Building at 14 North Seventh Street. In 1906, the office was moved to 111 South Twelfth Street, where it remained until the election of William L. Phillips as Grand Secretary in 1908, when operations were transferred to Washington, D.C., to the George Washington University chapter house at 1433 Rhode Island Avenue, N.W. In 1911, the Headquarters was relocated in Richmond in the American Building, and has remained in this city ever since. From 1915 to 1927, offices were maintained in the Virginia Electric and Power Building.

In 1927, the Fraternity occupied its first Headquarters building at 518 West Franklin Street at the corner of Belvedere Street. It was the second headquarters building of a college social fraternity owned by the organization. The property was sold in 1946, and in the intervening nine years, the Fraternity rented a suite of offices in the Sauer Building at 1900 West Broad Street and the Chamber of Commerce Building at 15 North Sixth Street in downtown Richmond. In 1955, the Fraternity purchased a building at 209 West Franklin Street, only three blocks from the first building, staying there until 1967, when the Headquarters moved into a building built by Sigma Phi Epsilon expressly for fraternity operations. The classic structure served SigEp well for 21 years on the north side of Richmond at 5711 Chamberlayne Road.

In 1989, operations returned to the Fan District of Richmond, at 310 South Boulevard, near the Fraternity's founding site. Streamlined operations allowed the Fraternity to move to a smaller, more functional facility. The Chamberlayne property, which was built to hold printing presses and punch-card computers, was no longer needed. SigEp's professional staff remains the largest, most respected staff in the business.

Sigma Phi Epsilon's new home was dedicated as "Zollinger House" on May 19, 1990, in honor of Past Grand President and Order of the Golden

J. Edward Zollinger, William & Mary '27

Heart recipient J. Edward Zollinger. "Zolly," and his family after his death, supported Sigma Phi Epsilon in substantial ways through the Educational Foundation with programs like the Zollinger Outstanding Senior Award and the Zollinger Leadership Awards.

National Housing Corporation

The National Housing Corporation (NHC) is a wholly owned subsidiary corporation of Sigma Phi Epsilon Fraternity which administers the Fraternity's housing loan program. There are seven Trustees of the Corporation who are appointed by the National Board of Directors. These Trustees, like the Board of Directors, are volunteers.

Southern Methodist University's expanded Residential Learning Community, opened fall 2005.

In addition to providing loans for housing, the Trustees of the NHC serve as consultants to the Alumni and Volunteer Corporations on matters relating to fraternity housing and fraternity house financing.

There are three types of loans the NHC can make:

1. Loans for furniture and equipment

2. Improvement loans

3. Purchase/construction loans

In limited situations, the National Housing Corporation can also assist alumni corporations in the purchase of new facilities by guaranteeing a first mortgage loan. There are restrictions on these guarantees and each situation is independently evaluated. The NHC can be a valuable asset to your Alumni and Volunteer Corporation.

Questions regarding the National Housing Corporation should be directed to the Fraternity's Director of Real Estate.

Chapter Investment Fund

Sigma Phi Epsilon is the only national fraternity which operates its own savings fund for undergraduate chapters to set aside long-range savings. The Chapter Investment Fund (CIF) was established by the Grand Chapter in 1959 to provide a means for judicious and profitable savings for future housing needs of Sigma Phi Epsilon chapters. Since its first deposits were received in 1960, the value of the fund has grown to more than $10 million dollars.

Every chapter of Sigma Phi Epsilon has benefited (or will benefit) from this innovative method for accumulating savings. Without this national program, it is doubtful that the undergraduate chapters of Sigma Phi Epsilon would have anywhere near the $10 million dollars they have in long-range savings.

The Educational Foundation

The Sigma Phi Epsilon Educational Foundation is the vehicle through which resources of the brotherhood are concentrated to meet the changing needs of today's undergraduate Brothers. The Foundation provides a variety of benefits and a wealth of support to the Fraternity.

The Sigma Phi Epsilon Educational Foundation is classified by the Internal Revenue Service as a 501(c)(3) public charitable and educational foundation. The Sigma Phi Epsilon Educational Foundation is a resource for chapters and an endowment in perpetuity for scholarship and leadership programs that benefit the development of the individual Brother. The Foundation has assets approaching $10 million with $3 million in chapter restricted funds and $6 million in scholarship and leadership resources for nationally based programs.

Anurag Kashyap won the 2005 Scripps National Spelling Bee, and a $5000 college scholarship from the SigEp Educational Foundation.

It is a Virginia non-stock, non-profit corporation incorporated in 1943 as the William L. Phillips Foundation. The name was changed in 1968 as its assets grew beyond the Phillips estate and to reflect its special relationship to the scholarship and leadership activities and programs of Sigma Phi Epsilon Fraternity.

The corporation has a 15-man Board of Trustees who serve staggered six-year terms. Officers are elected annually by the Board of Trustees. Life Trustees are elected to serve as advisors.

THE SIGMA PHI EPSILON EDUCATIONAL FOUNDATION IS A RESOURCE FOR CHAPTERS AND PROVIDES SCHOLARSHIP AND LEADERSHIP PROGRAMS THAT BENEFIT THE DEVELOPMENT OF THE INDIVIDUAL BROTHER.

The Foundation derives its resources from contributions of alumni and friends of Sigma Phi Epsilon and utilizes these resources for the scholarship and leadership development programs of the Foundation and the Fraternity.

Funds of the Foundation are allocated in three categories: **chapter funds**, which are restricted for use by a specific chapter; **endowment funds**, which are designated by the donor for a specific purpose; and **unrestricted funds**, which provide for programs at the discretion of the Trustees.

The President of the Educational Foundation is responsible for its day-to-day operation and is located at Zollinger House, the Fraternity's Headquarters.

Purposes of the Educational Foundation

1. To promote the education of undergraduate and graduate student members of Sigma Phi Epsilon Fraternity in colleges and universities located throughout the nation.

2. To bring student objectives and activities into accord with the aims and purposes of the several institutions of learning with which they are affiliated.

3. To promote in such students and in groups of such students, conduct and attitudes consistent with and conducive to good morals and constructive citizenship.

4. To create in such students and student groups an atmosphere which will stimulate intellectual progress and superior intellectual achievement.

5. To foster and develop such students and student groups so that each individual will be encouraged to the highest possible degree to develop physically, morally, intellectually, and socially.

6. To accomplish the foregoing purposes by promoting better understanding of the common interests of colleges, universities, social organizations, and students in the United States and elsewhere, in matters relating to the moral, physical, mental, and social education of youth.

7. To accomplish said purposes also by encouraging students in groups of their own choosing to organize and maintain such organizations for the accomplishment of all said ideals, and by promoting means for the solution thereof.

8. To accomplish said purposes by acquiring, utilizing, applying, and disposing of property, both real and personal, exclusively for establishing, maintaining, improving, and extending the benefits and usefulness of the corporation in the attainment of its said purposes, and also by such other methods or means as shall not be inconsistent with the aforesaid objectives of this corporation.

The Foundation accomplishes its purposes by creating and maintaining endowments. Endowments provide annual income for awards to inspire and recognize scholarship and to fund leadership educational programs of the Fraternity.

In addition, the Foundation maintains a scholarship fund for each chapter which provides annual income to be used for its educational programs. Each chapter's fund operates under a working agreement which sets forth the program designed for the chapter.

The Annual Fund

Each year, the Sigma Phi Epsilon Educational Foundation offers alumni an opportunity to contribute to the Annual Fund which is the backbone of Foundation giving and provides the resources for undergraduate support.

Specific uses of the Annual Fund proceeds are for National Competition Scholarships, Resident Scholar grants, Balanced Man Scholarship, Carlson Leadership Academy, academic recognition, Zollinger Awards, and Conclave leadership programs.

Summary of Foundation Funds

Chapter Funds

▶ Restricted to specific chapter

▶ Invested in pooled fund

▶ Annual return for award is 8 percent

▶ Working agreement specifies use

Sources of funds

▶ Alumni contributions

▶ Chapter fund raising

▶ Investment return (annual average is 16 percent)

Endowment Funds

▶ Donor instructions for use

▶ Invested in pooled fund

▶ Return for award is 6 percent

Sources of funds

▶ Contributions of alumni and friends

▶ Trusts, bequests, planned gifts

▶ Special fund raising

Unrestricted Funds

Sources of funds

▶ Annual Fund

▶ Board of Governors

▶ Contributions of alumni and friends

A relatively new donor said, "Alumni of Sigma Phi Epsilon, and that means alumni from the day they graduate, need to be aware of the importance of supporting the work of the Foundation; they shouldn't put off this decision. I did for too long and missed being involved which has proven to be a great thing for me to do."

By aggregating the contributions of alumni from across the country, resources which keep Sigma Phi Epsilon strong are directed to support the scholastic and leadership development of undergraduate Brothers. Because the aggregate effect is so powerful, the individual contribution becomes more important as a part of the whole. Young alumni should decide as soon as possible after graduation how they can become a part of the Foundation's program. Your first year gift will become an important part of the total Foundation effort.

There can be no doubt the quality of the Sigma Phi Epsilon experience is worth the investment of its alumni. The Educational Foundation is charged to preserve the legacy and help to create, for future generations, a fraternity experience still better than the one entrusted to our care by our predecessors.

Foundation Support

The Educational Foundation provides funding for the following programs:

Scholarships

▶ Chapter Scholarships

▶ Zollinger Scholarships

▶ National Competition Scholarships

▶ Balanced Man Scholarship

Student Loans

▶ Yancey Student Loans

▶ Bradford Student Loans

▶ Voit Student Loans

Leadership Programs

▶ The Carlson Leadership Academies

▶ The Balanced Man Program

▶ Resident Scholars

▶ Regional Director Training

▶ Conclave Leadership Programs

Chapter Programs

▶ Chapter Libraries

▶ Centers for Excellence

▶ The Added Dimension Program

Brothers participate in a roundtable discussion at the Carlson Leadership Academy in Des Moines, Iowa.

Communications & Giving

The Educational Foundation publishes a regular newsletter, *Kleos*, that is mailed to all alumni who support the Foundation on a regular basis. Young alumni are encouraged to begin participating as a member of the Foundation donor family at the time they enter the alumni ranks. The *Corinthians* is a recognition group for young alumni that builds recognition at the Virtue, Diligence, and Brotherly Love levels as a young alumnus establishes his record of participation with the Educational Foundation.

> **"IF A MAN IS PROUD OF HIS WEALTH, HE SHOULD NOT BE PRAISED UNTIL IT IS KNOWN HOW HE EMPLOYS IT."**
>
> ~ SOCRATES

To begin participating, contact the Sigma Phi Epsilon Educational Foundation at Zollinger House in Richmond and ask for a sample *Kleos* and donor materials.

Carlson Leadership Academies

In 1972, Sigma Phi Epsilon began conducting its annual leadership education meetings on a regional basis. Prior to 1972, the academies had been held in conjunction with a Grand Chapter Conclave as one national meeting during the summer. The reason for inaugurating Carlson Academies was to enable a larger number of members to participate in leadership programs *every* year.

The Carlson Leadership Academy program has been successful to the point where more than 1,900 members, and many alumni, attend every year. The academies are held in February after chapter elections, and chapters are encouraged to bring all new officers, and their Chapter Counselors, as well as other chapter leaders. The Academy program provides practice in management skills, goal development, and academic and career planning. The Headquarters staff and the Fraternity's National Leadership Committee plan and conduct the Academies. Carlson Leadership Academies are also used to present chapter awards for outstanding achievements in operational areas, and to present individual awards to undergraduate and alumni leaders.

The Sigma Phi Epsilon *Journal*

Launched in 1904 when the Fraternity was three years old, *The Journal* serves in many areas. As an illustrated news publication, it covers the activities of chapters; it reports the programs of the Fraternity, individual achievement of alumni Brothers, and the highlights of national and district activities, including Educational Foundation projects. As an educational publication, it carries features which have a basis in the Balanced Man Ideal.

While you are an undergraduate, *The Journal* is mailed to your home address, as reported on your membership form. After you graduate, it is important that you send Headquarters your new address, so that you may continue to receive *The Journal.*

Brothers and alumni of the Delaware Alpha Chapter at the University of Delaware.

YOUR CHAPTER'S OPERATIONS

"It is amazing how much we can accomplish when no one cares who gets the credit."

~ HARRY S. TRUMAN

With some basic information about Sigma Phi Epsilon and historical perspective, you are ready to understand what makes a chapter and its brotherhood a quality experience. While chapter dynamics and environments are complex, there are common characteristics among strong chapters with true brotherhood.

The following questions have been developed specifically to assist those responsible for fraternities to evaluate their situations. How well does your chapter rate? These are the "big picture" questions you should keep in mind as you strive to build the best possible chapter experience.

The Big Picture

▶ Does life in your chapter support the educational missions of the college?

▶ What do you do to orient freshmen to the values and customs of the college?

▶ How does your chapter promote the Balanced Man Ideal of developing a Sound Mind in a Sound Body?

▶ Do you have libraries and other resource rooms available in your chapter house?

▶ Does your chapter interact with faculty on a weekly basis? Is there dedicated academic space in your chapter house?

▶ What is being done to eliminate sexism, racism, and religious bigotry?

▶ Have you measured the development that results from membership in your chapter?

▶ Is participation in service projects an integral part of the fraternal experience?

▶ Is your chapter the largest fraternity on campus?

▶ How many men remain in the chapter throughout their collegiate career?

Strategic Plan & Your Chapter

Sigma Phi Epsilon's strategic plan was first adopted in 1989. The original strategic planning committee consisted of many leaders in the Fraternity, including undergraduates and alumni, who felt it was necessary for the Fraternity to have a plan that would frame our future.

The current plan was adopted in August, 2001, and continues to define the fundamental objectives of the Fraternity's operations. The plan is built on the foundation of the Fraternity's core values in pursuit of the Balanced Man Ideal and defines the long-term objectives and major activities for the Fraternity.

The plan is a valuable tool as it serves to ensure consistency for the Fraternity. Moreover, through its measurement system, the plan provides a record of progress and helps make the Fraternity's efforts tangible.

SigEp's 2nd Century:
Building Balanced Leaders for the World's Communities

ISSUE	AMBITION	STEPS TO SUCCEEDING	IN 2011
Being the best	Be so successful that other fraternities move to emulate us.	• Implement and advance the Leadership Continuum to encourage and support chapter environments that underpin Sound Mind, Sound Body and leadership life skills. • Continue to promote and expand the adoption of the Balanced Man Program at all chapters. • Lead in campus grades, intramurals and student government.	90 percent Balanced Man Program chapters Nat'l GPA 3.15
Volunteers	Become a volunteer-based organization.	• Have the best-trained volunteers. • Produce a quality quarterly Journal for all SigEps. • Use chapter plans to engage volunteers in continuous improvement.	2,000 volunteers, with five engaged per chapter.
Strong staff	To have the best professional staff.	• Lengthen the average term of employment on professional staff. • Utilize advanced education incentives. • Provide staff with professional volunteer management training.	Average tenure on SigEp staff: Four years.
Growth	Grow every year in chapters and members.	• Be among the largest on every campus. • Achieve SigEp presence on all prominent U.S. Campuses. • Execute manpower plans that provide growth for all chapters.	285 chapters with 50 at 90+ members and attain/maintain the largest average chapter size among fraternities.
Housing	Each SigEp facility among the best on campus.	• Maintain houses as quality living/ learning environments. • Residential Learning Communities as the benchmark for Greek housing. • Funding, fund raising and property management assistance for local housing corporations.	10 significant facility improvements per year.

Being Relevant

Our first and most important responsibility is academic performance. It is each chapter's business to positively affect each member's grades. Under the strategic plan, all chapters will have a grade point average above the all-campus average. Many fraternities compare their performance to the all-men's average. This vision is short sighted. When a man graduates, he will compete for a job or graduate school against all students—men, women, Greeks, and unaffiliated students. So, Sigma Phi Epsilon prepares its members by benchmarking their performance against the all-campus average.

All chapters should develop programming that provides learning opportunities for a member throughout his fraternity experience. It is important that an undergraduate learn as much through his association with the Fraternity as a junior and senior as he did as a freshman and sophomore. And, all chapter programming must be consistent with the "Statement on Chapter & Individual Responsibility," to ensure safety of Sigma Phi Epsilon members and guests. By providing for all members of your chapter, you ensure their continued involvement and participation.

Men join a fraternity for a variety of reasons—among them to have fun. One of your responsibilities is to ensure that the chapter's activities are safe and productive at the same time. The Balanced Man Program is central to this effort. The program requires a significant attitudinal shift in a chapter. Members accept equal membership in the Fraternity from the day they join; in return, they also accept membership expectations until the day they graduate and beyond. It is not easy to run against the norm for fraternities on campus. Few things worth doing come easily. The chapters who are proficient with the Balanced Man Program are proud to differentiate themselves on their campus, and have improved their membership retention, membership recruitment, campus involvement, and ability to attract quality volunteer support. They display better attitudes toward alcohol, and provide a safer

The University of Wisconsin SigEps keep its brothers involved with volunteer activities that reach out to their community and develop Sound Body. Brothers raised over $7,600 for the University of Wisconsin Children's Hospital.

experience. The chapters that have implemented the Balanced Man Program for several years are demonstrating that people want to join a chapter that lives its values. Balanced Man Program chapters are recruiting more men and academic performance is markedly improved.

November of 2002 marked the establishment of SigEp's chapter at Yale University. It is our first time on campus in our 104-year history.

Financial Operations

One of the realities in any fraternity is that you have to pay to play. The cost is an investment in the experience you will have for a lifetime.

Financial stability is the result of three factors: manpower, pricing, and collections. First and foremost, experience has shown that a chapter must be in the top quartile in manpower among fraternities and have at least 40 men to have sufficient resources for good programming.

Chapters must ensure they are charging fees in the top quartile on campus, and room and board should be priced above the residence halls. This results in resources to enhance chapter programming and maintains chapter facilities.

High accounts receivable and low occupancy rates cripple a chapter. Chapters and Alumni and Volunteer Corporations (AVCs) should have

lease agreements signed in February. Strictly adhering to the 30/60-day bylaw for dues collection will safeguard your chapter's future.

By remaining in the top quartile of manpower, pricing at a fair value, and collecting payments, you will build a prosperous chapter that has the resources to compete.

Volunteer Support

Over time, the support of volunteers has proven to be instrumental in the health and vitality of a chapter. Every chapter that performs over time has an effective Chapter Counselor and Alumni and Volunteer Corporation (AVC). The AVC should have enough people involved to manage the facility, if the chapter has one, and to provide mentors for important areas of chapter operations such as recruitment, academics, finances, and membership development.

Developing volunteer support from faculty and community members, in addition to local alumni, is invaluable. Resident scholars and housemothers continue to prove beneficial. The value of having a residential advisor, whether it be a resident scholar or housemother, is indisputable. By involving volunteers from outside the chapter in meaningful activities, your chapter will create a resource base that will benefit each member of the chapter.

Chapter Environments

Creating a chapter environment that is a home-away-from-home should be the aim of every Sigma Phi Epsilon chapter. Such an environment provides positive support for members to learn and succeed. A quality chapter environment means that the chapter home is clean, safe, and well-maintained. Your chapter house is your home-away-from-home and must be treated as such.

Home sweet home. If your chapter house looks and feels clean, safe, and well-maintained, you and your Brothers will have a place to be proud of.
COURTESY OF THE MISSISSIPPI BETA CHAPTER AT MISSISSIPPI STATE UNIVERSITY.

Sigma Phi Epsilon chapter facilities will be treated like your homes if they are not already. Clean up after yourself. Take out the trash when it overflows. Have all residents and out-of-house members participate in regular cleaning. Hold people accountable for damage they cause, especially alumni. These are the expectations of Sigma Phi Epsilon. The key to a good chapter environment is personal responsibility. Do not wait to be asked to do something. If you know it is right, take the initiative and do it yourself.

> **BY INVOLVING VOLUNTEERS FROM OUTSIDE THE CHAPTER IN MEANINGFUL ACTIVITIES, YOUR CHAPTER WILL CREATE A RESOURCE BASE THAT WILL BENEFIT EACH MEMBER OF THE CHAPTER.**

Maintaining chapter houses costs money. Chapters must save three percent of the property value annually to afford needed long-term maintenance. Rental rates must be set with the need for long-term savings in mind. Properties need to be properly insured, and the facilities must be filled. The benefit for you will be a top-notch place to live and learn.

Sigma Phi Epsilon will strive to meet the objectives outlined in the plan to maintain our position of leadership on the college campus. The strategic plan is the tool we will use to guide and measure our progress, and the full participation of every chapter and every member will make it possible. Right now, Sigma Phi Epsilon is a leading fraternity. It is up to you to keep us there.

Your Responsibility

You and your chapter share in the responsibility of fulfilling the objectives of Sigma Phi Epsilon's strategic plan. In doing so, you ensure a safe, fun, top quality experience for yourself and your Brothers while building a foundation for long-term success and superiority. You are meeting your expectations when you:

YOU HAVE AN OBLIGATION TO YOURSELF AND TO YOUR FUTURE BROTHERS TO LOOK INTO YOUR CHAPTER'S OPERATION, LEARN ALL YOU CAN, AND MAKE YOUR MOST EFFECTIVE CONTRIBUTION.

▶ Have a grade point average above the all-campus average, and worthy of the Phi Beta Kappa Wheelhouse.

▶ Are among the largest in manpower with a minimum chapter size of 40.

▶ Compete actively for campus leadership positions and do well in intramurals.

▶ Charge dues that are in the top quartile among fraternities on campus.

▶ Charge room and board equal to or greater than the residence hall on your campus.

▶ Have a Chapter Counselor and Alumni and Volunteer Corporation actively involved in maintaining the facility and helping the chapter plan responsible programming for all members.

▶ Have a development program based on a universal respect for self and others, that improves all members, and is consistent with the "Statement on Chapter & Individual Responsibility."

You Hold the Key

Your chapter and the 256 other Sigma Phi Epsilon chapters are the foundation of the Fraternity. From your membership and your programs and activities comes a feeling, an image, an attitude, and a public awareness of Sigma Phi Epsilon. Each individual member in each chapter shares a large part of the responsibility of making Sigma Phi Epsilon the most rewarding experience an undergraduate can have. The personal integrity and commitment of each member will determine the standards of achievement in Sigma Phi Epsilon.

Over the years, your chapter has created its own identity within Sigma Phi Epsilon. You have a body of alumni who have gone before you and who have a special interest in the chapter. As well as establishing your chapter, your national Fraternity has invested time, effort, and resources over the years in assisting your chapter and providing services. Your Headquarters staff has a special interest in your success because it has made a commitment to do everything within its ability to help you maintain a balanced, successful, excellence-oriented operation.

You have an obligation to yourself and to your future Brothers to look into your chapter's operation, learn all you can, and make your most effective contribution. Without your alumni, and national Fraternity, there would be no Sigma Phi Epsilon experience for you today. Without you and your contribution, there might not be that quality experience for tomorrow.

Chapter Leadership

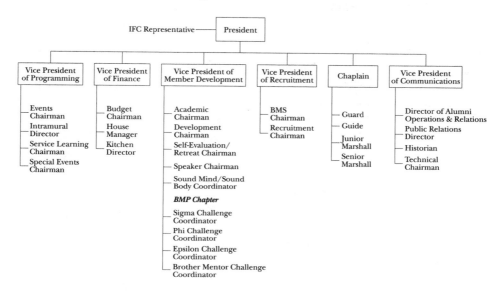

Overview of Structure

The chapter's management system is composed of two bodies: the executive committee, which guides chapter operations, and the standards board, which makes judicial decisions, manages chapter awards, and reviews risk management at events. The executive committee consists of the President, Vice President of Programming, Vice President of Finance, Vice President of Member Development, Vice President of Recruitment, Vice President of Communications, and Chaplain (note, the Chaplain is an ex-officio, non-voting member of the executive committee to ensure that he can fulfill his standards role without conflicting objectives). These officers are elected and take office annually between November 1 and February 1. The cabinets for each executive officer are appointed or elected within two weeks of the executive committee taking position.

The Executive Committee

The purpose of the executive committee is to provide vision and leadership for the chapter. Through goal setting and creating an action plan, the group moves the chapter forward in all its endeavors. The executive committee must be creative, task-oriented, and forward-thinking. Through clear communication with the chapter membership, the executive committee will see that the chapter's mission is achieved.

The executive committee's primary functions are:

1. To hold preliminary discussions on important business to provide recommendations to the chapter;

2. To provide direction and leadership for various cabinets;

3. To assure the effectiveness of the organization with planned follow-through on chapter activities and programs;

4. To communicate effectively with the chapter members so everyone is aware of plans, programs, and events.

The President is the leader of the chapter and executive committee. The Secretary takes the minutes of the chapter meeting, and the Vice President of Programming takes the minutes at the executive committee meeting. In the absence of the President, the Vice President of Programming fills his role.

The Standards Board

The standards board is the spiritual arm of the chapter. It is the conscience and the guide. The standards board, through use and understanding of the Ritual, serves a dual role—to discipline or expel members who fail in their obligation to the Fraternity, and to recognize members who excel in their dedication to Sigma Phi Epsilon. To be successful, the board must make difficult decisions, stand for what is right—not necessarily easy or popular—and move forward in the hope of accomplishment.

THE STANDARDS BOARD IS COMPRISED OF THE CHAPLAIN, WHO CHAIRS THE BOARD, SENIOR MARSHAL, JUNIOR MARSHAL, GUARD, AND GUIDE.

The standards board is comprised of the chaplain, who chairs the board, senior marshal, junior marshal, guard, and guide. This board is the judicial branch of the chapter and has the responsibility for all disciplinary measures, including suspension and expulsion of membership.

Areas of responsibility for this important committee are:

1. To enforce Grand Chapter and chapter bylaws, resolve disputes between Brothers, determine sanctions up to and including expulsion as authorized in the Fraternity's Trial Procedures;

2. To ensure that membership agreements and standards codes are signed, and ensure that fraternity and chapter standards are upheld;

3. To manage the chapter's awards and scholarship program;

4. To review proper risk management for upcoming events;

5. To plan the next use of the Ritual, inspect the Ritual equipment, and practice the Ritual.

The standards committee should make sure that the chapter's standards are reviewed and updated regularly, and that members are educated on them. The board should promote the Ritual in chapter programs and in chapter life.

Then-Grand President James F. Robeson, U. of Cincinnati '59, with the executive board of the New York Alpha Chapter at Syracuse University.

The Chapter Officers

The officers of the chapter, in order of succession are: President, Vice President of Programming, Vice President of Finance, Vice President of Member Development, Vice President of Recruitment, Vice President of Communications, and Chaplain.

PRESIDENT: The Chapter President is responsible for overall operations and the proper conduct of the members. He presides at all chapter meetings, communicates with those outside the chapter who have an interest in its progress (alumni officers, SigEp Headquarters, college officials, other fraternities, and SigEp chapters), knows all expectations of the chapter, and guides and directs the chapter toward meeting its goals. His cabinet consists of the public relations chairman and IFC representative. The cabinets of the Vice Presidents carry

on the work of the chapter, and it is the President who must direct the chapter and provide leadership.

VICE PRESIDENT OF PROGRAMMING: He is in charge of chapter functions and programs. It is his responsibility to keep the chapter calendar and promote attendance at chapter meetings and events. It is also his responsibility to ensure the members of the chapter have a positive and safe social experience. Members of his cabinet might include: events chairman, philanthropy chairman, intramural chairman, special events chairman, and risk management chairman.

VICE PRESIDENT OF FINANCE: He works closely with the Alumni and Volunteer Corporation (AVC) Treasurer and is responsible for the financial stability of the chapter and planning for the future financial needs. He and his cabinet, which might include a house chairman, kitchen director, and budget chairman, prepare the chapter's budget, distribute statements to members, collect dues, collect room and board, pay bills, and prepare monthly reports to the AVC and Headquarters. This Vice President is the chapter's business manager.

VICE PRESIDENT OF MEMBER DEVELOPMENT: He is the man in charge of activities that affect the development of chapter members. He is responsible for finding facilitators, planning chapter retreats, scheduling guest speakers, coordinating experiential learning activities, and tracking individual academic records. Members of his cabinet include the retreat chairman, academic chairman, speaker chairman, and in Balanced Man Program chapters the Sigma, Phi, Epsilon, and Brother Mentor challenge coordinators.

> **"FRIENDS ARE AS COMPANIONS ON A JOURNEY, WHO OUGHT TO AID EACH OTHER TO PERSEVERE IN THE ROAD TO A HAPPIER LIFE."**
> ~ PYTHAGORAS

VICE PRESIDENT OF RECRUITMENT: His main responsibility is to secure new members for the chapter. He is responsible for all recruitment events, alumni events, updating alumni addresses, extending bids to prospective members, publishing the chapter newsletter, and conducting the Balanced Man Scholarship. Members of his cabinet may include the recruitment events chairman, recruitment committee, and the Balanced Man Scholarship chairman.

VICE PRESIDENT OF COMMUNICATIONS: His main responsibility is to oversee the communications cabinet which may include the director of alumni operations and relations, public relations director, historian, and technology chairman. He strengthens relationships with alumni and communicates the positive actions of the chapter to the campus community and Headquarters while preserving the history of the chapter. He calls the roll and keeps the minutes of each meeting. He conducts all correspondence and brings all legislation before the chapter.

CHAPLAIN: His main responsibility is to lead the standards committee which is his cabinet, schedule committee meetings, and see that the ideals of the Fraternity are upheld. He is the man who, in addition to ritualistic duties, is responsible for maintaining an attitude in the chapter which is consistent with the principles of the Fraternity. He develops recognition programs to enrich brotherhood and the "fraternal" education of chapter members. He sets an example and maintains Sigma Phi Epsilon's Cardinal Principles: Virtue, Diligence, and Brotherly Love. It is his responsibility to counsel the executive committee in this area.

STANDARDS BOARD: The Ritual officers are also elected annually by the chapter and include: senior marshal, junior marshal, guard and guide. These officers form the standards committee and the cabinet of the chaplain. These members also have responsibilities for the chapter's Ritual equipment and proper conduct of the Ritual.

CABINET MEMBERS: Each member of the executive committee may determine any additional positions he will need to fulfill his responsibilities and the President makes appointments. For example, the Vice President of Programming may determine he needs an events chairman to work with social events and another man to work specifically with homecoming. Each of these chairmen may form his own committee to help with the details of the various events. These chairmen will report to the Vice President who will update the chapter at the weekly meeting as to how the responsibilities are being carried out.

Chapter Meetings

Weekly chapter meetings are designed to inform all chapter members of upcoming events, to hear committee and financial reports, and to have the chapter make decisions on important business. These meetings are not to debate minute details—that is the job of the committees and officers.

The order of business is standard and parallels that of any business meeting you will encounter during your professional career.

Order of Business

1. Roll call (Secretary)

2. Reading of the minutes of the preceding meeting (Secretary)

3. Vice President of Finance report

4. Vice President of Programming report

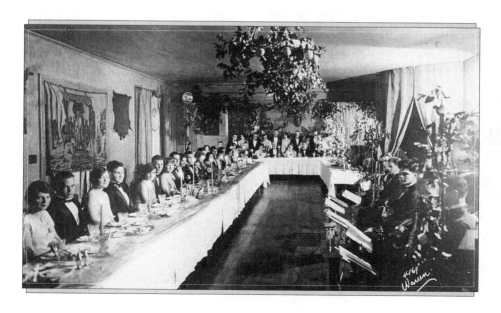

5. Vice President of Recruitment report

6. Vice President of Member Development report

7. Vice President of Communications report

8. Standards board report

9. Reading of notices and communications

10. Unfinished business (Secretary)

11. New business

12. Proposals for membership

13. Reports of sickness

14. Remarks for the good of the Fraternity

15. Distribution of membership cards and certificates

16. Installation of officers

17. Reading or discussion of Ritual

18. Closing

All members should attend chapter meetings.

The chapter should approach these meetings not as a social outlet, but as the key component in chapter communication. Excessive disruption or frivolity will lead to poor attendance at future chapter meetings and at least a week of chaotic events. Parliamentary procedure should be followed, but not abused to the point of absurdity. These meetings should be held in a place well suited for meetings—adequate seating for all, proper

WEEKLY CHAPTER MEETINGS ARE DESIGNED TO INFORM ALL CHAPTER MEMBERS OF UPCOMING EVENTS, TO HEAR COMMITTEE AND FINANCIAL REPORTS, AND TO HAVE THE CHAPTER MAKE DECISIONS ON IMPORTANT BUSINESS.

heating or cooling, well lit and prepared in advance for the meeting. An appropriate dress code should be established by the chapter, such as coat and tie or collared shirt and slacks. The chapter should also conduct a monthly Ritual meeting.

No alcohol should be present, and members who have been drinking should not be allowed to attend the meeting.

How to Conduct a Standard Business Meeting

An important skill that can be learned in the chapter is how to run and participate in a meeting. Conducting an organized, productive meeting will be valuable to you throughout your life.

▶ Start on time and stop at a definite time or when interest is high.

▶ Always have a flip chart with posted agenda or distribute a typed agenda.

▶ Be sure you have a quorum before transacting business; have the Secretary take roll, inform the chair, enter this fact in the minutes.

▶ "Call" on people to make reports—DO NOT "turn the meeting over."

▶ Be sure those who are to give reports are prepared. Do this BEFORE the start of the meeting. Written reports are a must.

▶ Reports should be given to the Secretary in writing and a motion should be presented to have the report "adopted" or "filed" or "returned to committee."

The presiding officer should initiate items for consideration, facilitate deliberation, orient and guide the meeting, encourage free discussion, and be able to summarize, clarify and restate motions on the floor.

▶ The main responsibilities of the presiding officer are:

1. to INITIATE items or proposals for consideration.

2. to FACILITATE the deliberations and actions of the group.

   a. Know parliamentary procedure.

   b. Avoid making long explanations or speeches.

   c. Use the Secretary. Get motions in writing.

   d. Be alert to members and their reactions.

   e. Use your authority and use it wisely.

   f. Handle business by "general consent" when appropriate.

3. to ORIENT AND GUIDE. Explain procedure.

4. to ENCOURAGE FREE DISCUSSION. Harmonize heated debate.

5. to SUMMARIZE, CLARIFY, and RESTATE motions.

▶ Minutes, motions, and reports should be distributed in a timely manner after the meeting.

"EVERYONE CAN BE GREAT BECAUSE EVERYONE CAN SERVE."

~ DR. MARTIN LUTHER KING

YOUR CHAPTER'S PRIORITIES

"Some of us will do our jobs well and some will not, but we will all be judged by only one thing—the result."

~ UNKNOWN

The quality operations of any chapter, whether on a large or small campus, public or private institution, residential or commuter population, can be narrowed down to four areas: manpower, finances, membership development and academics, and volunteer support. Any chapter that is performing well in these four areas of operation is likely to produce terrific results and provide a tremendous fraternal experience for its members. While every chapter and every campus retain their own unique traits, the fundamentals of fraternity operations do not change.

In this chapter, we will examine the four areas that predicate success and true brotherhood. A chapter that focuses on these goal-setting and daily operations will achieve a position envied by its peers.

Manpower

Recruitment, very simply, secures manpower and talent. It determines the quality of your chapter as well as the strength of SigEp nationally. It is a process that began before you arrived in the chapter and will continue long after you leave undergraduate walls. Recruitment is a year-round effort that must exist outside of the formal recruitment spectrum. Regardless of how many new members a chapter recruits or how many times per year new members join the chapter, the undergraduates must always be recruiting if we are to attract the most talented men on campus. Effective recruitment will help your chapter and Sigma Phi Epsilon thrive for decades to come.

Quality AND Quantity

Who are you and what do you stand for? Ask this question of Nike and you will likely hear about innovative sports and fitness equipment. Ask the same question of a church, synagogue, or mosque, and you will likely find a response based upon spiritual development. The point is, every organization offers some sort of "product." Fraternities are unique in that our "product," the very thing we offer, is our members. Our Ritual, member development programs, activities, leadership programs, the house, etc., are aimed at driving the quality of life for members, and our overall appeal.

RECRUITMENT DETERMINES THE QUALITY OF YOUR CHAPTER AND THE STRENGTH OF SIGEP NATIONALLY.

Recruitment standards, perhaps more than anything else, drive quality membership. Set recruitment standards high and go after men who meet SigEp's high standard, thus ensuring quality membership.

Likewise, the number of outstanding men in your chapter will be a key factor in success. Size is the single most distinctive attribute of fraternity success. Chapters with large membership offer more opportunities for friendship to potential members. Their membership is usually more diverse, contains more campus leaders, and represents power to outsiders. Think about the top fraternities on your campus (not including SigEp). Are they large in relation to competitors? Chances are the answer is yes.

OUR FRATERNITY VIEWS RECRUITMENT NOT JUST AS A MEANS OF GETTING MEN, BUT A VEHICLE TO ACTIVELY AND STRATEGICALLY RECRUIT THE BEST MEN.

Potential members often join student organizations in search of support behind their collegiate and life ambitions. Chapters with large manpower in relation to competitors offer greater perceived support behind their objectives. Large chapters also live *The Ritual and Guide of Sigma Phi Epsilon*. Our Ritual states that no man should absorb greater responsibility than he can bear. Large chapters can divide work among a greater number of people, offering members a better shot at achieving balance.

If your chapter is one of the largest on campus, you already realize the power of size. Your chapter should set its sights on consistently being 10 percent larger than the second-largest fraternity on campus. If your chapter is small, or average, in size relative to competitors, achieving a competitive size should be a top priority. Chances are your chapter consists of many quality members, but is suffering from insufficient quantity. Over the long term, a small chapter will have greater difficulty competing with larger chapters. Just as a football team consisting of only 11 men would tire over four quarters in competition with a squad boasting a 50-man roster, so will the chapter. Diligence in recruitment requires you to act swiftly.

At outstanding SigEp chapters, recruitment is a consistent, top priority. Our Fraternity views recruitment not just as a means of getting men, but a vehicle to actively and strategically recruit the best men, to develop the best "product." We strive to recruit the best men in dominant size. Whether your chapter is already number one on campus in manpower or is setting its sights on moving up, this guide is designed to help you achieve your goals.

Quality and quantity...achieve the best of both.

Skills + Process + Execution = Results & Positive Attitude

The equation above shows the key ingredients in recruitment success: plan, process, and skills. Whether you are member of a large state institution, or small private, whether your campus is 50 percent Greek, or less than five percent, year-round recruitment or deferred, recruitment results are dependent on these three factors.

Skills

In its most basic form, recruitment is the process of making friends. Perhaps the reason why so many famous alumni report NOT having been Chapter President, rather, in charge of recruitment, is because no other area of chapter operations is so focused on developing strong relationships and inspiring others to do the same. Talking to a new person can be a terrifying prospect for some people. Arming Brothers with the right skills about opening a conversation, talking accurately about SigEp, and handling objections will help the chapter put its best foot forward during recruitment and will help Brothers learn lifelong communication skills often not taught in the classroom. A good start is concentrating on listening. A potential member is going to choose the fraternity where he feels most comfortable and believes he has the most friends. Each recruiter must feel confident in his own ability to ask "leading" questions that promote

conversation and allow him to listen to the recruit and begin to understand what is important to him. Once we know what is important in a recruit's life and what his goals are, we can begin the process of aligning his goals and aspirations with those of Sigma Phi Epsilon. The best recruiters connect SigEp with where a recruit sees himself five years down the road, and explains to him how Sigma Phi Epsilon can aid him in his quest. These communication skills, combined with friendliness shown by Brothers, will help recruits come to the conclusion that SigEp is the fraternity of choice.

Process

To walk, you learn balance and put one foot in front of the other. To eat, you lift food to your mouth, chew, and swallow. Everything follows some sort of process, and recruitment is no different. The way you recruit is directly related to the quality and quantity of men you recruit. To execute a consistently strong recruitment process, get the right people working on the right jobs, be specific about task requests, follow up diligently, and hold Brothers accountable to their commitments. See the next section for a more complete recruitment process explanation.

Execution of Recruitment Plan

Like many membership organizations, chapters often struggle with the transition from one set of leaders to the next. Officer transition is a reality; therefore, it is important that chapters establish written plans of attack for important operations, like recruitment. Written plans encourage evolution versus the reinvention of the wheel. Chapters with written recruitment plans passed on from one officer to the next and revised as needed over time are more likely to be consistently outstanding. Another aspect of the great recruitment chapters is the presence of alumni in the recruitment process. Alumni often serve as mentors to the recruitment process, and for some alumni, recruitment mentoring is their one function on the Alumni and Volunteer Corporation. This kind of dedication to the process and plan ensures that the best information gets transferred from one Vice President of Recruitment to the next. This experience, diligence and know-how can make good recruiters great and take a chapter to a higher level of overall performance.

Results & Attitude

The right plan, process, and skills drive recruitment results and overall

Executive board for the Missouri Beta Chapter at Washington U. in St. Louis

attitude, or morale, of the chapter. Chapters that permeate a winning attitude are most likely to achieve strong recruitment results. Likewise, the attitude of the chapter is highly dependent upon recruitment results. Recruitment success drives morale up. It tells members that what they believe is right and solidifies their belief that SigEp is the fraternity of choice. As a leader, it is important you recognize this relationship and work diligently to achieve recruitment results and a winning attitude among chapter members. As recruitment results are achieved and momentum is gained, it is important that you capitalize on the opportunity to push for the best of both results and attitude.

Always, Maybe, and Never Joiners
The Recuitment Process of Sigma Phi Epsilon

SigEp has a long-held theory regarding incoming collegiate men's expectations about joining a fraternity. It states that a small percentage of men attend college under the premise that they will certainly join a fraternity, while another small percentage of incoming men say they will never join a fraternity. The largest percentage of men report they will "maybe" join a fraternity. Current studies of graduating high school males completed by the North American Interfraternity Conference now prove the above theory correct. Each category deserves special attention in devising recruitment and marketing plans.

Always Joiners

"Always joiners" are best described as men who are intent upon joining a fraternity as a part of their college experience. Some set of circumstances has attracted them to fraternity living. In some cases, they are legacies, men whose relatives were a part of a fraternity. Other times, they are men who are attracted to the negative perceptions of fraternity life, such as alcohol abuse.

In recruiting "always joiners," it is important to remember two things. First, strict application of standards is a must. High standards ensure the men attracted to those negative perceptions do not join your chapter. Second, it is important to reach these men early, such as the summer prior to arrival on campus. Since they are looking to join a fraternity, often the first fraternity that approaches them will be the one they end up joining. Caveats to this rule exist, but you should manage for the rule, not the exception.

CHAPTERS THAT PERMEATE A WINNING ATTITUDE ARE MOST LIKELY TO ACHIEVE STRONG RECRUITMENT RESULTS.

Never Joiners

"Never joiners" are men who, no matter what the circumstances, will not be attracted to joining a fraternity. "Never joiners" are a small percentage of the total on most campuses. It is important to routinely talk about the positive things your chapter is doing via various forms of communication, so these men, at the very least, have a positive view of Sigma Phi Epsilon and Greek life as a whole. Chapters often make the mistake of poking fun at this group due to a lack of confidence in their fraternity. If you are truly confident in the brotherhood and experience offered by Sigma Phi Epsilon, you will not need to compensate for perceived deficiencies held by "never joiners" by using childish insults. Instead, you will respect their decision to explore other avenues to achieve a satisfying college experience.

Maybe Joiners

Since "maybe joiners" represent the largest portion of the potential member pool on all campuses, your chapter's efforts should be concentrated on this category. "Always joiners" will be interested, so long as they are met early. "Never joiners" will likely never be attracted to Greek life. "Maybe joiners" are men who need convincing and require SigEp to take the initiative to meet them and communicate to them our Fraternity's values, thus initiating the recruitment process of Sigma Phi Epsilon. "Maybe joiners" tend to be top students on campus, and once convinced to join, often blossom into the best, most active Brothers. There are three key steps to recruit "maybe joiners" for SigEp:

THE KEY TO RECRUITING MAYBE JOINERS IS CONNECTING WITH THE RECRUIT ON A PERSONAL RELATIONSHIP LEVEL.

▶ BUILD A PROSPECTIVE MEMBER LIST. First, it is up to the chapter to take initiative to find and contact these men. The Balanced Man Scholarship, soliciting recommendations from sororities, faculty, and coaches often yield strong leads to "maybe joiners." On the average, a chapter will need to have about five times as many men on its list as it is trying to recruit. If the recruitment goal is 30, then the chapter needs around 150 men on the list.

▶ ARTICULATE THE MESSAGE. Second, these men require that members are able to articulate the values of Sigma Phi Epsilon. "Maybe joiners" need to be convinced; therefore, the accomplishments of your chapter and individual Brothers must be known and well explained. The key to this stage is connecting with the recruit on a personal relationship level, and almost any venue will work to implement this stage of the recruitment process. Events, casual meals, visits to apartments or dorm rooms, even a professional interview have the potential to be a recruitment opportunity. While important, it's not enough to say what your chapter doesn't do (i.e., haze, abuse drugs, alcohol, etc.), Brothers must be able to explain what your chapter does to live the Balanced Man Ideal. You must be specific! Highlight successful events or programs that promote our ideals so we are walking the walk. In short, this is where you answer the question, "So what's so good about SigEp?"

▶ CLOSE THE DEAL. Third, it is essential that the recruitment process be well explained so they understand how the joining process works. Since many of these men have not given a thought to joining a fraternity, the chance of misunderstanding is high. Words like rush, ritual, and bid can be confusing and intimidating if not properly explained. Finally, just as the chapter must make the first move in finding and contacting "maybe joiners," it will be left up to the chapter to make the offer clear for membership. While "always joiners" will often give indications that they are interested in joining, "maybe joiners" may not. If the man in question meets the chapter's recruitment standards, and the chapter has done its part in showing him all SigEp has to offer, an invitation for membership will surely be accepted.

Leave no doubt in the recruit's mind that SigEp is the place for him and that you want him to join the chapter. Hesitation in inviting a quality man to join the chapter may turn him off, or worse, provide an opportunity for a competitor to recruit a quality man whose top choice was SigEp all along.

Recruitment Helps Us Win

If your chapter is going to be successful in any other activities or programs, scholarship, intramurals, or membership development, you must first recruit the best men to manage and participate in these programs. For this reason, the Vice President of Recruitment has, next to the Chapter President, the most important responsibility in the entire chapter. He should take pride in the position and use it as a source of personal motivation.

Recruitment is the ultimate competition. The fraternity that recruits men with Sound Minds will typically win the Scholarship Cup. The fraternity that recruits men with Sound Bodies will usually win the intramural honors. The fraternity that recruits the hardest working leaders will maintain a leadership presence on campus. The fraternity that recruits the best balance of leaders with Sound Minds and Sound Bodies will undoubtedly be the top fraternity on campus.

On any given campus, the best fraternities will be comprised of not just the best men on campus, but the most men on campus. A simple rule of competition is that you must have the resources to compete. For fraternities, this means you need to have enough good men to draw upon. The ultimate

Make sure your recruits know what a great chapter you have. Include them in chapter activities and introduce them to other interesting brothers in your chapter.

aim is to have the best and the largest number of men join on campus. Visit any campus across the country, and you will find that the best fraternity on campus is usually one of the largest.

With this in mind, your goal is to recruit men who will allow your chapter to reach the top or stay on top if you're already there. You are not recruiting to "fill the house" or "to replace graduating seniors," you are recruiting to win. Make no mistake, your aim is to get the best recruits on campus and the most Balanced Men.

Bear in mind that you will be competing for these men. You will compete against other student organizations, dormitories, and general disinterest among many students. You will compete with other fraternities for men considering joining, but the biggest challenge is going to be recruiting the top men

who are not interested in a fraternity. To compete effectively in both situations, you must continuously improve your brotherhood through the Balanced Man Ideal. That is, continuously improve what you have to offer and market it wisely. If you are the best fraternity, you must constantly improve if you want to maintain that position, because you can bet the competition will be doing everything they can to catch you. If you are not the best fraternity, you should identify who is, and use them as a benchmark. Then, develop a specific plan to compete effectively with them until you surpass them as number one. Once you have, continue to improve so you remain there.

Complacency is an ugly situation. Sloth is evil. Truly dominant chapters continuously seek ways to improve the experience offered members.

The Long Range

The Vice President of Recruitment has to be able to think long term. Decisions made now will have a huge impact on your chapter's success next year, and even four to five years down the road. If you recruit the top Balanced Man this year, the impact on next year is obvious. But, the impact five years from now should be obvious as well. After all, a fraternity is only as good as the men in it. Once you recruit the right men and provide them with strong member development, they will be able to carry out successfully the mission of the Fraternity in future years and presumably recruit more outstanding men to continue the tradition after they are gone.

Sigma Phi Epsilon remains one of the strongest national fraternities in the world thanks to the efforts of our Brothers. A national fraternity is as strong as its collective chapters. Your approach to recruitment will impact the national Fraternity. Our challenge is to remain a leader in the fraternity world. You play an important role in this effort.

The resources offered will provide you with the tools and concepts necessary to compete effectively on your campus. These tools and concepts can be applied to any campus situation with a little creativity and initiative. If you employ them diligently, your chapter will achieve even greater success, and more men on your campus will reap the benefits of the SigEp experience.

Your recruitment program should provide an opportunity for prospective members to get to know members. The program should make each member think about the benefits of his fraternal experience so he can relate them to potential members.

The recruitment program must be "dry," meaning without alcohol. Dry recruitment has been an integral part of Sigma Phi Epsilon's recruitment program since the 1985 Grand Chapter Conclave in San Antonio. Dry recruitment shows chapter members at their best and says the chapter is comfortable with its offerings without depending on alcohol.

Know and sell the nature of Sigma Phi Epsilon and your chapter. The quality of your chapter will attract the right men and your chapter will gain performance, power, and prestige.

Remember, be interested, not interesting. A potential member needs to be heard and feel a part of the group. He can only do this by letting you know who he is and how he feels.

Besides, how else can you find out if he is SigEp material or what his objections may be? Listen.

Some Recruitment Tips

For a comprehensive list along with other recruitment resources, visit *www.sigep.org/recruitment/default.asp*

ASK QUESTIONS FIRST. Get to know a potential member by asking questions about him before talking about SigEp.

BE ARTICULATE. Make sure all Brothers know HOW to talk accurately about the SigEp experience. Does everyone in your chapter know how to discuss Sound Mind, Sound Body? SigEp's Cardinal Principles? Are the activities your chapter has accomplished or is planning attracting the best men on campus? Don't allow SigEp to be just like everyone else. The things your chapter VALUES and DOES sets you apart from competitors. Talk about what makes you different, a cut above. Successful people gravitate toward success. You must quantitatively show just how successful you really are as a chapter in order to attract the best men.

"IN UNION, THERE IS STRENGTH."

~ AESOP

DEVELOP A WRITTEN RECRUITMENT PLAN. This will define the step-by-step process of recruitment to the Brothers and the recruitment committee.

HOLD A CHAPTER RECRUITMENT CLINIC. At least once a year, on a night, weekend or other appropriate time, teach the recruitment plan, its technique, role-playing, what to say and how to say it. New member development should also include recruitment skills education. Talk to your Regional Director about how to set up a skills education workshop.

FORM AN OUTSTANDING RECRUITMENT COMMITTEE AND GIVE COMMITTEE MEMBERS TIME TO LEARN—The recruitment committee is a small group of Brothers who extend membership bids to potential new members. Select four to six Brothers who will devote the necessary time and who have the necessary commitment to excellence. Appoint at least one experienced Brother to the committee. If the team is inexperienced, name them far enough in advance of the "big" recruitment time to enable them to gain the knowledge they need to compete against your rivals. Be sure to include adequate transition.

SET RECRUITMENT GOALS. Make them high, but attainable—with a winning effort. Determine your target by striving to be at least ten percent larger than the next largest fraternity. Hit the recruitment mark and watch brotherhood, participation, excitement, and many other chapter characteristics take off.

RECRUIT MEN WITH HIGH GPAs. Have a written set of recruitment standards and follow them. Part of your chapter's recruitment standards should include a GPA requirement, and that requirement should at least be a 3.0.

SELECT YOUR TARGETS. Identify and go after the best, the ones that everyone else wants, the "Blue Chips." This means starting early. Recruit men who have the potential to make a difference in your chapter and after graduation.

SUMMER RECRUITMENT. Organize a team early in the year. Start gathering names in March. Invite high school seniors to a pre-recruitment weekend during the spring term and/or host events during summer orientation.

"ALL FUNCTIONS ARE RECRUITMENT FUNCTIONS." A potential member can be invited to virtually all chapter functions. Remember: Recruitment is 24/7, 365.

BE AGGRESSIVE. Beat competitors to the punch. Convince the recruit that joining SigEp is the best decision for him.

Hold a chapter meeting and go over recruitment strategies and goals. Make a list of target recruits and decide who is best to make the initial contact.

Finances

Quality finances are the combination of good manpower, competitive pricing, and strict collections. The more a fraternity runs like a business, the more it runs like a fraternity.

The sound financial operation of your chapter depends on the cooperation of each Brother. On many Vice Presidents' of Finance doors there is a sign which says, "*Brotherhood* is no excuse—it's the *reason* you need to pay." If you have a financial problem, there are several avenues to a fair payment option, but one of these is not to live on the "brotherhood excuse." Conversely, *you* will have to pick up the bills of your Brothers who choose to not pay.

A good Brother does not want to take away from anyone else's experience. He cares about helping the chapter, and sees money owed to the Fraternity as one of his first responsibilities so the chapter can provide services and programs to him and his Brothers.

The Vice President of Finance will want to assist you if you have financial problems and avail yourself to work with him before you are behind in your financial obligations; he has the resources of the Alumni and Volunteer Corporation which can extend payments, make loans, or execute promissory notes. Loans are also available from the Sigma Phi Epsilon Educational Foundation.

Grand Chapter Bylaws provide that a member whose debt to the chapter is 30 days past due is automatically suspended from the Fraternity. When a debt becomes 60 days past due, the member is expelled. With all the avenues available to assist a Brother in need, such a situation should rarely arise.

Academics & Membership Development

The first and most important membership development topic for every chapter to address is academics. Academic performance is the best indication of quality in a chapter. Sigma Phi Epsilon members and chapters should be above the all-campus average each term. Taking time to see that members are setting academic goals, posting their schedules, and attending class is the business of the Fraternity. Sigma Phi Epsilon exists to advance the mission of the college or university where it has a chapter.

Ensuring a quality environment is the best policy. Study tables do not work. In fact, they are counter-productive, creating a bureaucracy that is stifling. Instead, the chapter should be focused on creating an environment that makes it easy to do well, and difficult to do poorly. Through the enforcement of academic standards, members are aware of the expectations they must uphold. The chapter provides an environment conducive to academic success, and the members are personally accountable for their results through the decisions they make and their application to studies.

> "BY BELIEVING PASSIONATELY IN SOMETHING WHICH STILL DOES NOT EXIST, WE CREATE IT."
>
> ~ NIKOS KAZANTZAKIS

Phi Beta Kappa Wheelhouse

At the 46th Grand Chapter Conclave in Chicago, Illinois, Sigma Phi Epsilon established a new benchmark for academics, the Phi Beta Kappa Wheelhouse. Phi Beta Kappa is the oldest, most respected honor society in America. Phi Beta Kappa's minimum GPA requirement is a 3.5 and chapters that have a cumulative GPA that is within 10 percent of that standard (a minimum 3.15) are in the Wheelhouse. For the Fall of 1999, SigEp had 19 chapters in the Wheelhouse, and for the Fall of 2002, that number grew to 35. By 2011, the fraternity plans to have a nationwide GPA of a 3.15.

Part of membership development in Sigma Phi Epsilon is the expectation that each member of the chapter will become involved with an organization on campus or in the community. If your chapter is not helping you become a better citizen, student, and fraternity man, then you must influence a change, or future Brothers of your chapter will also have a stagnant experience.

IN THE SPRING OF 2005, SIGMA PHI EPSILON ACHIEVED A 3.02 NATIONWIDE GPA, THE HIGHEST NATIONAL AVERAGE OF ANY AMERICAN FRATERNITY.

Make sure your chapter offers regular programming for all members, freshmen through seniors. Make sure alumni are a part of the workshops and discussions held in your chapter. Make sure your needs for a balanced education are being met. It is your responsibility.

Alumni & Volunteers

The Story of Mentor

The story of Mentor comes from Homer's Odyssey. When Odysseus, King of Ithaca, went to fight in the Trojan War, he entrusted the care of his household to Mentor, who served as teacher and overseer of Odysseus's son, Telemachus. In time, the word mentor became synonymous with trusted advisor, friend, teacher and wise person. There are many examples of helpful mentoring relationships, such as Socrates and Plato, Coach Bill Walsh and Joe Montana, and Robin Williams and Matt Damon in the movie Good Will Hunting.

Today, Sigma Phi Epsilon volunteers serve as vital mentors to your undergraduate experience. Of the more than 200,000 living alumni, many are serving our Fraternity as a Chapter Counselor, President of an Alumni and Volunteer Corporation, or as an advisor to one of our Brothers. Upon your graduation, it will be your responsibility to carry on the tradition of a lifetime experience within Sigma Phi Epsilon.

Alumni

Sigma Phi Epsilon alumni are an invaluable resource. Yet, so too, is the wealth of community leaders, university administration, and even parents who are willing to join you in your journey of brotherhood.

Sigma Phi Epsilon's first traveling secretary, Clarence H. Freeark, Illinois '23, often said, "The chapter is not good because the alumni take an

Foyer of the Kansas Gamma Chapter house at the University of Kansas

active interest; the alumni take an active interest because the chapter is good."

Today, it's a little of both. The interest of your chapter's alumni is vital because Sigma Phi Epsilon is a lifetime experience. And with age comes experiences our alumni may share with you as you grow in the Fraternity. Throughout your fraternity experience, you will make many contributions to it and many close friends. The Fraternity will become an important part of your college years. After you graduate, that relationship continues.

An active, involved presence by chapter alumni is fostered through communication with your Alumni and Volunteer Corporation and your alumni at-large. It is sharing the successes of the chapter, but, even more importantly, it is offering alumni Brothers the opportunity to reconnect with Brothers of their era. A good start

to fostering alumni involvement includes: ask for donations of time and talent, not money; publish at least two alumni newsletters per year concentrating on alumni news; report regularly to the *Journal*; contact alumni by telephone or personal visits; maintain an accurate address for each alumnus; host special alumni functions at homecoming in the fall and a spring alumni day; or participate in Ritual activities.

Our volunteers must balance work, family, friends, and other activities much like you balance your course schedule, part-time jobs, and other activities. It is essential to plan alumni activities well in advance, giving alumni the opportunity to make plans before their schedules fill with other obligations. It is discourteous to wait until two weeks before an event to send invitations. At a minimum, invitations should be mailed six weeks prior to the event.

SigEp alumni are very special Brothers, and they are to be treated accordingly when visiting the chapter house or meeting place. Every Brother should greet an alumnus, or any visitor, warmly, and so show him that SigEp is genuinely happy he is visiting. An alumnus who does not receive a warm welcome will soon stop visiting and donating his time and talents. At the same time, an alumnus is expected to act in accordance with his Oath of Obligation and the policies of the Fraternity when visiting the chapter. SigEp alumni should serve as role models of the Balanced Man Ideal.

Planning a quality alumni program requires careful attention and advance preparation. Your chapter's alumni operations director's responsibility is to guide your chapter in these plans. He should coordinate his activities with those of the Alumni and Volunteer Corporation to assure that the alumni program meets the needs of its audience.

MAKE ALUMNI CONTACT AN AUTOMATIC PART OF THE CHAPTER'S ANNUAL PROGRAM WITH CONCENTRATION ON ACTIVITIES FOR ALUMNI THROUGHOUT THE YEAR.

To be effective, implement year-round alumni planning systems, making plans at the beginning of each academic year. Coordinate an annual strategy session with your Alumni and Volunteer Corporation President. Make alumni contact an automatic part of the chapter's annual program with concentration on specific activities for alumni throughout the year.

The benefits to the chapter, and to individual Brothers, of good alumni programming are numerous. Alumni are among the greatest resources for you, your chapter, and Sigma Phi Epsilon.

Volunteers

Mentors can also be found beyond the Fraternity. Throughout America, there are thousands of community leaders, faculty and university administrators, and local businesspeople who seek out opportunities to give time to the development of today's college students. And they are not all SigEps. A relationship with someone outside of the Fraternity can begin simply by asking.

Are you interested in a particular profession or field of study? Chances are your local community has people already engaged in those areas.

Oftentimes, your university faculty is an overlooked resource. At some point in time, a faculty member chose this profession for the chance to help you develop as a person and build your knowledge base. It is quite common that they become quite busy working toward a tenure-track or on research in their field. Given SigEp's Balanced Man Ideal of Sound Mind and Sound Body, the Fraternity is uniquely positioned to engage faculty.

Across the country, chapters are hosting professors of philosophy, religion, ethics, art, business and various other disciplines to discuss current events, cultural appreciation, and learning. Take time and include faculty as a regular part of your chapter meetings. Ask them to speak to your chapter and provide for question and answer sessions. Host a faculty dinner and award an outstanding person the Professor of the Year Award. By making positive outreaches to the university faculty and administration, your chapter can be an integral part of the campus community. There are chapters today, like the Ohio Iota Chapter at the University of Toledo, where it is not uncommon to see the University President at a chapter event.

Parents

While you may have waited several years for the chance to be independent, parents provide a large group of people who are interested in your success. Numerous chapters are supported by the efforts of a Mom's Club, Dad's Club, or a Parents' Association. Parents have been active in supporting chapter home cleanups and maintenance, scholarship programs, and now a few even sit on our Alumni and Volunteer Corporations. Regular communication on the progress of the chapter can provide a great deal of excitement about the Fraternity for parents.

Goal Setting & Smart Management

The executive committee and Chapter Counselor have the direct responsibility of working with the Brothers and developing goals for the chapter.

Goal setting is the key to any successful organization. You will be introduced to goal setting in practically all fields of endeavor. Chapter goals help ensure a tighter brotherhood, greater success on campus, and a better fraternity experience.

Successful goal setting is "SMART." Good goals require five ingredients:

SENSE: A goal must make sense and be clearly understood when it appears in written form.

MEASURABLE: Some quantitative number or measure attached to each goal so that members will know when it is achieved (e.g., recruit 35 men).

ATTAINABLE: But not a part of "normal" operations. The goal must be within reason, yet one that pushes the chapter beyond its "comfort zone."

RESPONSIBILITY: Clearly assigned. Someone must have the responsibility to see that it is achieved.

TIME: Set a timeline for achieving the goal. Be specific.

Chapter Goal Setting

To provide you with a better understanding of the process of goal setting, review this outline for organizational planning:

1. Determine the chapter's greatest areas of concern.

2. Visualize: "What would it look like without the problem."

3. Establish priorities (manpower, academics and development, finances, and alumni and volunteers).

4. Set a specific and identifiable goal for each priority.

5. Select the best method to achieve each goal.

6. Monitor and re-evaluate priorities, goals, and projects or methods.

7. Evaluate progress weekly, monthly, and semi-annually. Written evaluations should be used to establish a foundation for the next year.

Georgia Delta Residential Learning Community at the University of Georgia

BUILDING BALANCED LEADERS

If you removed the insignia from your house, would our Founders be able to tell that you are a SigEp by your actions?

~ STEPHEN B. SHANKLIN,
Former Chairman of the Member Development Committee, National Director

Sigma Phi Epsilon stands for high ideals to be sought after and served. Our values are the Cardinal Principles of Virtue, Diligence, and Brotherly Love. Our Ritual is both a celebration of the values we share and guide to how we ought to live our lives and conduct our affairs. As a SigEp, you have an obligation to uphold these values, and it is the Fraternity's responsibility to see that you are properly prepared to receive these lessons as a member of the Fraternity. Education in Sigma Phi Epsilon, then, starts with the Ritual and an understanding of the importance ceremony plays in our lives.

The Significance of Ritual

Why must we have ritual in our lives? It is through ritual that we bring purpose into our lives. Our rituals reveal to us, with intense moments of meaning, opportunities to display the powerfully operative forces that shape the way we live. It is by ritual that we embody why we live and celebrate what we believe.

All brothers are inspired by the Ritual in one way or another, whether they joined 24 hours or 24 years ago.

The concepts presented are excellent guidelines around which one can base his entire life. By striving to attain those ideals we profess, we can develop empathy, personal contentment, and the motivation to strive for excellence. Our Ritual unveils to us the secret of self-knowledge.

A System of Values

Edward King from Bradley University puts fraternity rituals in perspective. He states that they are essentially one thing, a system of values. These values do not change very much because they are the product of history and the spirit of man and how he relates to his fellow man and to his

OUR RITUALS REVEAL TO US, WITH INTENSE MOMENTS OF MEANING, OPPORTUNITIES TO DISPLAY THE POWERFULLY OPERATIVE FORCES THAT SHAPE THE WAY WE LIVE.

god. This relationship between man and man, and man and god, has never been a static one. It is confusing and illuminating, painful and exciting, a separation and a reunion. Man is both animal and spiritual in nature, and to reconcile the two can often be painful, confusing, and frightening. That is why it is essential and critical that man, and in our context, our Brothers, understand what the Ritual is and its purpose.

As a system of values, the Ritual is an instrument of self-evaluation. The stated values are clear and absolute and often difficult to emulate. These values may be expressed by other fraternities under the terms honor, courage, integrity, fidelity, courtesy, and humility. Religiously speaking, the three main values which have resounded since the beginning of time are truth, honor, and love. We express these same values in the Cardinal Principles of Sigma Phi Epsilon— Virtue, Diligence, and Brotherly Love. Our Founders took the idea of friendship and fused that with commitment and gave birth to our Fraternity. If there were nothing significant about the commitment to these ideals,

RELIGIOUSLY SPEAKING, THE THREE MAIN VALUES WHICH HAVE RESOUNDED SINCE THE BEGINNING OF TIME ARE TRUTH, HONOR, AND LOVE.

then it is not likely that our Fraternity would have extended beyond the boundaries of Richmond College, much less become the great Fraternity it is today.

Symbol or Substance

A question arises, "Why do some members become so positively affected by the Fraternity's Ritual and others do not?" To some, the message goes deep, while for others it barely scratches the surface. When symbol must replace substance, the meaning is lost. At all times, the meaning and application of the Ritual must be sought. If not, the Ritual becomes just a ceremony.

Why are we not reaching all of our Brothers? Probably because we are not preparing them properly for their first introduction to our Ritual, and that it is kept in secrecy to the extent that we seldom use it or discuss it. How you prepare and educate members on the ideals and principles of our Ritual will determine how effectively they will emulate and use the guidelines and values which have sustained our Fraternity over the years.

A SigEp alumnus said, "My introduction to the Ritual of Sigma Phi Epsilon was clothed in mystic secrecy. I had not been prepared for any of the symbolism, vocabulary, or basic concepts of the ceremony. Thus, my initial exposure was one of partial dread, and, in the 22 minutes of the individual portion of the ceremony, my mind was in a labyrinth, trying to put all the actions and words together to make meaning. Fortunately for me, my chapter spent a portion of each meeting discussing components of the Ritual, and, over the remainder of my undergraduate experience, I was enriched by the contents and concepts of our Ritual.

Having been prepared with familiarity with the symbols and vocabulary would have allowed the ceremony to have greater meaning as the secrets of the Fraternity were revealed."

Challenge of Brotherhood

Interview with Father Raymond K. Ackerman, National Chaplain

Brothers must be willing to talk with one another about the challenges of life.

Brotherly love is an elusive term to many. But it is not to Father Raymond K. Ackerman, Oklahoma '79, Sigma Phi Epsilon's National Chaplain, "Brotherly Love is a heartfelt affection that looks to another with acceptance of differences, sees potential, and calls us beyond ourselves to be accountable to one another. It requires us to take action on one another's behalf, not to be passive."

Brotherly compassion is the easiest to see and understand. The friendships we share are a reflection. Unfortunately, all too often, chapters and chapter members fail to move beyond it. You may have heard someone say, "He can do anything. He is a Brother."

According to Ackerman, "Because he is a Brother is precisely why he cannot do whatever he likes. He has vowed to uphold certain standards and ideals within Sigma Phi Epsilon."

Does your chapter ever have a problem collecting the chapter dues on time, or enforcing academic standards, or upholding proper conduct of fellow members? Brother Ackerman believes this is a reflection of priorities, both of the chapter and the member.

"Our priorities flow out of our values. People that float by, don't pay their bills, just show up to socialize—they don't share our values. Likewise, a chapter must understand its identity, its values, its goals, and its purpose. This must be clearly communicated and expected of all members. How will your actions show that you uphold our Cardinal Principles?"

Brotherly Love requires us to be both compassionate and firm. "Being compassionate means challenging and confronting. A member who does not uphold his obligation must be confronted out of our heartfelt desire to see him succeed. A member who is not living to his potential must be challenged to do and be more."

"The challenge of Brotherly Love is not to take for granted what we can achieve together. It is to seize the day; to live so as not to let the precious moments slip by. The real tragedy is when we aren't true to ourselves, when we don't confront, and when we don't challenge. We must demand more of ourselves. We must demand more of our Brothers."

Ritual Orientation

Planning and preparation are key components of good Ritual education. Additionally, there are some things you and your chapter can do to enhance this part of the fraternity experience.

▶ Include Ritual education events and ceremonies throughout the year in which all members practice and participate.

▶ Conduct a service project organized and carried out by the chapter for the benefit of a needy person, a family, or a group.

▶ Have members write essays on one or more of the following subjects:

> ▶ "True brotherhood."
> ▶ "What the Fraternity means to me."
> ▶ "My performance as a member."
> ▶ "The Cardinal Principles in my life."

▶ Hold regular mini-retreats with discussion topics such as:

> ▶ What is a workable solution for apathy?
> ▶ How are the founding principles of the Fraternity relevant today?
> ▶ How can the chapter improve, and what is its direction for the future?

▶ Attend a religious service as a group and discuss its relevance to the chapter.

▶ Hold a pre-Ritual discussion of symbols to make the ceremony more meaningful.

▶ Discuss the Oath of Obligation to prepare for commitment to Sigma Phi Epsilon.

▶ Discuss unusual vocabulary in the Ritual so meaning is clear during ceremony.

Questions for Personal Consideration

1. How does your chapter use the Ritual in daily interactions?

2. What programs of Ritual orientation/education are offered by your chapter?

3. Does your chapter respect the Ritual? Is it conducted properly?

4. How is membership in the Fraternity like a journey?

5. How does the Ritual call us to enforce standards for all members?

6. How does the Ritual outline clear expectations for all members?

7. Why is preparation and practice of the Ritual important?

8. What do the Cardinal Principles mean to you?

9. How are you practicing Sigma Phi Epsilon's values in your life?

Educating for Brotherhood

Educating our brothers is a process that has come full circle, to once again following the ways of our Founders. We have returned to continuing education as a goal and primary function of the chapter.

Sigma Phi Epsilon's Founders, like the founders of Phi Beta Kappa—the first Greek-letter fraternity in America—believed that the purpose of their organization was to round out, or balance, the formal education of the members. They sponsored discussions of current topics in all fields from art to literature, to politics and business. Issues that were not covered in the classroom were covered by the Fraternity. These students were the best students in their respective fields of study and came together to enhance and balance their education through the resources offered by a superior group of their peers.

Continuing education in fraternities went beyond college as alumni returned to lead or teach sessions for the benefit of their fraternity. As time wore on, and colleges and universities broadened their curricula and outside activities, some fraternities and chapters became indifferent in their contribution to a man's education. This attitude deterred some students from joining fraternity chapters because they felt they could enhance their learning through other avenues. This cycle was destructive because the education offered by the chapter became limited to the new members, and centered on fraternity history and trivial information. Essentially, some men were throwing away educational opportunities by joining a fraternity. Some chapters even used an oppressive system of forced "learning" (often enforced by hazing) that turned away good students and quality men.

As this spiral of indifference toward education caused other problems in chapters (i.e., a dependence on alcohol, poor academics, low retention of members), it also was a warning signal. It called good students in fraternities to stand up for true education and a return to the ideals of their founders. This awakening, and movement to return to continuing education, is now in full force. Those chapters who never lost the value of programming for all members are leading the way for those chapters who are restructuring their programming.

SIGMA PHI EPSILON'S FOUNDERS BELIEVED THAT THE PURPOSE OF THEIR ORGANIZATION WAS TO ROUND OUT, OR BALANCE, THE FORMAL EDUCATION OF THE MEMBERS.

Sigma Phi Epsilon is a firm believer that chapter programs are meant to balance a man's education...health and fitness awareness, relationship-building, cultural awareness and appreciation, career development, Ritual education, community participation, etc. These issues and others affecting the students of today must be a part of the programming of SigEp chapters if they are to be a reflection of the values and intentions of our Founders.

As a college fraternity, Sigma Phi Epsilon must be aware of the needs of our student brothers, and work to make our Fraternity a true enhancement to a man's education. Colleges and universities may never be flexible enough to fully meet the needs of their students, but fraternities have the resources to be a partner in student education.

Total Programming

"WHAT YOU DO SPEAKS SO LOUDLY I CANNOT HEAR WHAT YOU ARE SAYING."

~ HARRY S. TRUMAN

Fraternity programming should offer a wealth of experiences for all members from the time they join until they graduate. From teaching basic information, such as chapter operations, study skills, etiquette, and Ritual education, to covering such topics and issues as sex education, career development, leadership skills, and community service, no better avenue exists to round out an education than through the Fraternity.

Getting Started

New members of the chapter should be treated and educated as the top-quality men they are. Your chapter asked these men to join because they were the best students, and to treat them as anything else is unacceptable.

The best way to educate and assimilate new members into any group is through the examples set by all members. You have a responsibility to show these men what brotherhood and Sigma Phi Epsilon are all about.

New members of any group, and certainly a SigEp chapter, will act by the precedent set within the group. If your chapter values superior academic performance, respect for others, and responsible behavior, then your new members will also.

Programming for All Members

The goal of educating the chapter members is to prepare them for leadership, inside and outside of the Fraternity, in a fashion that treats them as the future leaders they are. Poorly planned programs or hazing will destroy brotherhood and chapter operations swiftly.

All chapter members need education outside the classroom. The following list offers a sample of programs your chapter should offer all members:

Sound Mind:

▶ All members attend a music performance (symphony, bluegrass, a cappella group, etc.).

▶ All members tour an art museum.

▶ Invite a philosophy professor to speak to the chapter on the origins of the Balanced Man.

▶ Have a poetry recital in the chapter house.

▶ Have students of different religions educate the chapter on their beliefs.

▶ Have a professor teach a class in the chapter house.

▶ Have sign language education.

▶ Have CPR certification for members of the chapter.

▶ Academic success seminar facilitated by a professor:

> ▶ "Why Scholarship?"
> ▶ "How to Study."
> ▶ "Tips on Taking Exams."

▶ Time management seminar.

▶ Etiquette seminar.

▶ Presentations by Greek advisor, university officials, and professors.

▶ Presentation by a coach or sports official on gentlemanly behavior.

▶ Ritual education discussions on the meaning of the Ritual.

Sound Body:

▶ Chapter members get a physical annually.

▶ Chapter members consult with a personal trainer to design a work-out plan for their fitness goals.

▶ Have dance lessons with a sorority (Samba, Tango, Swing).

▶ Have a Yoga instructor work with the chapter.

▶ Nutrition and health seminar by campus health center.

▶ Attend or host a stress management workshop.

▶ Chapter hosts a wellness day on campus.

▶ Train for a mini-triathlon.

▶ Have a healthy menu for chapter meals.

▶ Track mileage (running, biking). Set a goal for the chapter to reach.

Leadership & Career Preparation:

▶ Public speaking seminar facilitated by a faculty member or qualified alumnus.

▶ Professional letter-writing seminar facilitated by campus career placement service.

▶ Presentation and discussions on leadership by guest speakers:

> ▶ "The Art of Leadership."
> ▶ "Attributes of a Leader."
> ▶ "When to Lead; When to Follow."

▶ Workshop on counseling skills facilitated by professional counselor.

▶ Résumé-writing workshop by professional from the community.

▶ Dress for success seminar by local clothier.

▶ Graduating seniors pool résumés to send in special mailing to chapter alumni.

▶ Interview skills workshop facilitated by a professional.

▶ Dinner with alumni to practice etiquette and simulate interview situation.

▶ Discussion of leadership and business-related books or articles.

▶ Finance professional discusses IRAs, 401k's and investments.

▶ University loan officer talks to the chapter about consolidation of debt.

2005 Senior Dinner at the New Hampshire Alpha Chapter at Dartmouth College

Questions for Personal Consideration

1. Are new members given a proper example of the Fraternity? Are the requirements of big brothers helping to set this example?

2. What needs to change to provide an ideal example?

3. What educational programs are currently offered by the chapter?

4. Is the chapter programming meeting the needs of the members?

5. What programs, issues, or topics would benefit you?

6. What programs could benefit the entire chapter?

7. What programs from the list given should your chapter implement?

8. How could you be instrumental in implementing this program?

9. Are chapter educational programs well-planned? Balanced?

10. How can chapter programming be enhanced for all members?

Balanced Man Program

While the first chapter to implement the Balanced Man Program (BMP) did so in 1992, the foundation was created when 12 men gathered in the tower of Ryland Hall in 1901. The Balanced Man Program is a return to the values and principles on which Sigma Phi Epsilon was founded. The program, as initially envisioned and in practice today, addresses the following chapter needs: sustained involvement of older members; extensive community and campus involvement; greater understanding of the values articulated in the Fraternity's Ritual; development of Sound Mind and Sound Body programs; and increased focus on good leadership practices. These are among the earliest visions of Sigma Phi Epsilon. Since its creation, the Balanced Man Program has become the standard for membership development in Sigma Phi Epsilon.

The Journey Begins

Formally, the BMP was born in 1989. During Sigma Phi Epsilon's strategic planning process, the Strategic Planning Committee adopted the vision statement, *Building Balanced Leaders for the World's Communities*. To ensure that the Fraternity achieved this vision in undergraduate chapters, fraternity leaders gathered to develop a new membership development program. Soon, the group was struck with the notion that what they needed was something more than just improved new member programming—what was needed was an all-encompassing program that affected fraternity culture by involving all chapter members.

At the 42nd Grand Chapter in Washington, D.C., 1991, the results of this group's work were presented to undergraduate leaders of the Fraternity. In response, the voting delegates passed a resolution directing the Fraternity to transform the pledging process from that of proving worthiness, to developing universal respect for self and others and continuous growth and development.

First implemented in the Fall of 1992, the Balanced Man Program is the Fraternity's leadership development program. It is a self-determined membership experience based on achievement in the chapter and community. A "journey" is the best way to describe the Balanced Man Program, as it is based on the concept of life as a continuous journey. Many chapters in Sigma Phi Epsilon are using the Balanced Man Program to better prepare members to face and surmount the many challenges faced in college and beyond.

THE BALANCED MAN PROGRAM IS THE FRATERNITY'S LEADERSHIP DEVELOPMENT PROGRAM.

Values & Vision

The BMP differs from other development programs in a number of ways:

1. The focus of the program centers on six fundamental concepts: mentoring, the Balanced Man ideal of developing a Sound Mind and a Sound Body, community involvement and service learning, brotherhood and chapter unity, single-tier continuous development, and experiential learning.

2. Mentors help members make decisions and set goals. These mentors are recruited from both the undergraduate chapter and the surrounding community.

3. The BMP uses experiential learning, such as ropes courses, and service learning in addition to a chapter's current programs to create a strong development program.

4. New members in the Balanced Man Program are extended all of the rights and privileges of membership. And, there exists no point at which a chapter member is "finished" with meeting expectations. Members are fully integrated from the day they join, and are held accountable for continued leadership and involvement throughout their journey.

The Balanced Man Program has the two goals of improving the development of all members individually, and strengthening chapters. The Balanced Man Program builds brotherhood and chapter unity by developing individual members through mentoring and community service. Brotherhood is also strengthened by developing the group through chapter experiential learning activities and enhanced Ritual ceremonies. As members progress through the challenges, their ability to lead and serve will be tested and, through mentoring, nurtured.

THE BALANCED MAN PROGRAM HAS THE TWO GOALS OF IMPROVING THE DEVELOPMENT OF ALL MEMBERS INDIVIDUALLY, AND STRENGTHENING CHAPTERS.

Excellence in Programming

Implementing the Balanced Man Program provides chapters with many advantages including:

◗ Increased group activities provide better opportunities for brotherhood and fun.

◗ Many different mentors throughout college, in addition to a big brother.

◗ Opportunities to have an impact in the community through service learning.

◗ Improved academic support through mentoring and goal setting.

◗ The SigEp QUEST AND BALANCED MAN PROGRAM LEXICON which provide guidance for the personal development of each member.

◗ Utilization of community mentors in addition to alumni volunteers.

◗ Enhanced Ritual presentations and opportunities for discussion, which lead to a greater comprehension of the ideals of the Fraternity.

Sigma Phi Epsilon has been commended for its ability to make these long-held desires a reality. The Fraternity has been recognized with several honors that highlight the value of the Balanced Man Program. First, in 1994, the Balanced Man Program was awarded a $250,000 Department of Education grant designated for the promotion of highly innovative efforts in higher education. Also in 1994, the Association of Fraternity Advisors bestowed the "Excellence in Educational Programming Award" on Sigma Phi Epsilon for the BMP. And today, many other fraternities are acknowledging Sigma Phi Epsilon's leadership by creating their own, often similar, versions of a four-year, continuous membership development program.

Chapters, in adopting the BMP as their standard for member development, have found a way to consistently perform by adhering to high standards, and providing exceptional programming. Balanced Man chapters are achieving the intended results as they out-perform their peers in academics and recruitment, have seen increases in campus and community involvement,

The youngest and the oldest: Ken Maeda, South Carolina '08, with Dr. George E. Meetze, South Carolina '30. At 95 years old, Brother Meetze is the oldest living alumnus of the South Carolina Alpha Chapter.

and enjoy the benefits of their ability to attract additional volunteer support.

The Building Blocks

The Balanced Man Program builds brotherhood by developing individual members through mentoring, sound mind and sound body programming, and service learning. Brotherhood is also strengthened by developing the group through chapter experiential learning activities and enhanced Ritual ceremonies. As members progress through the challenges, their ability to lead and serve will be tested and, through mentoring, nurtured.

Six major components are used in the Balanced Man Program for leadership development, and to strengthen your chapter. They are mentoring, the philosophy of Sound Mind and Sound Body, community involvement and service learning, brotherhood and chapter unity, single-tier continuous development, and experiential learning. Each of these components has corresponding expectations in each of the challenges. Together they provide insight and experiences necessary for effective personal development. The following is a synopsis of how each component is used in the Balanced Man Program.

Mentoring

A mentor is an individual who serves as a positive role model and is a source of support and guidance. A mentor oversees the development of his mentee by teaching, counseling, and supporting him in his endeavors.

When searching for a mentor, seek a person whom you respect because of his talents, values, and experience.

Your mentor may be older or younger, but always choose someone from whom you can learn and who will provide you with honest feedback and advice.

After the Sigma Challenge, you will have the opportunity to select a mentor. He will aid you in setting personal goals and establishing action plans. Frequently, he will become a lifelong friend. The best mentor/mentee relationships involve regular communication, clear expectations, and the sharing of dreams and aspirations. Mentoring is brotherhood in action!

THE MIND HOUSES YOUR HUMANITY, AND, THEREFORE, AN EXERCISE OF THE MIND IS JUST AS IMPORTANT AS THE EXERCISE OF THE BODY FOR FULL MATURING AND DEVELOPMENT.

As a mentee, you will have the opportunity to learn. As a mentor, you will have the opportunity to teach and positively influence a member of Sigma Phi Epsilon. Mentors are the stewards of the Fraternity's Cardinal Principles.

The Philosophy of Sound Mind and Sound Body

The ancient Greeks believed that a body's good health was vital as the vessel of the mind. The mind houses your humanity, and, therefore, an exercise of the mind is just as important as the exercise of the body for full maturing and development. The purpose of a human's time on earth is to live the best, balanced life and to explore the unexamined facets that make us better men.

SigEp chapters use the Balanced Man Ideal of developing a Sound Mind and a Sound Body to frame its programming ideas. To help develop the Sound Body, chapters do not simply participate in intramural sports, but are also encouraged to sponsor annual physicals that measure cholesterol, blood pressure, and screen for different types of cancer. Many chapters have also begun to educate their members on how to prepare healthier meals, which begins by serving healthier meals in the chapter facilities.

To pursue a Sound Mind, we look to a high GPA as only the beginning. SigEp takes the next step by inviting political candidates and university professors to speak to the chapter. SigEp promotes greater diversity understanding by inviting historically African American fraternities and sororities to chapter meetings, and by volunteering at the university's international houses. SigEp chapters are committed to providing an intellectual atmosphere that benefits themselves, their university, and their community, and strives to center on the Balanced Man.

Sigma Phi Epsilon continually exhibits its dedication to helping a man develop not just a sound physical body, but moreover a healthy, lasting vessel for the mind.

Community Involvement and Service Learning

By defining your community as your campus and the area surrounding campus (whether it is a city, town, or rural area), expectations for community involvement open a world of activity and opportunity. Community involvement gives you exposure to many people of different backgrounds and diverse experiences. Through such contact, you will learn what issues face your community, how you can be helpful to your community, and how to work well with others.

The Balanced Man Program encourages community involvement in a variety of arenas. Specifically, you have opportunities to be involved in campus organizations as both a participant and as a leader, in intramurals, in community operations awareness, and in service learning.

Service learning is community service that involves direct contact and personal effort in meeting the needs of the community. Service learning provides you with the opportunity to learn from others.

A service learning project could mean working to feed the homeless, providing day care for the children of working mothers, or tutoring adults in a literacy program. It could also mean building a house, driving an elderly neighbor to the grocery store, or working in an animal shelter. Whatever the size or type of community, the opportunities for service learning are plentiful and varied.

Combined with personal reflection and discussion, service learning can teach you much about yourself and your community. For instance, ask yourself:

▶ What am I learning about and from the people I am working with in my community?

▶ What am I learning in relation to my on-campus experiences both inside and outside the classroom?

▶ What am I learning about society and myself?

SigEp brother Scott R. Erwin, Richmond '04, is surrounded by many of his students. He worked to bring democracy to Iraqi youth.

Many chapters partner with YouthAIDS to make a difference in their communities.

Service learning and other elements of community involvement are critical to leadership development. Through such involvement, you will become a balanced individual who has developed empathy for his neighbors, a broader world view, and a dedication to responsible citizenship for a lifetime.

Single-Tier Continuous Development

The Balanced Man Program supports the concept of single-tier continuous development whereby all members from the moment of joining the organization are considered equal and share all the rights of privileges of membership in Sigma Phi Epsilon. Additionally the Balanced Man Program removes the concept of pledgeship and that of proving worthiness for acceptance of membership.

Continuous development was designed to provide older members continued developmental opportunities throughout their college experience. For example men in the Epsilon and Brother Mentor Challenges begin preparing for their professional careers with workshops on résumé writing, dress for success, and interview skills. The role of mentoring also provides older members with specific tasks during their final terms in college.

Experiential Learning

From every experience you have in life, you can learn a valuable lesson. Some of these experiences are more structured than others, with experiential learning activities being one of the more structured. An experiential learning activity is a planned challenge that requires chapter participation, problem-solving, and cooperation. SigEps create brotherhood through individual contributions to these group activities. Examples of experiential learning include high ropes courses, team-building activities such as trust falls, and problem-solving activities.

The frequency of these activities contributes to the leadership development of a chapter's members. Experiential learning enhances your self-awareness and increases your self-confidence. This, in turn, will sharpen your leadership skills.

Another benefit of experiential learning activities is that they nurture brotherhood by improving chapter communication, motivation, and cooperation. Experiential learning builds and maintains a strong brotherhood!

Balanced Man Stewards

Balanced Man Stewards act as development mentors for the Vice President of Member Development and the Development Cabinet. The Steward helps provide ideas for Sound Mind and Sound Body programming. In a Balanced Man Program Chapter, the Steward ensures the chapter is operating the challenges of the Balanced Man Program, helps evaluate the progress of the program, and works with the Development Cabinet to ensure continued success.

Balanced Man Stewards are trained volunteers enabled to make a significant impact on the development of both individual members and the collective chapter. Stewards can be SigEp alumni, university officials, parents, men or women.

The SigEp Quest

The SigEp Quest, a guide for the Balanced Man Program, was created as a development tool for both the individual member and for the challenge groups to implement a fun and healthy Balanced Man Program. The Quest is a **FOR MORE INFORMATION ABOUT THE SIGEP QUEST, GO TO WWW.SIGEP.ORG/ MEMDEV/RESOURCES.ASP.** skeleton model for the Balanced Man Program and also helps track the performance of members through the guidelines of each challenge.

Utilizing the Quest helps support the progress of the program and ensures that your chapter is building men both individually and collectively. Members will have the opportunity to track their goals throughout college, keep track of their overall development throughout the challenges, and reflect upon the ritual and experience within Sigma Phi Epsilon.

"Give me a stone to stand on and I can move the world!"

~ ARCHIMEDES

The Grand Plaza of Zollinger House during the 2004 Ruck Leadership Institute

PROTECTING YOUR FUTURE

"Don't think there are no crocodiles because the water is calm."

~ MALAYAN PROVERB

You are Responsible

Responsible behavior starts with you. "Tradition," pride, and egos are tough to change. Even the best chapters may struggle to step back and get a good look at themselves and their peers, but the old adage, "Boys will be boys," is not acceptable anymore. Fraternities have an obligation to protect themselves and their members. Your future, that of the chapter, and Sigma Phi Epsilon depends on responsible behavior. Consequently, risk management must be enacted, or chapters will not be around to make excuses.

Upon entering the world of college and Sigma Phi Epsilon, you accepted a tremendous responsibility. *You are responsible for your actions.* It has been charged that fraternities are losing their credibility as part of America's system of higher education. Campus administrators, boards of trustees, faculty and opinion leaders are not as willing to allow fraternities to be irresponsible. The general lack of good behavior on campus, combined with the prevalence of drugs and alcohol abuse among college students has heightened community awareness. Fraternities are targets for criticism. The way to contest this is to act responsibly.

Risk management is a phrase once limited to the business world, but is now one that you will hear throughout your college career. It is the act of reducing risks through responsible behavior. Substance abuse, hazing, negligence, poor community relations, sexual abuse, and sexually transmitted diseases are all risks prevalent on college campuses and unacceptable in Sigma Phi Epsilon. Be aware of these risks and take steps to protect your future and that of your chapter.

Risks of Alcohol

For the most part, the law will determine what is and is not risky behavior insofar as alcohol is concerned. The minimum drinking age in the United States is 21. Note, however, that even though you may be of legal age, irresponsible use of alcohol places you and your chapter at risk.

YOU ARE RESPONSIBLE FOR YOUR ACTIONS.

Alcohol combined with your brotherhood development activities is unacceptable. The chapter may incur criminal and civil liability if injury or death results from any chapter activity, not to mention the possibility of surcharge and charter withdrawal. Your brotherhood development must be managed in a way which conveys care and concern for the well-being of each new chapter member. Alcohol has no place in any Sigma Phi Epsilon brotherhood development activity.

Hazing & the law

If a chapter hazes, it exposes the chapter, its officers, alumni, the housing corporation, and the individuals who perpetrate or condone the hazing to a myriad of consequences. Hazing may result in surcharge,

HAZING IS THE PHYSICAL OR PSYCHOLOGICAL DEGRADATION OF ANYONE.

charter suspension, or charter withdrawal. Lawsuits are also possible as well as criminal prosecution. Such consequences are devastating to a chapter or individual.

In university judicial codes and most state laws, hazing is typically defined in terms of psychological as well as physical abuse. Detailing each type of hazing activity is senseless. Simply put, anything you would not do in front of an individual's parents, girlfriend, and professors is probably hazing.

HAZING: Hazing is the physical or psychological degradation of anyone. Hazing has no place in Sigma Phi Epsilon. It is not in line with the principles of the Fraternity and has done nothing but destroy men and their chapters. Sigma Phi Epsilon has banned hazing.

Article I, Section 4, of the Grand Chapter Bylaws states, "Any pre-initiation activity shall be of a constructive nature in accordance with the purposes and objectives of the Fraternity, and all forms of hazing are prohibited."

Pursuant to a resolution adopted at the 1975 Grand Chapter Conclave, all undergraduate chapters of SIGMA PHI EPSILON FRATERNITY are required to review this Bylaw at the beginning of the academic year and to adopt a motion supporting this policy.

Do not haze or allow yourself to be hazed. Call 1-800-767-1901. Sigma Phi Epsilon Headquarters can help stop it.

Hazing can only lead to the loss of integrity and trust. The loss of these ingredients will lead to the loss of friends and your chapter. Develop strict disciplinary actions against those in your chapter who feel the need to haze. Remove them from your chapter. Realize the difference between labeling hazing as a "tradition" and what hazing actually is—a secret bad habit. If hazing is a problem, address the subject in the presence of a respected alumnus who is an attorney and report it to fraternity officials, your Chapter Counselor, Alumni and Volunteer Corporation, and Headquarters.

The Truth of the Matter

"MY HUSBAND AND I WALKED INTO THAT COLD STERILE ROOM AND SAW OUR 6'2" STRAPPING SON, CHUCK, LYING ON A STAINLESS STEEL TABLE COVERED WITH A SHEET. WE KNEW HIS BLUE EYES WOULD BE CLOSED TO US FOREVER. THAT WAS THE MOST DEVASTATING MOMENT OF OUR LIVES."

~ EILEEN STEVENS, FOUNDER, C.H.U.C.K., PARENT & ANTI-HAZING ACTIVIST

Hazing is generally a function of people with low self-esteem who, through putting others down, try to build themselves up. Several years ago Eileen Stevens' son, Chuck, was killed by a fraternity in a mindless hazing activity involving the forced consumption of alcohol. Since that time, Stevens has been speaking to universities and Greek organizations. A supporter of fraternities, Stevens' proposes:

If the Greek world is to remain in existence, it must rid every chapter on every campus of hazing in all its ugly forms! The very survival of fraternities and sororities depends on that simple fact.

The past decade has seen dramatic, precedent-setting change. Nearly every state has outlawed hazing—and these laws are being tested in the courts. Multimillion dollar lawsuits have jolted the financial foundation of national fraternities resulting in an insurance crisis. University boards are seeking the abolishment of Greek-letter organizations

Regular risk management seminars should be held at least once a year for all members.

on their campuses and some have succeeded in doing just that!

The ever-present media continues to print the hard facts—ugly, frightening facts that can't be justified—blemishing the innocent along with the villains.

Everyone who cares about Greek life has been affected by the adverse publicity and there is a crisis—Greek life is in jeopardy—make no mistake! Young innocent adults have been maimed, killed, injured physically and emotionally by insidious, secret, hazing practices. Too many have looked the other way for too long. The safety of students should be our number one priority! We must challenge them—arm Greek organizations with as much information and educational programming as possible. This is our only hope.

Ask Yourself This

Dr. Will Kiem, longtime fraternity advisor and member of Delta Upsilon, has a simple self-test to determine if your chapter's activities are appropriate.

1. If you have to ask if it is hazing, it is.
2. If in doubt, call your national office.
3. If you will not pick up the phone, you have your answer.
4. Do not fool yourself!
5. If you haze, you have low self-esteem.
6. If you allow hazing to go on, you are a "hazing enabler."
7. Failure to stop hazing will result in the death of fraternities.

Illegal Drugs

The drug scene is no longer behind closed doors. When you encounter drugs in the fraternity, more often than not, you will encounter a campus where drugs are more or less socially acceptable.

THE FINANCIAL DRAIN OF DEALING WITH THE USE OF DRUGS IN THE JUDICIAL ARENA CAN LEAD TO CHAPTER CLOSINGS.

Nonetheless, using drugs on fraternity premises or at fraternity functions is unacceptable and a violation of the law. The possession, use, distribution, and manufacturing of illegal drugs are serious crimes. They must be dealt with or your chapter will suffer the consequences. Such consequences can take several directions:

▶ A person can be convicted of drug possession under the doctrine of "constructive possession," meaning YOU can be convicted of drug possession because your roommate has drugs in your room.

▶ An officer who is lawfully present can seize any illegal drugs which are in plain view and arrest everyone in the room under the "plain view" doctrine.

▶ Under criminal nuisance laws, chapter officers and house corporation officers can be charged with maintaining a house, lodge or apartment in which illegal drugs are distributed, stored, concealed or habitually used. The penalties for such offenses can reach up to 20 years imprisonment.

The use of drugs in the chapter can lead to serious judicial matters. Even if the chapter "wins" the case, the financial drain will usually be too great to overcome, and the chapter will lose in the long run.

Failure to Maintain Chapter Property

Negligence in maintaining the physical property of your chapter may lead to injury and lawsuit. Your chapter owes it to its members, alumni, and guests to keep the house or lodge in good condition. If a person gets hurt because your chapter or Alumni and Volunteer Corporation fails to fix a problem, the costs of going to court will far exceed the costs of fixing damaged property before harm is done. Your Alumni and Volunteer Corporation maintains a regular procedure to evaluate and maintain your chapter house as a safe environment.

National Housing Corporation President and National Director Bert J. Harris, III, Florida '74, meets with undergraduates during a Carlson Leadership Academy.

Neighborhood Relations

The neighbors have more power than you think! A serious problem develops when fraternities become bad neighbors. If your neighbors tire of your chapter, they can make your life miserable, and they may be justified in doing so.

The neighbors can get zoning laws changed so that your house does not conform to the law. When this happens, you cannot renovate, improve, or repair anything without asking permission from a city which can freely deny you. A community can attack you financially. They can adopt special property laws, excise or income taxes, as well as heavy licensing and inspection fees which could destroy a chapter financially. A community can send in a fire marshal or building inspector to present the chapter with a mandatory list of improvements. A community can see that strict parking, noise, and alcohol laws are enforced. As a member of the community, you have a responsibility to be a good neighbor.

This idea of being a good neighbor transcends your chapter and your members. If one chapter on campus is a bad neighbor, then all chapters suffer. Look to improve chapter/community relations through a public relations program involving community service projects, and regular, two-way communication with your neighbors. Be a good neighbor and ask your Brothers to set the example for the Greek community on your campus.

Sexual Abuse

Today's woman understands that she has an equal share in the decisions regarding sexual activity. The legal fibers of our society—the courts—have also undertaken to reinforce this change. Rape, as defined by law, does not happen only at the muzzle of a gun or at knife point. Any attempt to deprive a woman of the rational ability to refuse to participate in sexual activity is now viewed as rape. Such rational deprivation certainly includes the misuse of alcohol or drugs.

ANY ATTEMPT TO DEPRIVE A WOMAN OF THE RATIONAL ABILITY TO REFUSE TO PARTICIPATE IN SEXUAL ACTIVITY IS VIEWED AS RAPE.

You must be aware of the social and legal implications of involving yourself (and potentially the entire chapter) in such activities. Each Brother must be fully informed of the local and state laws that relate to abusive behavior and must be fully cognizant of the potential personal and group liabilities. To have a greater impact, have an outside law enforcement officer come to the chapter and consult with the membership on the reality of the problem.

Preventing sexual abuse starts with being personally responsible for yourself and other brothers in your chapter.

As a young man, it may be time for you to analyze personally and with your chapter Brothers just what form of relationships you have with women. Is your chapter a place where women are degraded in word or deed? What about themes for chapter parties, how are women depicted on chapter t-shirts or during recruitment events and how are women addressed when they visit the chapter? Perhaps your chapter prides itself in gentlemanly behavior, where women are treated as friends or guests, and as equals deserving the same respect as a Brother. You may find yourself reporting to a woman in your first job, likely marrying one who has a college degree—making more money than you. The behavior you choose today will influence your future success and happiness.

The ultimate step to prevent sexual abuse is for each fraternity member to be personally responsible for himself and other Brothers in the chapter. If it becomes obvious that a member might be doing something that could involve him in an allegation of "date rape," other Brothers should be responsible enough to confront the man in an effective manner. By doing so, they could be preventing a great deal of pain and misunderstanding. Every fraternity member has taken an oath to help another member should that be necessary. Preventing a problem before it happens is an expression of Brotherly Love and responsibility. Remember, no means no.

Difficult Decisions

As an undergraduate, you will make important decisions. You will be presented with choices which will affect your academic success, your degree and your life after college. You will make decisions which will affect your friends and your chapter. Approach these decisions with responsibility. Your future and that of your chapter is in your hands. Act in a way which reflects maturity and high standards.

Brotherhood in Sigma Phi Epsilon is based on mutual respect and Brotherly Love. Demonstrate your love for your brothers through your responsible actions...and ask for help when you need it.

Crisis Management Procedures

When risk is not managed, it becomes a crisis in many situations. What should you do immediately after a crisis occurs? We, as fraternity leaders, must be prepared to cope quickly and effectively should the unforeseen happen. For these reasons, we strongly encourage you to review this section carefully.

Crisis Defined

Webster defines crisis as a "decisive moment, or turning point, during an unstable state of affairs." For a fraternity member, crisis means that particular state of uncertainty, panic, or chaos which develops when media, police, campus officials, or who knows what descends on your chapter as a result of an incident. Actual examples of crises which many fraternity chapters have faced in recent years include:

▶ Members hurt in an auto accident.

▶ Members being arrested for selling drugs.

▶ Members being hospitalized after a hazing incident.

▶ Members dying from alcohol/drug abuse in the chapter house.

▶ Members gunshot by uninvited guests at a party.

▶ Fire destroying a chapter house.

▶ Fights leading to a riot between two fraternities.

▶ Members killed in a drunk-driving incident.

▶ Suicide.

Steps to Take

CALL THE CRISIS HOT LINE IF YOU HAVE AN EMERGENCY, 1-800-767-1901, 24 HOURS A DAY.

Initial Steps

1. The President or his appointee should take charge in every emergency situation. If the President is not available, the next ranking officer should take charge.

2. The President's first phone call should be to emergency officials if necessary—911 in most communities. Make certain emergency phone numbers are located near each telephone.

3. Notify the Chapter Counselor and Alumni and Volunteer Corporation of the events as soon as possible. Also, as soon as practicable, report the incident to the Fraternity's Headquarters. Seek the experience of the national fraternity staff in managing the remainder of the crisis period. Headquarters should be informed as soon as possible to provide the right amount of support. Not reporting an incident to Headquarters exacerbates the situation to the point where little support can be provided.

4. Contact appropriate campus officials.

5. Close the chapter house at once. Permit only members and appropriate officials to remain on the house and grounds.

6. In case of fire, tornado, hurricane, or earthquake, have a pre-designated meeting place away from the building. Take a head count and report any missing members to fire officials at once.

7. The President should gather the facts of the incident as soon as possible. Never speculate or engage in rumor spreading.

8. Also, as soon as it is practical, assemble the chapter. Remind the members to:

   A. Stay calm.

   B. Follow instructions.

   C. Make no statements outside the chapter—with the exception of emergency officials.

   D. Do not speculate or spread rumors.

   E. Be aware the President is the chapter's sole spokesman, and he will keep others apprised of all developments.

   F. Never admit/accept fault or liability for the incident.

Subsequent Steps

1. Complete an "incident report form" and forward to Headquarters. To download a copy visit www.sigep.org/documents/incident-report-form.pdf.

2. Work with the national staff, campus officials and local alumni to manage the remainder of the crisis period.

Managing the Media

1. As soon as practicable, prepare a statement to be released to the press. At best, this statement should be developed with the input of alumni and the Chapter Counselor, as well as Headquarters.

2. Instead of "no comment," provide an initial statement such as: "We are cooperating fully with the university and police in conducting an investigation of the incident. Subsequent comments will be made when we are certain of all the facts. We will announce information as soon as it is practicable."

3. Consider holding a press briefing away from the fraternity house. You should involve your Chapter Counselor, Alumni and Volunteer Corporation, Headquarters staff, and Greek advisor.

4. Establish a distribution list for one-page updates or releases: alumni, other IFC members, media, Headquarters, etc.

5. Other considerations:

   A. Again, have one designated spokesman—introduce this person to the media and refer all calls to the spokesman.

   B. Do not release any names until an alumni advisor or Headquarters believes the timing is appropriate.

   C. Seek the advice of the campus public relations staff.

   D. Update the media consistently; yet, only when there is something to say.

The ideal SigEp chapter offers a home away from home, a moral and intellectual atmosphere, and a place where men are brothers to each other.

THE IDEAL
SIGEP CHAPTER

SigEp at Its Best

Joining Sigma Phi Epsilon in 1918, Ulysses Grant Dubach had already started to make his mark on the Fraternity. As Dean of Men at Oregon State College, Dr. Dubach advised a group that would form the Oregon Alpha Chapter. That chapter and many others have achieved success by following the simple outline left by U. G. Dubach. According to Dr. Dubach, Sigma Phi Epsilon will provide four things to its members.

"A Home-Away-from-Home"

A home, to Dubach, is more than a place to hang your hat. A true Sigma Phi Epsilon home is a place in which to live. It is a place where our members can talk about anything. A place that is safe. A place that is welcoming. A place that offers a man proper guidance and direction in his life.

"A Moral Atmosphere"

Dubach states that Sigma Phi Epsilon must provide a moral atmosphere that makes it easy for a man to do right and difficult for him to do wrong. A moral atmosphere requires that we are respectful toward others at all times. Sigma Phi Epsilon, at its best, will provide its members a moral compass with which to make smart decisions.

"An Intellectual Atmosphere"

In a Sigma Phi Epsilon home, the Fraternity must provide an intellectual atmosphere that is compelling. After all, the first duty of a SigEp is to earn his degree. Therefore, academics are absolutely the business of the Fraternity. And, Sigma Phi Epsilon must act as a partner with the university in the attainment of that education.

"A True Brotherhood"

The Fraternity is a place where men are Brothers to each other. A true brotherhood means tough love. When a Brother fails to meet his obligations, he has jeopardized his membership. A true brotherhood in Sigma Phi Epsilon welds men together, not for four months, nor for four years, but for life.

Sigma Phi Epsilon, at its best, will provide a home away from home, a moral atmosphere that makes it easy to do well and difficult to do poorly, an intellectual atmosphere that is compelling, and a true brotherhood. Now, how are we going to do it? Dubach identified four components that will ensure success.

Ulysses Grant Dubach was Dean of Students at Oregon State University and "Mr. Scholarship" for Sigma Phi Epsilon for several decades. He traveled to countless chapters and district meetings to reinforce that "character and brains" were the two main qualities a SigEp needed.

"Recruit the Right Men"

U. G. Dubach outlined the qualities essential to membership in Sigma Phi Epsilon: character and brains. If a man has these two things, the Fraternity can teach him anything else he needs to know to be successful. If a man does not have both of these characteristics, he may wear a SigEp pin, but he will never be a true SigEp. As U. G. Dubach said, "You can't carve rotten wood."

A TRUE SIGEP COULD NEVER HUMILIATE ANOTHER PERSON AND SUCCEED.

"Teach Them Right"

The new members will be right if you are right. There is no substitute for leading by example. That goes for all aspects of the chapter, from good academics to pervasive campus involvement, extensive community service to intense intramural competition. If members are living according to the Ritual, a new member will learn to be a great SigEp.

"Induct Them Properly"

Before beginning any Ritual ceremony, the officers must be prepared mentally and spiritually. There is no place for hazing, and a true SigEp could never humiliate another person and succeed. These new men must be alert and know that they are safe in the company of Brothers. Sigma Phi Epsilon stands for high ideals, and the Fraternity's Ritual is its embodiment and celebration.

"Live the Right Way"

Finally, after being inducted, a member of Sigma Phi Epsilon must live right, every day. We pursue the Balanced Man Ideal, developing a Sound Mind in a Sound Body.

Sigma Phi Epsilon Fraternity, at its best, will make for all these things. As U. G. Dubach emphasized, if you have it in your heart to make SigEp great, it will be great. A team that won't be beaten can't be beaten. Strive to live above the common level of life. Choose the harder right instead of the easier wrong, and never be content with the half-truth when the whole can be won.

SigEps always strive to be their best, by living according to the Ritual and by broadening their mind through intellectual pursuits.

The Ideal Chapter House

Picture this...green lawn, landscaping, red door. You look up and see a large house with the elegant letters spelling out, "Sigma Phi Epsilon."

You approach the front and walk inside. Someone greets you and shakes your hand. Through the doorway, you turn and look to your left. In this room, there are sofas, with members of the chapter sitting and listening intently to a story being told. The speaker is a classics professor, and he is relating why the founders of Phi Beta Kappa in the late 1700s chose Greek letters to represent their organization, and not another name.

Turning your attention to the right, you peer into another room and see a woman. In front of her are two long tables of sitting men. She has been invited by the Brothers to lead an etiquette dinner. You watch as they practice holding a knife, fork, and spoon properly, so in the future, they will be prepared for any formal meal functions.

SigEps at the Valparaiso Residential Learning Community utilize their chapter house for educational opportunities by hosting speakers, alumni and faculty at events throughout the year.

You turn back and look straight ahead. In front of you, there is an open door. It is the resident scholar's room, and inside are two Brothers conversing with the resident scholar. They are looking at their grades for the semester and making plans for what classes to take next year.

Off to the side is a staircase leading up. You take it to the second floor. You notice the clean steps along the way and are glad your feet are not sticking to the floor. In fact, you haven't smelled any lingering smoke or alcohol. You walk down the hallway, looking at the walls, floors, and ceiling. It's clean. Not because new members just finished cleaning this morning, but because clean people live there.

You are in a home of Sigma Phi Epsilon. This is the place where members, alumni, parents, and guests continually take pride in the living environment, where school and life meet with dynamic activity. This is your regular experience when passing through the red door.

Does this description match your environment? If not, what are you doing to make this vision a reality?

Social Fraternity?

By Gary E. Griffith, Texas, '70, Grand President 1995-1997

During the 1960s, while I was an undergraduate, the term "social" was being redefined. The country was in chaos while the Vietnam War flared and Civil Rights efforts marched forward.

Our Founders understood "social" to mean fellowship. The term was characteristic of upper-class culture. Leaders and intellectuals bonded together for the purpose of improving the *society* in which they lived. Virtue, Diligence, and Brotherly Love—SigEp's Cardinal Principles—were the means by which this service was to be accomplished. Sigma Phi Epsilon was a way of life.

In the 1960s and 1970s, the age of anti-establishment changed "social" to mean something different. Traditional values were abandoned in many parts of society. Being social rather than acting socially became the norm for many Greeks, Sigma Phi Epsilon included. Alcohol and partying became synonymous with the new definition of the word.

The 1980s saw that new meaning pushed to the limits. Huge keg parties, hazing, and liability nightmares raged. People died. Some were our Brothers. Universities, parents, law enforcement and communities at large raged back.

Look at many chapters today and you can still see evidence of why people's impression of a "fraternity" is "Animal House" or "Old School."

Ask yourself this: are your chapter's grades above the all-campus average? Do you have development programming for upperclassmen? Who's your faculty advisor or faculty fellow? Are alumni and volunteers involved? How long since the last newsletter or news release? Have you had a non-alcoholic event this month? How about this year? Do you sing as a chapter? How many members are involved on campus? Do members know the chapter's standards?

In the late '80s under the directive of undergraduates, Sigma Phi Epsilon began to search for its roots. Sigma Phi Epsilon is currently leading the Greek world in reclaiming our past, our values, and our traditions through initiatives like the Balanced Man Program, Residential Learning Communities, and the strategic plan.

Sigma Phi Epsilon will become a way of life again, if it is not already. That's for sure. As we build balanced leaders for the World's communities, we will be the *societal* fraternity our Founders meant us to be. The ideal SigEp chapter is just that.

Members of the Texas Beta Residential Learning Community at the University of North Texas collect canned goods for a chapter-wide food drive.

*Mike Powers, Oregon State '07, standing atop the ruins of Mycenae
during the 2005 Tragos Quest to Greece.*

LEADERSHIP ESSENTIALS

"Two roads diverged in a wood, and I took the one less traveled by, and that has made all the difference."

~ ROBERT FROST

True leadership can be identified through the choices we make. With each choice comes consequence; with each success, joy; and with each failure, knowledge. Today, fraternity men face numerous choices that will impact their lives and build habits to last a lifetime. As a result, Sigma Phi Epsilon has positioned its leadership development programs as an opportunity to gain knowledge and skills in order to make effective decisions that will contribute to the well-being of each member.

Through a natural progression of leadership programs, Sigma Phi Epsilon offers the Leadership Continuum as the vehicle for leadership development. Starting from the very day a new member joins, he will be offered opportunities to better himself personally and to build his ability to lead teams toward a common purpose. As he progresses in his chapter experience, a member's SigEp experience must progress as well. He will build individual skills, learn how to apply these skills, impact the Fraternity, and be a lifelong contributor to our world's communities.

To take this road less traveled, Sigma Phi Epsilon provides leadership development focused upon self-development and team dynamics.

Self-Development

▶ Perspectives/prejudices as individual.

▶ The relationship of the follower and leader — How and when to be whom.

▶ Motivation/goal-setting — Organizing your team toward a common purpose.

▶ How to treat yourself and others — Sound Mind and Sound Body.

Team Dynamics

▶ Apply knowledge of self to personal style of leadership.

▶ Recognize the need for change.

▶ Develop and foster a vision for a common purpose.

▶ Form clear objectives and well-functioning teams to execute the vision.

▶ Measure progress, make adjustments, satisfy the team — continual improvement.

▶ Mentoring to fellow members.

Each successive program builds upon the fundamentals of the previous in order to build a greater sense of self-awareness and an ability to make a difference in fellow chapter members' lives. As a result, Sigma Phi Epsilon has programming that reinforces and teaches the tangible skills necessary to *"Build Balanced Leaders for the World's Communities,"* the mission of Sigma Phi Epsilon.

Leadership Continuum Programs

EDGE: SigEp should be one the greatest experiences of your life. As such, the Fraternity offers its own innovative program for first-year members, EDGE. EDGE is about making healthy choices that match your personal values and those of Sigma Phi Epsilon. Participants

build greater self-awareness about the consequences of their actions and those around them through interactive discussions and reflective activities. Participants have fun through challenging experiences such as ropes courses, physical challenges, and activities based upon camaraderie. Participants choose the lifestyle they wish to lead and receive training on overcoming obstacles with regard to alcohol and drug abuse, personal wellness, and goal achievement. The program involves a highly regarded faculty of senior undergraduates, distinguished alumni, and renowned guest speakers.

CARLSON LEADERSHIP ACADEMY: The Academy program is the central component of the Leadership Continuum, providing hands-on training to more than 1,900 under-graduates and volunteers annually. The Academies are held in February after chapter elections, and chapters are encouraged to bring all new officers, Chapter Counselors, and rising chapter leaders. The academy program provides practice in management skills, goal development, and academic and career planning. Put on by the National Leadership Committee and the Headquarters staff, the Academies provide an appropriate venue for the presentation of chapter awards for notable achievements in recruitment, development, and scholarship and for individual achievement in student leadership or volunteer involvement. The academy program is named for Brother Curtis L. Carlson, Minnesota '37, Founder and Chairman of The Carlson Companies, a global leader with various holdings such as T.G.I. Friday's, Radisson Hotels, and Carlson Wagonlit Travel.

GRAND CHAPTER CONCLAVE: Sigma Phi Epsilon's national convention, the Conclave is attended by more than 1,400 SigEps and friends every two years. The Conclave takes place in August of each odd-numbered year.

At this grand event, the Fraternity elects its national board, enacts legislation, and celebrates the accomplishments of the Fraternity over the previous two years. The Fraternity awards its most renowned accolades at the Conclave: the Buchanan Cup for Chapter Excellence, the Citation for distinguished career achievement, and the Order of the Golden Heart for dedicated, selfless service to Sigma Phi Epsilon. The Conclave is the ultimate SigEp experience.

RUCK LEADERSHIP INSTITUTE: The Ruck Leadership Institute is the Fraternity's premier leadership development experience, the "Top Gun" of SigEp. The nation's best and brightest gather in Richmond, Virginia, for a four-day program focused on personal leadership and the Balanced Man Ideal. Competition for entry into the program is fierce as hundreds of notable undergraduates apply annually. Once on-site, they can expect constant motion, activity, and energy. Attendees see first-hand how Sound Mind and Sound Body can become a tangible part of chapter life through competitive challenges, theatrical productions, etiquette sessions, and facilitation by prominent SigEp alumni.

TRAGOS QUEST TO GREECE: The Greeks believed in arête, or being the best that you can be, striving for excellence. It is only proper that your Fraternity offer the opportunity to live and learn at the very site of the birthplace of Greek antiquity. Each summer, SigEp undergraduates walk in the footsteps of Plato, Aristotle, and Socrates. These special Brothers gain valuable insight into the Balanced Man Ideal of Sound Mind and Sound Body. This 11-day program is a scholarship opportunity generously provided by the Sigma Phi Epsilon Educational Foundation.

Five Practices of Exemplary Leadership

Being a leader is a difficult task. When problems arise, everyone turns to you. On the other hand, when the chapter succeeds, everyone wants part of the glory.

As Dr. Barry Z. Posner, California-Santa Barbara, '70, wrote in *The Leadership Challenge*, there are five practices of exemplary leadership:

Model the Way

▶ Credibility is achieved with consistency in words and actions.

▶ Understand the values outlined in the Cardinal Principles and the Oath of Obligation.

▶ Confront members acting inconsistently with the Fraternity's principles.

▶ Recognize small improvement so continued improvement will follow.

Inspire a Shared Vision

▶ Be positive about the future and motivate people so they can make a difference.

▶ Envision the future and set goals to achieve the desired result.

▶ Ensure all members know the chapter's goals and are contributing to their achievement.

Challenge the Process

▶ Maintaining the status quo only breeds mediocrity. Do not listen to the chapter if the result is inconsistent with the Fraternity's principles.

▶ Insanity is doing the same thing over and over again and expecting different results. Experiment and take risks by implementing innovative programs.

Enable Others to Act

▶ Leaders build teams with spirit and cohesion.

▶ Make sure committees are functioning well.

▶ Listen to all members.

▶ Groom future leadership to take over after you are gone.

▶ Give credit instead of taking it.

Encourage the Heart

▶ Make people feel like heroes. Let other members take the credit for accomplishments.

▶ Thank those who help you. Recognize volunteers and their families every year.

▶ Celebrate achievements.

▶ Spend 30 minutes every week writing thank-you and congratulatory notes to individuals who have helped the chapter.

By following these five practices, you will be well on the way to being an effective leader.

The most common failures and omissions of leaders are:

1. Too often, they do not establish realistic goals and do not set action steps or time schedules for reaching these goals.

2. Too often, they do not successfully sell the members of the organization on the importance of reaching particular goals; they do not motivate or involve all members.

3. Too often, they delay replacing incompetent people and hope that something or someone else will shape them up instead.

4. Too often, they do not recruit enough competent people with management potential.

5. Too often, they do not educate enough people for more responsible positions.

6. Too often, they do not pre-judge changing market conditions soon enough to allow time for new product development.

7. Too often, they do not recognize changes in marketing and distribution soon enough to allow shifts in sales policies.

8. Their greatest failures are in the misjudgment of people and their capabilities, desires, ambitions, and loyalties.

All of the above situations can easily be applied to a fraternity chapter in the areas of membership recruitment, member development, leadership development, member involvement, etc.

Spotting Leadership Potential

The following are some traits to look for in future chapter leaders:

▶ ACADEMIC BASE: Chapter leaders have their personal priorities in line. The student leader is a student first.

▶ DEDICATED WINNER: A leader is willing to dig in to improve the chapter. If he hates to lose and is willing to work harder, then he is dedicated.

▶ WORK ETHIC: A leader does not stop working until the task is done. Then he is looking for the next task to complete.

▶ CAN TALK/WILL LISTEN: A leader must be able to communicate, first by listening, and then by articulating his ideas.

▶ DEDICATION: A leader must be tough, willing to take constructive criticism, correct mistakes, and make a second effort.

SigEps at the Ohio State Residential Learning Community relaxing in the chapter house formal room.

▶ HONESTY: A leader must be able to admit mistakes, seek help, realize his own limitations, and be truthful.

▶ PRACTICAL: Being able to prioritize tasks is essential for a leader, tackling the immediate needs with a plan for the future.

▶ SELF-CONFIDENCE: Having faith in himself, a leader knows when to ask for help and will accomplish objectives on time.

Because a chapter's leadership changes annually, and its membership turns over every four years, it is vital that members be educated from the day they join on how the chapter operates and how they can contribute. Only then can a chapter be consistent in its programming and capable of building on its achievements.

Questions for Personal Consideration

Consider the following questions. Where does your chapter need to improve, and how will you act to improve your chapter's weaknesses? It is your responsibility to see that the chapter runs properly, achieving and even surpassing its goals.

1. Are your chapter officers good LEADERS? How? How are they not?

2. Are all members involved in some aspect of chapter operations? How could they be better involved? How are committees performing?

3. How does your chapter evaluate its performance? Are plans readjusted for the future? When was the last chapter retreat?

4. Are members educated properly on chapter operations? Could other members run the chapter if they had to?

Evaluating Your Chapter's Operations

Evaluate your chapter's operations and determine its strengths and weaknesses. With other chapter members, design goals and an action plan to improve the weaknesses. Present your plan to chapter leaders and present it to the chapter members for their participation. Make the goals S.M.A.R.T. and monitor them weekly when your plan is underway.

The Art of Solving Problems

If SigEp chapters never had problems, there would be little challenge in being a member. It would be like living somewhere where everything was done for you and you didn't have to make tough decisions, very unrealistic, and certainly something you will not experience throughout your life. Your chapter will have problems.

Every Chapter Encounters Problems

Almost all chapters move through cycles of quality. For example, a chapter will see a need to improve its recruitment results. A few men will work very hard and do a great job, and, over two years or so, the chapter's quality will rise steadily. Then men may become complacent with their success and feel it comes without effort. They begin to coast, and when you coast, it's always downhill. Two years pass, the decline becomes obvious, dissatisfaction sets in, and the men roll up their sleeves and get back to work.

The difference between an average chapter and a *consistently* good chapter is the good ones recognize the **WHEN YOU ENCOUNTER A PROBLEM OR WARNING SIGNS ON THE HORIZON, REMEMBER THAT ALL CHAPTERS HAVE PROBLEMS.** warning signs early, and act right away to short-circuit the decline. There's still a cycle, but the amplitude is reduced, and the chapter maintains a higher level of quality.

When you encounter a problem or warning signs of problems on the horizon, remember that all chapters have problems, your chapter has survived problems before, and ask yourself the following questions:

1. What is the real problem?

2. What are the possible solutions?

3. What resources are available?

4. What are the priorities in resolving the problem?

5. What immediate steps can you take to get started?

6. How can you plan a long-term course of action?

7. How will this lead to solving the problem?

Chapter problems are solved by "doers" and not by complainers, whiners, or people who get in the way of what is right and needs to be done. Do not become a part of the problem by dwelling on it. Be a part of the solution. Ask yourself and your Brothers, "What would it look like without the problem?" And make plans to get to that goal.

Tackle a Problem Now

Using the questions below and the other six questions in this section, outline a solution to a chapter problem. Big or small, problems must be handled, and the experience of solving them will benefit you and your chapter.

▶ What is an immediate problem facing your chapter?

▶ Who is responsible for this managing the problem?

▶ What are your objectives in solving this problem?

▶ What action steps are necessary to solve this problem?

"The credit in life does not go to the critic who stands on the sidelines and points out where the strong stumble, but rather, the real credit in life goes to the man who is actually in the arena, whose face may get marred by sweat and dust, who knows great enthusiasm and great devotion and learns to spend himself in a worthy cause, who, at best if he wins, knows the thrill of high achievement and, if he fails, at least fails while daring greatly, so that in life his place will never be with those very cold and timid souls in the gray twilight who know neither victory nor defeat."

~ THEODORE ROOSEVELT, 1899

RESPONSIBILITY:
COMMUNITY

RESPONSIBILITY: COMMUNITY

"Be the change you want to see in the world."

~ MAHATMA GHANDI

In the first part of *The Lifetime Responsibility of Brotherhood,* the responsibility to "self" was discussed and guidelines for understanding, managing and respecting yourself were outlined as a foundation for self-esteem. Next, your responsibility to Sigma Phi Epsilon was discussed. As important as your relationship to Sigma Phi Epsilon is your relationships with others. Many different types of love and friendship will be experienced with others—acquaintances, friends, brothers, girlfriends and your family.

Part III will cover friendships and relationships, relationships and mentoring, care and concern, ethical decisions, diversity, interfraternalism, service and citizenship. As the founders believed, Sigma Phi Epsilon has a greater responsibility to the community and society at large. To live according to our Cardinal Principles, members of Sigma Phi Epsilon must be engaged in service to others while being good citizens. As you read this section, you should gain a better understanding of all these relationships and "brotherhood" beyond the Fraternity.

TO LIVE ACCORDING TO OUR CARDINAL PRINCIPLES, MEMBERS OF SIGMA PHI EPSILON MUST BE ENGAGED IN SERVICE TO OTHERS WHILE BEING GOOD CITIZENS.

FRIENDSHIPS & RELATIONSHIPS

"Go often to the house of a friend, for weeds soon choke up the unused path."

~ SCANDINAVIAN PROVERB

Make no mistake, Sigma Phi Epsilon is an organization based upon principles, aspirations, and purpose. Yet, it is the very people that make up its membership who make this Fraternity matter. In this age, we live in a world obsessed with "cool." That's cool, he's cool...we respect those who appear cool, people who have gadgets that are cool, people who are standoffish or seem above the situation.

"Cool" is hurting our organization. In an organization based upon people, the relationships we share are what matter most. Brotherly Love cannot be idle pretense. It must be a living, breathing passionate concern for your well-being, but, more importantly, for those around you. As the Scandinavian proverb says, "Go often to the house of a friend, for weeds soon choke the unused path."

We must embody Brotherly Love not as a crutch to lean upon, but rather as a shield that encourages us to show our inner passion for life and for SigEp. For it will be the very friendships you make within the halls of Sigma Phi Epsilon that will ring in your hearts for years to come. It is necessary for you to express your care and concern for a Brother, to rejoice with him in success, to aid him in his sorrow, to be a true friend and Brother.

▶ Did you know that loneliness is a problem for many college students?

▶ Did you know that frequent contact helps develop friendships?

▶ Did you know that it is possible to increase the number of friends you have?

▶ Would you know what to do if you felt unworthy of friendship?

There are many things you can do to increase the number and quality of your friendships and the amount of warm support you get from your family. It is not necessary to struggle through school in a rather lonely existence, hoping that things will get better later on. College life provides a tremendous opportunity to develop a wealth of friendships.

BROTHERLY LOVE CANNOT BE IDLE PRETENSE. IT MUST BE A LIVING, BREATHING PASSIONATE CONCERN FOR YOUR WELL-BEING, BUT, MORE IMPORTANTLY, FOR THOSE AROUND YOU.

Developing Friendships

As with success in school, you have choices about how many friends you have. Having friends is not a matter of luck or having money or having a great personality. Friendship develops between people as a result of a combination of variables that you can influence.

Make Frequent Contact

Research into the sources of feelings of friendship shows that the main contributing factor is *frequency of contact.* Research in colleges, housing projects and neighborhoods shows a consistent relationship between friendship and how often people have contact with each other. To have more frequent contact with other students, get involved in one or more of the many extra-curricular activities on campus.

Many activities are available to you that will bring you into contact with other students with similar interests. Keep in mind that it is not unusual for a beginning student to feel lonely. Loneliness is a normal experience when in a totally new situation without contact with old friends and family.

ALLOWING PEOPLE TO KNOW MORE ABOUT YOU IS THE ONLY WAY TO GAIN THE FRIENDSHIPS AND ACCEPTANCE YOU NEED.

The Fraternity provides unlimited opportunities for friendship in an atmosphere that actively provides support and brotherhood. As a member of Sigma Phi Epsilon, you have already given yourself a big first step toward lifetime friendships.

Be Assertive

Can you walk up to someone who looks interesting and initiate a conversation? If you are in the cafeteria, can you go to a stranger, ask permission to join that person, and ask several questions that will help you get to know each other? Can you voluntarily offer your opinions or thoughts in a way that lets others get to know you? By being assertive, you will find numerous opportunities to build your relationships with others.

Once you decide to take initiative and make a reasonable effort to create what you would like to have, you will find your life works better. One important lesson in life is to learn how to develop friendships, be a good friend, and gain the support of other people. It could be that learning these basic skills of human interaction will prove to be one of the most valuable abilities you learn in college.

If you sit back passively and hope that others will go out of their way to be friends with you, you are likely to be disappointed. Be assertive.

Be a Good Listener

People like being listened to. They feel friendly toward a person who has a sincere interest in them. How do you accomplish this? Ask questions and listen with an open mind. Do not be judgmental. A judgmental person, even though remaining silent, eventually communicates through facial expressions, body language, and other reactions.

Good listeners have a wide range of acceptance for what they learn about others. This is why so many people feel friendly toward a person who is accepting and tolerant.

If the person you are listening to has attitudes and opinions that you dislike, the chances are poor that you will be a good friend of that person. You can have empathy for the individual, but you probably will not have much in the way of friendship.

Your behavior is contagious. Positive behavior creates positive reactions; negative behavior gets negative reactions.

Something Interesting to Say

Listening is not enough, however. Read up on current events that could help you prompt an interesting discussion. You might read, for example, about the use of steroids by student athletes and ask people what they know firsthand.

Let People Know You

If you want people to accept you and like you, you have to let them know what you feel, think, and do. If people have very little experience of you as a person, there is little for them to relate to. Accept the fact that when some people learn about your feelings and thinking, they won't like what they hear. That's okay. No matter what you are like as a person, some people will like you and others dislike you. That is the way the world works. Trying to avoid being disliked will prevent you from being liked. Allowing people to know more about you is the only way to gain the friendships and acceptance you need.

Putting on an act that impresses others creates a barrier to friendship. How? Because when people smile and show that they like you, a part of you knows it is your act they like. This makes their response emotionally dissatisfying. You tend to question how much you can really respect anyone who falls for an act such as yours. And you still end up feeling lonely because you have private thoughts and feelings that others don't see. Trying to come up with the perfect act is not the way to avoid feeling lonely. It is guaranteed to make you stay lonely behind a happy front.

Manage Conflict

Anger between friends is often hard to handle. There are ways for people to express anger to each other yet remain friends. If you feel angry at someone, here is how to manage the conflict:

▶ First, ask the person's permission. Ask if you can get angry at him.

▶ If he says to go ahead, then say, "I feel angry because you..."

▶ Start by saying, "I feel..." not "I am...." Anger is an emotion, not who you are.

▶ Ask if he knew his actions had such an effect on you. He may not have known.

▶ Listen to what he says about his behavior. Have some empathy for him.

▶ Ask for resolution. What will work for you? What can be done now?

▶ Discuss and negotiate a solution that is satisfactory for both of you.

▶ Thank the person for listening. Do this even if he shrugged and didn't care.

▶ The bottom line is that it is your problem. Don't close the door for good.

When some people feel angry, they "fight dirty." They react in ways that prevent resolving the difficulty. Some reactions destroy relationships. Avoid the following:

▶ Don't catch the person by surprise and let him have it unexpectedly.

▶ Don't blame him for your emotions and say, "You made me angry."

▶ Don't swear and turn him into something he is not. "You are a…"

▶ Don't refuse to talk face-to-face about what is upsetting you.

▶ Don't give him the silent treatment or talk behind his back.

▶ Don't conspire to try to get others to agree with your perception.

▶ Don't decide never speak to him or spend time with him.

"You…" statements are often hurtful and lead to a permanent loss of friendship. "I feel…" lets you express your feelings and gives you a chance to work things out. Anger is a normal part of any relationship. Even when people like each other, there are bound to be moments of dislike.

WHEN A FRIENDSHIP CAN SURVIVE MOMENTS OF ANGER, THE FRIENDSHIP BECOMES MORE DURABLE, MORE LASTING, AND RICHER.

Closing off, suppressing, or "stuffing" unpleasant feelings does not work well. When you suppress unpleasant feelings, you shut down positive feelings as well. The challenge is to handle unpleasant feelings in a productive way when they occur. It may take some practice if you were raised to hide and avoid angry feelings, but you can learn how to do it. The benefit is that when a friendship can survive moments of anger, the friendship becomes more durable, more lasting, and richer.

Conflict-Resolution Strategies

Conflict is a daily reality for everyone. Some conflicts are relatively minor, easy to handle, or capable of being overlooked. Others of greater magnitude, however, require a strategy for successful resolution if they are not to create constant tension or lasting enmity in home or business.

The ability to resolve conflict successfully is probably one of the most important social skills that an individual can possess. Yet there are few formal opportunities in our society to learn it. Like any other human skill, conflict resolution can be taught; like other skills, it consists of a number of important sub-skills, each separate and yet interdependent. When resolving conflict, one must consider the importance of the relationship and the importance of the outcome.

RELATIONSHIP: How you handle a conflict situation is highly dependent upon the value you place on the relationship you share with that individual. If you value the relationship highly, you will be more likely to work toward a solution that is agreeable to both of you. If you do not, you may work more toward your objective in resolving the conflict.

OUTCOME: The desired outcome plays an enormous factor in conflict resolution. If the outcome is trivial to you, you will be inclined to acquiesce to the other's resolution strategy. However, if the outcome is important, you are more likely to engage in more competitive strategies.

Your balance between the importance of the relationship and the outcome will play a significant role in how you will approach a conflict situation. Conflict-resolution strategies may be classified into three categories—avoidance, defusing, and confrontation.

AVOIDANCE: Some people attempt to avoid conflict situations altogether or to avoid certain types of conflict. These people tend to repress emotional reactions, look the other way, or leave the situation entirely, for example, by quitting a job, leaving school, or getting a divorce. These people either cannot face such situations effectively, or they do not have the skills to negotiate them effectively.

Avoidance strategies are successful when cooler heads must prevail. Do not play a resolution during a heated moment. Seek out time when the other is more apt to be agreeable to conflict resolution. Intervening when the other is impaired is highly unsuccessful, though all effort must be made to ensure that the other party is safe from others and from himself.

Similar to avoidance, we often will accommodate the wishes of another as we value the relationship more or the outcome is simply not important. For example, the relationship shared between a parent and child. In order to preserve the relationship, one will accommodate the wishes of the other. While this can be an effective strategy when the outcome is unimportant to you, one should not willingly accommodate when the outcome is important.

Although avoidance strategies do have survival value in those instances where escape is possible, they usually do not provide the individual with a high level of satisfaction. They tend to leave doubts and fears about meeting the same type of situation in the future and about such valued traits as courage or persistence. An avoidance strategy will not lead to a satisfying conflict resolution.

DEFUSION: This tactic is essentially a delaying action. Defusion strategies try to cool off the situation, at least temporarily, or to keep the issues so unclear that attempts at confrontation are improbable. Resolving minor points while avoiding or delaying discussion of the major problem, postponing a confrontation until a more suitable time, and avoiding clarification of the main issues underlying the conflict are examples of defusion. Again, as with avoidance strategies, such tactics work when delay is possible, but they typically result in feelings of dissatisfaction, anxiety about the future, and concerns about oneself.

CONFRONTATION: The third major strategy involves an actual confrontation of conflicting issues or persons. Confrontation can further be subdivided into *power* strategies and *negotiation* strategies. Power strategies include the use of physical force (a punch in the nose), bribery (money, favors), and punishment (withholding love, money). Such tactics are often very effective from the viewpoint of the "successful" party. One person wins and the other person loses. Unfortunately, however, for the loser, the real conflict may have only just begun. Hostility, anxiety, and actual physical damage are usual byproducts of these win-lose power tactics.

CONFLICT-RESOLUTION STRATEGIES MAY BE CLASSIFIED INTO THREE CATEGORIES— AVOIDANCE, DEFUSING, AND CONFRONTATION.

With negotiation strategies, unlike power confrontations, both sides can win. However, the degree of satisfaction will depend upon the negotiation strategy employed: competition, compromise, or collaboration.

In a competitive situation, one must win at the expense of the other, a zero-sum game. Competitive negotiation strategies are useful when there can be only one winner of the relationship with the other is unimportant. A competitive negotiation situation, like a power strategy, can be satisfying for the "winner" and dissatisfying for the "loser."

In compromise, both parties agree to forego some benefit for the situation in order to preserve a common ground between the two. Both parties will essentially "win" by splitting the perceived benefit equally among the parties. This strategy is useful when looking to resolve a situation quickly.

If we are able to collaborate, we are able to find new approaches to resolve the situation. Collaboration requires creativity, communication, and problem-solving skills. In a collaborative approach, you compete against the conflict rather than the other person. A quick resolution is not likely, yet collaboration will bring about a more satisfying result for each party.

The aim of negotiation is to resolve the conflict with a compromise or a solution which is mutually satisfying to all parties involved in the conflict. Negotiation, then, seems to provide the most positive and the least negative byproducts of all conflict-resolution strategies.

Feel Worthy of Friendship

If you do not feel worthy of friendship, none of the recommended actions will work for you. How do you react when people like you? Is it enjoyable or do you get embarrassed? When people tell you they like you, do you say, "Thank you," or do you feel uncomfortable?

What is your opinion of people who like you? Is it positive or negative? Do you respect them or do you question their judgment? If you feel uncomfortable when people make efforts to be friends with you, take a little time to make as long a list as you can in answer to these questions:

▶ What are all the good reasons people would enjoy being my friend?

▶ What are all the ways that am I a nice person to be around?

▶ What are all the things I like and appreciate most about myself?

If you are uncomfortable answering such questions for yourself, you may have been raised to avoid feelings of self-esteem. Conscious self-esteem is essential for any person to function well in the world. Self-esteem acts as an insulating buffer against unfounded criticisms. Self-esteem allows you to accept people's praise and affections as legitimate.

Thinking well of yourself is not conceited. Conceit means to feel superior to others and inform them about it. Self-esteem means to feel good about yourself even though you still have a lot to learn.

Left to right: R. Major Sharpe, Tennessee '05, Alumni and Volunteer Corporation President and Order of the Golden Heart recipient G. Burl Rainwater, Tennessee '58, and W. Jacob Rasnick, Tennessee '05, at the 2003 Conclave in San Antonio.

RELATIONSHIPS & MENTORING

"We are not achievers until someone expects something of us."

~ ANONYMOUS

Relationships with your Brothers are special and require special attention. Maintaining friendships without fostering "cliques" is a challenge, but the greatest challenge for Brothers is to love each other, without future fallout, when times are tough.

A Faithful Friend

One of the most critical relationships you can have within the community or the chapter is a relationship with a mentor. This is a person who will give you support, provide encouragement, and offer information to assist you in making good, responsible choices. Most successful people today will attribute a measure of their success to their mentor. Without the help of a guide along the way, life's journey is much more difficult.

Finding and utilizing the right mentor can make all the difference in the world to a young man. It may have a far-reaching impact on the rest of his life.

As a teenager in rural Mississippi, Walter Payton found himself in a troublesome situation. Although he was on his high school football team and was a good student, Walter feared he would not be able to go to college.

Sensing his anxiety, Walter's football coach, Charles Boston, encouraged him to improve and distinguish himself in football. Boston's continued support and guidance led Payton to Jackson State University and to a successful life as a professional football player and distinguished businessman.

This mentoring relationship had a life-changing impact on Payton. There was no magic button that needed to be pushed, no endless hours of consultation, only someone older and wiser giving a little time and encouragement to a young man.

THE GREATEST CHALLENGE FOR BROTHERS IS TO LOVE EACH OTHER WHEN TIMES ARE TOUGH.

Choosing A Mentor

When you search for a mentor, seek someone whom you respect because of his talents, values, and experience. Your mentor may be older or younger, but always choose someone from whom you can learn and who will provide you with honest feedback and advice. He will aid you in setting personal goals and establishing action plans. Frequently, he will become a lifelong friend. The best mentoring relationships involve regular communication, and clear expectations. Mentoring is brotherhood in action

A solid relationship will be vital to your success. You have a right to expect that your mentor will undertake this relationship in earnest and provide you with the necessary guidance to become comfortable in the chapter. Your first mentor should:

▶ Be your friend, first and foremost.

▶ Spend at least five hours a week together.

▶ Eat at least two meals a week together.

▶ Become acquainted with your family.

▶ Discuss the Cardinal Principles with you.

▶ Review academic success tips with you.

▶ Help you set academic goals and priorities.

▶ Help you learn time management skills.

▶ Study together at least five hours a week.

▶ Introduce you to other members.

Being A Mentor

When the time comes for you to become a mentor, you must remember many things. As a mentor, you will be a role model and the one who can foster a love for the Fraternity and community. You can be the difference between Sigma Phi Epsilon being a genuinely positive experience, or one that does not encourage growth and development.

The man you are mentoring needs your guidance on being a good member. Remember:

▶ He may lack good study habits and skills.

▶ He may fear competition with other students.

▶ He may fear disappointing his parents and friends.

▶ He may be shy or homesick.

▶ He may have problems with his new freedom.

▶ He may need help managing his time.

▶ He may worry about choosing the right major.

▶ He may fear being rejected by the chapter.

▶ He may have difficulties with his roommate.

▶ He may have difficulties with a relationship.

You do not have to be Charles Boston to be a good mentor. You have to be yourself and show that you care. As a member in Sigma Phi Epsilon, you will be called upon, whether formally or informally, to serve as a mentor to other members. You should feel honored. It is an important job. No special skills, or even any knowledge of the Fraternity, are required. Just be yourself!

▶ Provide encouragement.

▶ Review goals and progress.

▶ Provide academic support.

▶ Give honest feedback.

▶ Be a positive role model.

▶ Serve as an inspiration.

▶ Listen and be a friend.

As a mentor, it is very important that you are understanding and supportive. Remember your responsibilities. This is one of the most important roles you will play for the life and future of the Fraternity.

Critical Considerations

▶ Do not try to do more than you are qualified to do. If you are not a trained counselor, do not try to deal with major emotional problems. Make sure he seeks professional assistance. The first call should be to the counseling center of the college or university.

▶ Always remember that you are responsible to the young man, not responsible for him.

▶ Be clear about your motives. Know what you want from the relationship and what you are willing to give.

▶ Although you may feel more comfortable with people who are similar to you, consider an occasional long shot. It may be even more rewarding.

▶ Do not try to force him to follow in your footsteps. If he aspires to follow your general path, encourage him to add his own personal touch.

▶ Find the motivational "hot spots" in the young man and use them.

▶ Be prepared for departure day. If you have done your job well, he will outgrow your help. This does not mean that your friendship must come to an end, it only means the relationship takes on a different note.

▶ Use your own style and be yourself.

Adult Definition of Honesty

By Ron Smotherman

To manifest adult honesty requires an adult definition. Most of us operate from a child's definition.

As children we are told to be honest, and we are told that means not to lie, cheat, or steal. Rarely is a child told why not to lie, cheat, or steal, and when told, the reasons given insult the child's intelligence. Further, honesty is presented to children as a passive quality—actions one does not take. We do not teach honesty as an active quality—something one does as an act of honesty, or otherwise one is not honest. The result is a world full of passive liars—people who will not tell the truth when it is time to tell the truth.

TO BE A MENTOR, YOU HAVE TO BE YOURSELF AND SHOW THAT YOU CARE.

Being honest means much more than not telling lies. Honesty is also an action one takes. It is an act of telling the truth. Dishonesty, on the other hand, can be an act or a non-act. Telling untrue information is dishonest, and so is withholding the truth when it is time to tell it. But this goes deeper than information.

Honesty requires truthful representation of your experience, as well as the information at hand, expressed for no other purpose than the expression itself. There are situations when it is time to express the truth of how you feel, and if you withhold that, you are a liar, and will pay a liar's price. Also, if you use telling the truth of your experience as a weapon to punish others, you are lying, and will pay a liar's price.

There is another realm of honesty which is harder to define. It is the realm of being honest, which goes beyond doing honest. Being honest is represented by telling the truth to the best of your knowledge and experience, at your own responsibility.

HONESTY IS THE ACT OF TELLING THE TRUTH.

If you are being honest for someone else, or if you are being honest for something you believe in, or if you are being honest for a reward, or to avoid punishment, or to reward or punish others, then you are not being honest, although you may be doing honest.

Being a mentor requires using the adult definition of honesty.

On Tough Brotherhood

By George W. Spasyk, Former Executive Vice President, Lambda Chi Alpha Fraternity

Not too long ago, I ran across the expression "tough brotherhood" in one of the reports of Educational Leadership Consultant Brent Judge. I thought it was an unusual combination of words—almost an oxymoron, which Webster describes as "a combination of contradictory or incongruous words (such as cruel kindness)." But the more I thought about it (and wished I had thought of it first), the more it made sense to me.

We think of a brother most often in terms of caring, sharing and brotherly love. Those who have blood brothers know what I mean—I had five of them when I was growing up—all older than I. And they did care for their kid brothers, and there was an abundance of brotherly love. But on further reflection, they were also tough on me. They never let me get away with my evil deeds without a word of caution or reprimand.

I would think nothing unusual about someone saying his parents were "tough" with him. In fact, I would think it tragic if they were not. Being a tough parent is a tremendous expression of love. Maybe we don't appreciate it while we're growing up, but we certainly do after we've left the nest. My father expressed his love in many ways. He came from the "old country," Eastern Europe, where men greet each other with a kiss on the cheek, or on both cheeks, and I was embarrassed as a teenager when he did that. What I wouldn't give today to have a kiss on the cheek from my Dad. But he also expressed his love for me when he would punish me. Tough love.

That kind of tough love should be present in all of our chapter houses, but too often it is missing. Instead, we often see a watered-down version of brotherhood, where so-called brothers back away from conflict, afraid to take a stand, afraid to challenge intolerable behavior. This only results in more conflict, more intolerable behavior. And the end result is an erosion of standards, loss of pride and respect, and then a complete absence of brotherhood.

A permissive society, a permissive home, or a permissive fraternity chapter reflects a lack of love. My equation of family and fraternity is

where the fraternity can provide one of the most valuable experiences for young men. Confront bad behavior and apathy. Uphold high standards. That's tough love. That's a fraternity.

Not only do we learn to work with each other in spite of our shortcomings, but by refusing to accept human frailty as inevitable, the crucible of experience which we call fraternity provides for us the opportunity to help each other to overcome our imperfections. And that means displaying, when it becomes necessary, tough brotherhood!

not made lightly. I truly believe it. In a very real sense, the fraternity creates a family relationship among its members. It aims to bring together in intimate association a group of young men who will be congenial, loyal and helpful to one another during some of the best years of their lives—the college years.

The fraternity offers its members the nearest possible equivalent to home that can be found on the college campus, and these close ties, this tough brotherhood, often bind men in friendship for life. You will not find that in the residence halls.

It must be remembered, however, that fraternity does not offer sanctuary from real life. We must acknowledge that man is not perfect, and, therefore, that no association of men can be perfect. We all screw up every now and then, and do stupid things. Rather than being disillusioned by the imperfections of some of our brothers, that is precisely

Questions for Personal Consideration

1. How can tough brotherhood improve your relationships with SigEps and others?

2. What steps will you commit to take to improve these relationships?

3. Why is tough brotherhood the mark of a true fraternal experience?

4. How does the "adult definition of honesty" play a part in tough brotherhood?

5. Why are adult honesty and tough brotherhood necessary to be a friend, mentor, and Brother?

6. Without tough brotherhood, men may wear fraternity letters, but there is no fraternity. Why?

CARE & CONCERN

"It is one of the most beautiful compensations of this life, that no man can sincerely try to help another without helping himself."

~ RALPH WALDO EMERSON

The Fraternity is not a place for any kind of abuse—not abuse of yourself and not abuse of others. Sigma Phi Epsilon has policies clearly stating the position of the Fraternity and the position its members should take. Anyone who disregards these policies is not "SigEp material" to be sure. Abusive behavior is behavior unbecoming of a Sigma Phi Epsilon member.

Treating all men and women with respect is common sense and the way of the civilized man. Sigma Phi Epsilon's Ritual calls for all members to honor the dignity of all men and women. Acting any other way is not only unbecoming of a SigEp, but is also a disgrace to the Fraternity and a setback to society and civil rights. "Do unto others as you would have them do unto you." This is a way of life for members of Sigma Phi Epsilon.

Respect for Self & Others

By Robert Fulghum, *Everything I Ever Needed to Know I Learned in Kindergarten*

Most of what I really need to know about how to live, and what to do, and how to be I learned in kindergarten. Wisdom was not at the top of the graduate school mountain, but there in the sandbox.

These are the things I learned: Share everything. Play fair. Don't hit people. Put things back where you found them. Clean up your own mess. Don't take things that aren't yours. Say you're sorry when you hurt somebody. Wash your hands before you eat. Live a balanced life. Learn some and think some, and draw and sing and dance and play and work every day some.

Take a nap in the afternoon. When you go out into the world, watch for traffic, hold hands and stick together. Be aware of wonder. Remember the little seed in the plastic cup. The roots go down and the plant goes up, and nobody really knows why, but we are all like that.

Goldfish and hamsters and white mice and even the little seed in the plastic cup—they all die. So do we.

And then remember the book about Dick and Jane and the first word you learned, the biggest word of all: *look*. Everything you need to know is in there somewhere.

DO UNTO OTHERS AS YOU WOULD HAVE THEM DO UNTO YOU.

The golden rule and love and basic sanitation. Ecology and politics and sane living.

Think of what a better world it would be if we all had cookies and milk about three o'clock every afternoon and

then lay down with our blankets for a nap. Or if we had a basic policy in our nation and other nations always to put things back where we found them and cleaned up our own messes. And it is still true, no matter how old you are, when you go out into the world, it is best to hold hands and stick together.

Resolutions on Behavior & Respect

Sigma Phi Epsilon adopted the following resolution regarding behavior and respect. It establishes expectations and standards for all members of the Fraternity. The resolution was adopted during the 41st Grand Chapter in 1989.

WHEREAS Sigma Phi Epsilon believes that the dignity of the individual is an essential element of a civilized society and that dignity comes from a feeling of self-worth; and

WHEREAS individual self-esteem is a necessary factor in establishing healthy relationships and brotherhood; and

WHEREAS Sigma Phi Epsilon chapters and members are encouraged to act in all matters consistent with the values of Sigma Phi Epsilon; and

WHEREAS Sigma Phi Epsilon seeks that which is good and just, and rejects that which is destructive, demeaning and abusive, and believes we can have a positive influence in the directions and achievements of society; therefore be it

RESOLVED: That we accept and rededicate ourselves to the concept that Sigma Phi Epsilon is a caring, collaborative, and learning commitment, and in this spirit adopt the following:

1. Members of Sigma Phi Epsilon are expected to exhibit high standards of conduct at all times and effectively deal with those who do not.

2. Each chapter is expected to provide educational programming directed toward life skills and interpersonal relationships.

3. Educational programs on alcohol and drug abuse must be presented at a minimum of two meetings a year.

4. Programs at the local and national levels must be developed and maintained to enhance the self-esteem of our members.

And be it

FURTHER RESOLVED: That Sigma Phi Epsilon Headquarters design and implement member development programs on a chapter, regional, and national level; and be it

FURTHER RESOLVED: That events, concepts, or materials which demean or degrade any member of society have no place in Sigma Phi Epsilon.

FURTHER RESOLVED: That each chapter and member be made aware of this resolution.

Position on Sexual Harassment

Sigma Phi Epsilon is concerned about the relationship between men and women on the college campus. We believe the change that is underway in society is good. We believe women are co-responsible for the quality of life we share.

Specifically, we want the public to be aware that this is a difficult time for the student population and all young people in general.

This issue is not restricted to fraternities, but because we deal with undergraduate students, it provides an opportunity for us, as well as other men's and women's fraternities, to demonstrate leadership in educating our members and other students, to develop an understanding, and to communicate.

We want our members to know that Sigma Phi Epsilon will not tolerate or condone any form of sexually abusive behavior (physical, mental, or emotional) on the part of its members.

Sigma Phi Epsilon will seek to educate its members about their proper relationships with women and to recognize in meaningful ways those chapters and individuals making tangible and visible steps toward the recognition of human dignity.

Both men and women need:

▶ Understanding as they redefine their relationships.

▶ Education on the changes underway.

▶ Clarity of the ramifications for unacceptable behavior.

▶ Support, care, and empathy as these changes take place.

Sigma Phi Epsilon is dedicated to providing a safe, healthy, and compelling chapter environment for its members and guests.

Sean Baran, U. of Richmond '07, speaks with media from around the world. Brother Baran, a volunteer EMT, had just spent three hours performing triage in a London hotel after the 2005 subway bombings.

ETHICAL DECISIONS

"In any moment of decision the best thing you can do is the right thing, the next best thing you can do is the wrong thing, and the worst thing you can do is nothing."

~ THEODORE ROOSEVELT

As a part of Sigma Phi Epsilon, you will have many opportunities to make decisions that affect you, your chapter, and other Brothers. These decisions will, in turn, affect other groups and individuals related to you and your chapter—including your school, your neighborhood, your family, local agencies and businesses, etc. You will have an opportunity with your decisions to make an ethical decision using the principles of Sigma Phi Epsilon as your guide. All SigEps need to be prepared to make ethical choices and balance all the components involved in ethical decisions; this section will give you guidelines for using ethics and morals to ensure decisions you make are true to you and the Fraternity.

Basic Ethics

A basic understanding of ethics is critical to any person. The concept of ethics can be broken into the answers to two questions:

1. What do I do?

2. Where do I turn to find out what I do?

The answers to these two questions give you the context in which to make ethical judgments or decisions. "Doing ethics" is the process of making decisions and choices based on a set of principles or one ultimate principle.

The answer to the first question is "morals." Morals are the acceptable and, by definition, unacceptable behaviors that we act out.

The answer to the second question is "ethics." Ethics are the principles or the principle by which we identify the rightness or wrongness of human behavior.

ETHICAL GROWTH IS REFERRED TO AS DEVELOPING MORAL MATURITY.

Another word that interchanges with ethics is values.

The process of ethical growth is referred to as developing moral maturity. There are two major developmental models on this process. The late Lawrence Kohlberg suggests six stages of moral development. The classic model presented here is tied to traditional religious and philosophical patterns and has four stages.

STAGE 1: Pre-rational—childlike, self-centered, self-directed.

STAGE 2: Rule obedient—follows and usually accepts others rules without much question or thought.

STAGE 3: Ethical maturity—the ability to raise questions with practices and beliefs, reflect on them, and relate higher values to decisions or actions to be or already taken. Looking at the consequences of an action before the consequences have to be dealt with and having to gather a fair amount of information to do this process.

STAGE 4: Meta-Ethics—the process of reflecting on why we study ethics. This is for moral philosophers and rarely for the rest of us.

All of this, although short in form, suggests that no decision is made in a vacuum and no decision is without consequences. Each of us makes about 1,500-2,000 decisions a day. Most do not require or involve ethical values. But, the important issues in our lives do.

Principled Reasoning

By Michael Josephson, *Ethical Decision Making & Principled Reasoning*

Basic moral education occurs during the process of growing up. We learn from parents, teachers, religious leaders, coaches, employers, friends and others, and, as a result, most of us reach adulthood with our character essentially formed and with a basic understanding of, and fundamental respect for, ethical values.

But, the presumptive values adopted in our youth are not immutably etched in our character. We know that values are constantly shuffled and prioritized, for better or worse, in response to life experiences. Thus, youthful idealism is tested as we are emancipated into a world where important and binding decisions must be made. Only then do we discover what we are really willing to do to get and hold a job and be

successful in a competitive society. By the same process, the blind competitiveness and materialism of young adulthood will later be challenged by life-changing experiences (e.g., illness, parenthood, divorce, death of a loved one) or the simple fact of maturation, causing one to reflect on the meaning of life (sometimes inducing a "mid-life crisis").

Ethical Norms

It is critical to effective ethics education to overcome the cynicism of ethical relativism—the view that ethics is just a matter of opinion and personal belief as in politics or religion. There are ethical norms that transcend cultures and time.

In fact, the study of history, philosophy and religion reveal a strong consensus as to certain universal and timeless values essential to the ethical life: 1) *Honesty*, 2) *Integrity*, 3) *Promise-keeping*, 4) *Fidelity*, 5) *Fairness*, 6) *Caring for others*, 7) *Respect for others*, 8) *Responsible citizenship*, 9) *Pursuit of excellence*, and 10) *Accountability*.

These ten core values yield a series of *principles*, do's and don'ts, which delineate right and wrong in general terms and, therefore, provide a guide to behavior. Individuals may want to edit or augment the list, but overall it has proven to be a valuable tool in examining the ethical implications of a situation and providing solid reference points for ethical problem-solving.

Ethical Principles

HONESTY: Be truthful, sincere, forthright, straightforward, frank, candid; do not cheat, steal, lie, deceive, or act deviously.

INTEGRITY: Be principled, honorable, upright, courageous and act on convictions; do not be two-faced, unscrupulous, or adopt an end-justifies-the-means philosophy that ignores principle.

PROMISE-KEEPING: Be worthy of trust, keep promises, fulfill commitments, abide by the spirit as well as the letter of an agreement; do not interpret agreements in a technical or legalistic manner in order to rationalize non-compliance or create excuses for breaking commitments.

FIDELITY: Be faithful and loyal to family, friends, employers, and country; do not use or disclose information learned in confidence. In a professional context, safeguard the ability to make independent professional judgments by scrupulously avoiding undue influences and conflicts of interest.

BE FAITHFUL AND LOYAL TO FAMILY, FRIENDS, EMPLOYERS, AND COUNTRY.

FAIRNESS: Be fair and open-minded, be willing to admit error and, where appropriate, change positions and beliefs, demonstrate a commitment to justice, the equal treatment of individuals, and tolerance for diversity. Do not overreach or take undue advantage of another's mistakes or adversities.

CARING FOR OTHERS: Be caring, kind and compassionate; share, be giving, serve others; help those in need and avoid harming others.

RESPECT FOR OTHERS: Demonstrate respect for human dignity, privacy, and the right to self-determination of all people; be courteous, prompt, and decent; provide others with the information they need to make informed decisions about their own lives; do not patronize, embarrass or demean.

RESPONSIBLE CITIZENSHIP: Obey just laws (if a law is unjust, openly protest it); exercise all democratic rights and privileges responsibly by participation (voting and expressing informed views),

> DO NOT BE CONTENT WITH MEDIOCRITY BUT DO NOT SEEK TO WIN "AT ANY COST."

social consciousness and public service; when in a position of leadership or authority, openly respect and avoid unnecessary secrecy or concealment of information, and assure that others have the information needed to make intelligent choices and exercise their rights.

PURSUIT OF EXCELLENCE: Pursue excellence in all matters; in meeting personal and professional responsibilities, be diligent, reliable, industrious, and committed; perform all tasks to the best of your ability, develop and maintain a high degree of competence, be well informed and well prepared; do not be content with mediocrity but do not seek to win "at any cost."

ACCOUNTABILITY: Be accountable, accept responsibility for decisions and the foreseeable consequences of actions and inactions, and for

setting an example for others. Parents, teachers, employers, many professionals and public officials have a special obligation to lead by example, to safeguard and advance the integrity and reputation of their families, companies, professions and the government; avoid even the appearance of impropriety and take whatever actions are necessary to correct or prevent inappropriate conduct of others.

The first question in ethical decision-making is: "Which ethical principles are involved in the decision?" Considering the above list is an excellent way to isolate the relevant issues involved.

Ethical Behavior

"WOULD THE BOY YOU WERE BE PROUD OF THE MAN YOU ARE?"

~ LAURENCE PETER

Ethics education works best when it builds upon our positive inclinations. Most people want to be ethical; they want to be worthy of the respect and admiration of others and they want to be proud of themselves and what they do for a living. Self-esteem and self-respect depend on the private assessment of our own character. Very few people can accept the fact that they are less ethical than others. In fact, most people believe that they are more ethical.

Common Misconceptions

Law abidingness is an aspect of responsible citizenship and an ethical principle especially important in a democracy. Often, we hear, "If it is legal, then it is ethical." We should not, however, confuse ethics with legality. Laws and written codes of ethics are minimalist in nature—they only establish the lines of consensus impropriety. Even though it is legal, it may not be ethical.

Ethics requires more of a person than technical compliance with rules. Everything that is lawful is not, *ipso facto*, ethical. Thus, the fact that certain conduct escapes the label of illegality, including the fact that a person has been formally acquitted of a criminal charge, does not, in itself, provide moral exoneration.

People we regard as ethical do not measure their conduct in terms of minimal standards of virtue. They do not walk the line, or consistently resort to legalistic rationales to circumvent legitimate standards of behavior or the spirit of their agreements. Ethical persons consciously advance ethical principles by choosing to do more than they have to and less than they have a right to do.

The fact is that an ethical person must often sacrifice short-term benefits to achieve long-term advantages. He or she must also be prepared to sacrifice physical or material gains for abstract intangibles such as self-esteem, the respect of others, reputation and a clear conscience. An ethical person must be able to distinguish between short-term and long-term benefits and costs.

Ethical Decisions

The first task of ethical decision-making is to distinguish ethical from unethical responses; the second is to choose the best response from the ethically appropriate ones. Although there may be several ethical responses to a situation, all are not equal.

Making the distinctions necessary is much more difficult and complex than is normally thought because, in so many real world situations, there are a multitude of competing interests and values, and crucial facts are unknown or ambiguous. Since our actions are likely to benefit some at the expense of others, ethical decision-makers also attempt to foresee the likely consequences of their actions.

We cannot solve all problems by resorting to some mechanistic formula, but we can be more effective if we have a structure. A process which systematically takes into account the ethical principles involved in a decision tends to prevent inadvertent unethical conduct and allows us to consciously choose which values to advance—to determine whom to aid and whom to harm.

When one is in the trenches, it is difficult, if not impossible, to analyze problems fully and objectively. While most people do not want more rules telling them what to do, they do want assistance in perceiving the ethical implications of their decisions and in developing realistic, morally centered approaches for resolving ethical dilemmas.

Used by permission. Taken from an article printed in "Ethics—Easier Said Than Done," Vol. 1, No. 1, produced by the Josephson Institute for the Advancement of Ethics in Los Angeles, California. Michael Josephson is a noted expert in ethics education and has spoken for hundreds of various groups across the nation, from politicians to clergy.

Ethics & Fraternalism

The North American Interfraternity Conference (NIC) has taken the lead in ethics education for all Greeks nationwide. You should confront the issues here by yourself and with your chapter. Only through discussion and contemplation can you begin to understand ethics and values in the fraternity experience and how they relate to the larger community.

The North American Interfraternity Conference Statement of Fraternal Values & Ethics

In an effort to lessen the disparity between fraternity ideals and individual behavior and to personalize these ideals in the daily undergraduate experience, the following basic expectations of fraternity membership have been established by the NIC:

I. I will know and understand the ideals expressed in my fraternity Ritual and will strive to incorporate them in my daily life.

II. I will strive for academic achievement and practice academic integrity.

III. I will respect the dignity of all persons; therefore, I will not physically, mentally, psychologically or sexually abuse or haze any human being.

IV. I will protect the health and safety of all human beings.

V. I will respect my property and the property of others; therefore, I will neither abuse nor tolerate the abuse of property.

VI. I will meet my financial obligations in a timely manner.

VII. I will neither use nor support the use of illegal drugs; I will neither misuse nor support the misuse of alcohol.

VIII. I acknowledge that a clean and attractive environment is essential to both physical and mental health; therefore, I will do all in my power to see that the chapter property is properly cleaned and maintained.

IX. I will challenge all my fraternity members to abide by these fraternal expectations and will confront those who violate them.

Fraternal Expectations

In addition to the NIC's "Statement of Fraternal Values and Ethics," the North American Interfraternity Conference has developed a list of basic expectations for every fraternity chapter.

Through the interactive process of small group discussion, find consensus on the best possible approach for your chapter to deal with each particular NIC expectation. Ideally, the discussion of these NIC basic expectations will lead the group to develop specific policies and programs in the areas covered by the expectations.

Format of Discussion

In order to achieve the maximum value from the discussion of these important issues, a Values and Ethics Workshop is best presented in a retreat format of at least a full day. Only in such a time frame can all expectations be covered adequately. If this is not practical, a series of workshops extending over a period of several weeks may be utilized. Each of these sessions, of at least two hours duration, may cover two or three of the expectations, but each session should include the NIC Statement of Fraternal Values and Ethics.

The North American Interfraternity Conference Nine Basic Expectations

EXPECTATION I: Develop safe membership activities for education on the ritual.

EXPECTATION II: Develop academic standards and support programs.

EXPECTATION III: Develop procedures for dealing with hazing violations.

EXPECTATION IV: Establish risk management procedures, AIDS education.

EXPECTATION V: Establish house rules and codes of conduct.

EXPECTATION VI: Develop and communicate a chapter budget.

EXPECTATION VII: Develop alcohol, risk management, and drug policies.

EXPECTATION VIII: Establish maintenance procedures for chapter facility.

EXPECTATION IX: Establish internal governance and disciplinary procedures.

SigEps at the University of Tennessee-Martin brought the "Writing on the Wall" project to campus. Student groups painted racial epithets on a wall erected on campus and then five days later helped destroy it.

DIVERSITY

"The tough minded respect difference. Their goal is a world that is safe for differences."

~ RUTH FULTON BENEDICT

Sigma Phi Epsilon prides itself on the diversity of its membership; diversity that is more than a difference in hair color or taste in music. Our diversity is rounded with members of all faiths, races, economic groups and geographical backgrounds. The Fraternity is also represented at a wide variety of colleges and universities in a multitude of locations, each with their own unique nuances. The common bond of our Ritual and Cardinal Principles breaks down discrimination against someone based on race, religions, and sexual orientation; and discrimination is not tolerated in Sigma Phi Epsilon.

When Brothers who have served as Regional Directors are asked, "What is the first thing you hear when visiting a chapter?" It is, "We're diverse!" In fact, many chapters are anything but diverse; members dress alike, share the same religion, are from the same economic background, etc. There is little diversity. Some chapters, however, when recruiting new men purposefully set out to select a spectrum of Brothers—and you see it. This spectrum reflects a true cross-section of society.

The challenge for the Fraternity and its members is to take this wide-ranging diversity and view it as an advantage rather than a hindrance, as it may be viewed by those close-minded members of our society. A respect for the differences between all people is the first step toward appreciating diversity. This respect must be inclusive. The only boundaries for membership in Sigma Phi Epsilon are those of a man's integrity, his willingness to embrace the principles of the Fraternity, and his ability to make positive contributions to the Fraternity and local chapter.

THE TRADITION OF APPRECIATING DIVERSITY AND AN UNCONDITIONAL WELCOME TO MEN OF ALL NATIONALITIES, RACES, RELIGIONS, AND SEXUAL ORIENTATION STANDS FIRM IN SIGMA PHI EPSILON.

The red door means welcome to all. In 1928, when remodeling their house, the Syracuse chapter found this symbolic gesture of welcome (painting their chapter house door red) only fitting for Sigma Phi Epsilon, a Fraternity with a proud history of diversity.

The tradition of appreciating diversity and an unconditional welcome to men of all nationalities, races, religions, and sexual orientation stands firm in Sigma Phi Epsilon. Anything less would not be in line with our Ritual and Cardinal Principle of Brotherly Love.

Being Inclusive

Many members remark that people are never excluded from chapter activities or events based on race, creed, ethnicity, sexual orientation, economic background, or geographic location. However, honoring diversity means being inclusive, too. Sponsoring events that actively include people of different races, creeds, and backgrounds is as important as opposing discrimination and bigoted behaviors.

An unfortunate reality is that many people stay away from the Greek community because they fear biased attitudes. To change this stereotype, members of the Greek community must not only open themselves to an array of people, but also actively seek to involve them with the organizations.

Eight Things YOU Can Do to Honor Diversity

From the Memorial Union Program Council, and Dr. Phyllis Lee, Director of Multicultural Affairs at Oregon State University

Speak Out:

Do not let racist, sexist, homophobic or other stereotypical comments continue in conversation without objecting to them. Ask that the comments be stopped, or walk away if they continue.

Learn About Other People:

Read about different cultures and lifestyles. Expose yourself to traditions, values and attitudes of others. Attend a multicultural event on campus or in the community.

Be Informed About Issues:

Attend lectures, read the newspapers, listen to public radio, and watch films which address discrimination, bigotry, and other complex issues.

Treat People as Individuals:

Do not make assumptions about others based on race, ethnicity, sexual orientation, economic status, religion, etc.

Celebrate Our Differences:

Eat new foods, listen to different kinds of music, and participate in events which honor other cultures within the U.S. and around the world.

Examine Your Attitudes:

Become aware of ideas, words, and actions which may dehumanize or devalue others and eliminate them from my life. Respect others for their similarities as well as differences.

Learn About Yourself:

Talk with family members about your cultural heritage, where your ancestors came from, and about the traditions and values which are important to your family.

Be Part of the Solution:

Form or join groups to educate yourself and others about the value of diversity, to promote positive social action, and to learn love and respect for one another.

Ashley Judd speaks about HIV/AIDS during the SigEp three-on-three basketball tournament at the University of Kentucky.

Questions for Personal Consideration

1. Is your chapter truly diverse?

2. What can you do to broaden your chapter experience?

3. What are the benefits of diversity?

4. What does your chapter do to ensure your broad base of members has brotherhood and meaningful experiences with each other?

Mississippi Alpha Chapter at the University of Mississippi

INTERFRATERNALISM

"Save for the wild force of Nature, nothing moves in this world that is not Greek in its origin."

~ JOHN ACTON

As members of Sigma Phi Epsilon, each man is responsible to the larger community beyond the Fraternity. One of the important constituencies to which Sigma Phi Epsilon belongs is the interfraternal community. Consequently, SigEp has a responsibility to be actively involved in the leadership and service to this part of the community.

Competition is the best source of motivation when tempered with respect. Sigma Phi Epsilon approaches interfraternalism from two equally important standpoints. First, all 66 fraternities that are members of the North American Interfraternity Conference have common backgrounds and strive for virtually the same high ideals. The choice between fraternities is a choice of which of the Greek-letter fraternities particularly appeals to an individual. This choice takes into account the perceived qualities offered by a particular chapter on a certain campus at a particular junction in a young man's life.

Fraternities were founded by the great students of their day, and Greek was a subject studied only by the best students. These great students named their organizations with Greek symbols and their values because they knew the distinguished place Greek history and tradition held. The fact that the Greek-letter fraternities flourish today shows that these great students founded organizations with long-standing value. Founders of all fraternities sought excellence and set out to have their members be part of the best "society" possible. The aims of Greek-letter fraternities center around the Greek word "arete," meaning excellence in every part of life.

The backgrounds of all fraternities are very similar, and with the exception of some misguided local chapters, all fraternities are to be respected for their intentions and records of good men and good deeds.

THE AIMS OF GREEK-LETTER FRATERNITIES CENTER AROUND THE GREEK WORD "ARETE," MEANING EXCELLENCE IN EVERY PART OF LIFE.

Secondly, Sigma Phi Epsilon believes healthy, "sportsmanlike" competition brings out the best in individuals, chapters, and Greek systems. However, this competition should in no way be malicious, vengeful, or reckless. Speaking poorly of other fraternities, fighting or feuding with other fraternities, or destroying their property is not acceptable behavior for SigEps. On the other hand, initiating an academic contest, sponsoring a reception (win or lose) after a championship sporting match or sending salutations or congratulations to other fraternities *is* what interfraternalism is all about. We are all striving to improve the lives of our members and our communities.

WE ARE ALL STRIVING TO IMPROVE THE LIVES OF OUR MEMBERS AND OUR COMMUNITIES.

Sigma Phi Epsilon chapters must also take the lead in making their local Greek system an organization of prominence and support for its member chapters. A strong Greek community will help the SigEp chapter reach its potential. Concurrently, the Greek system should be one that fosters and monitors competition and

outstanding performance by each of its chapters.

Serving on the Interfraternity Council is one way to ensure the Greek system is meeting the needs of its members. As an IFC officer, you will receive numerous rewards, both tangible and intangible. Tangible rewards include practical experience in an organization designed to serve a broad cross-section of constituents, contact with your school's administration and exposure to new ideas that will be useful to you and your chapter. Intangible benefits include friendships and a sense of satisfaction knowing you helped your school, other Greek organizations, and Sigma Phi Epsilon.

Part of interfraternalism also includes positive relations with the many other organizations and living groups on campus. Events with residence halls or the foreign student organization or honorary fraternities can be beneficial to both groups. Make friends and allies outside the Greek system, too.

Respect other fraternities and organizations as you believe Sigma Phi Epsilon deserves respect.

You and your chapter should also work to improve relations with your Greek advisor and university officials. All men and women serving Greek systems should be thanked and treated courteously as they can help your chapter and the Greek system excel.

Questions for Personal Consideration

1. What can your chapter do to foster interfraternalism?

2. Does your chapter understand the policies and guidelines of the Interfraternity Council? When does the entire chapter review these policies?

3. How should the chapter deal with members who violate IFC policy or act inappropriately toward other fraternities?

4. What IFC policies would your chapter like to improve? How can you improve them in the best interest of your chapter, other fraternities, and the school administration?

5. What can you/your chapter do to improve relations with the Greek advisor?

APPENDICES

SYMBOLS OF OUR FRATERNITY

Nearly every organization and institution has symbols which identify it and instill in its members a deeper understanding of its ideals. Our country has a seal and a flag, your college has a seal and a flag, and each state has a seal and a flag. Sigma Phi Epsilon's symbols include:

THE FOUNDERS BADGE: The original badge designed by the Founders had the "E" added below the skull and bones after the badges were made. On subsequent badges, the "E" was brought above the skull and bones to join the ΣΦ. This design, in a slightly smaller size and with 20 pearls bordering the black heart, remains the official badge today. The Grand President's badge is bordered by rubies, and the E is below the skull and bones as on the original badge.

At the 1973 Conclave in Denver, an additional official badge was authorized. This badge is of the same size and shape as the original Founders badge and is bordered by a band of gold. The 1973 Conclave also authorized that official badges may be made with heavy-duty gold plate, "golklad," in addition to white and yellow gold. The new Founders-size badge was designed by Past Grand President and Order of the Golden Heart recipient William A. MacDonough, Washington & Lee '29.

THE COAT OF ARMS: Nearly all fraternities boast a coat of arms. A heritage from the old days of feudalism and knighthood, it is an emblem which can become very precious to a SigEp. For a long time, however, Sigma Phi Epsilon displayed a coat of arms which was not heraldically correct. The original design was adopted in 1908 at the Chicago Conclave. Frederick M. Cutler, Massachusetts '30, called attention to the old emblem's inaccuracies. In 1933, Mark D. Wilkins, Oklahoma State '30, then a Field Secretary for the Fraternity, consulted Arthur E. DuBois, in charge of the heraldic work of the United States Government, and the new and revised coat of arms was subsequently accepted.

The badge and coat of arms are the official insignia of the Fraternity; their esoteric meaning is contained in the Ritual of the Fraternity. They are trademarks owned by Sigma Phi Epsilon, used only with permission, or by undergraduate chapters and members.

THE FLAG: The Fraternity's flag has a background of purple, with a red bar extending diagonally from the upper-left corner to the lower-right corner, this bar fimbriated on either side by a narrow band of gold for the purple background. In the center of the flag, mounted upon the red bar, appears a gold star of five points.

The 1955 Conclave in Cincinnati authorized an alternative form for the official flag. In this form, the Greek letters ΣΦΕ are placed in the upper-right corner of the regulation flag, while the Greek letter A, B, Γ, or whatever the chapter designation, is placed in the lower-left corner. The purpose is for clearer identification of the flag when it is used for display.

The flag with Greek letters is commonly called the "display flag" and the simplified flag is the "Ritual flag." Every chapter should have a display flag and a Ritual flag.

THE BALANCED MAN SYMBOL: Concurrent with the Fraternity's development of a strategy in 1989, the Balanced Man symbol was created as an expression of the values of our Greek-letter heritage, "A Sound Mind in a Sound Body." The Balanced Man symbol was created by the international advertising firm, TBWA/Chiat-Day, whose former chief executive and chairman is Past Grand President and Order of the Golden Heart recipient William G.

Tragos, Washington U. in St. Louis '57. The Balanced Man symbol is representative of the goals of each Sigma Phi Epsilon.

The Balanced Man pin is presented to all new members in Balanced Man Program chapters during the Sigma Rite of Passage. The pin is worn on the lapel of a suit or sports jacket and can be worn on collared shirts. All members are expected to wear the Balanced Man pin during Ritual ceremonies.

THE PLEDGE BADGE: The pledge badge is a gold rectangular shield of equal sides. Along the diagonal of the rectangle appears in gold the Greek word "eggua" (pronounced "engeea" which simply means "pledge"), above this is a crown and below is a five-pointed star, also in gold. The background is red enamel.

The word "pledge" denotes an *action* or vow that a member of the Fraternity has made to uphold the Cardinal Principles of Sigma Phi Epsilon. This badge is used by chapters not implementing the Balanced Man Program.

THE ALUMNI RECOGNITION PIN: The "Ducal Crown" (from the coat of arms) is worn as a lapel pin. This is recognized as the alumni pin, and chapters present them to graduating seniors at the annual senior banquet.

THE GREEK LETTER SYMBOL: Specially designed Greek letters form Sigma Phi Epsilon's official symbol. In color, the symbol is printed in purple (Σ), red (Φ), and gold (E). The Greek letters in bold colors speak to a new era in the Fraternity's life and to its history, traditions, and values. The letters, worn by all members, represent the motto of Sigma Phi Epsilon and its fundamental beliefs. The stages you go through during your growth in the Fraternity will coincide with the gaining of the knowledge of the Ritual of the Fraternity. The secrets of the Fraternity embody its Cardinal Principles of Virtue, Diligence, and Brotherly Love.

ΣΦΕ

SIGEP LOGO: It is the Fraternity's primary logotype and used in preference to the more internal Greek Letter symbol. It is designed in a contemporary adaptation of the classic Bodoni typeface. In color, it is printed in red.

SigEp

FRATERNITY COLORS AND FLOWERS: The fraternity colors are purple and red. The flowers are the violet and the dark red rose.

FRATERNITY WHISTLE: The fraternity whistle, as adopted at the 1912 Conclave in Detroit, is an adaptation of the first two lines of "The Letter Song" (Nadina), from "The Chocolate Soldier," by Oscar A. Straus, an Austrian composer. (It is also the whistle used by the soldiers in the movie "Bridge Over the River Kwai.") An official "whistle committee" sometimes appears at Grand Chapter Conclaves to remind the Brothers of the fraternity whistle.

THE RED DOOR: The tradition of the red door on Sigma Phi Epsilon chapter houses began with the New York Alpha Chapter at Syracuse University in the 1920s. The trend spread, and, as you travel to other college campuses, you will see the "red door" of Sigma Phi Epsilon. Wherever you find it, you will know members, new and old, are all welcome to walk through and share the brotherhood of Sigma Phi Epsilon.

FRATERNITY AWARDS

Individual Awards— Undergraduate

CLIFFORD B. SCOTT KEY: Awarded annually to the Brother in each chapter who has the highest academic average for the year. The award honors former *Journal* Editor and Order of the Golden Heart recipient Clifford B. Scott, Nebraska '13, who wrote the words and music to the Sigma Phi Epsilon Anthem. Nominations are made by the undergraduate chapter through Headquarters.

FRANK J. RUCK INTERFRATERNITY LEADERSHIP AWARD: Presented each year at Carlson Leadership Academies to the chapter or individual showing outstanding campus leadership and making a significant change on the campus as a whole. The award honors Past Grand President, Order of the Golden Heart recipient, and former President of the North American Interfraternity Conference, Frank J. Ruck, Michigan '46. Nominations are made by the Headquarters staff, District Governor, and local volunteers.

J. EDWARD ZOLLINGER OUTSTANDING SENIOR AWARD: Presented each year at Carlson Leadership Academies to the outstanding senior in each district of the Fraternity. Each District Governor makes a selection, based on nominations from the chapters, Chapter Counselors, and Alumni and Volunteer Corporations. The award is named for the late J. Edward Zollinger, William & Mary '27, Past Grand President, Order of the Golden Heart recipient, and longtime President of the Sigma Phi Epsilon Educational Foundation.

Zollinger Seniors are balanced men and role models of excellence. The award is based on outstanding scholastic achievement, campus leadership, and community involvement.

ZOLLINGER SCHOLAR: Cash awards of $500 for the junior year, and providing they maintain a 2.5 G.P.A. and stay active in fraternity and campus life, a $400 scholarship in the senior year from the Educational Foundation's Zollinger Leadership Fund, presented to each Zollinger Outstanding Senior's chapter. The award is presented to a sophomore Brother who, in the chapter's judgment, shows outstanding leadership potential.

RECRUITMENT EXCELLENCE AWARD: Awarded to the Brother in the chapter showing hard work and dedication to recruiting men who meet the high standards worthy of Sigma Phi Epsilon. Nominations are made by the undergraduate chapter through Headquarters.

SIGMA PHI EPSILON FELLOW: A Sigma Phi Epsilon Fellow is an undergraduate from a Balanced Man Program chapter who embodies the Cardinal Principles of Virtue, Diligence, and Brotherly Love, as exemplified by his excellence in academics, leadership, and, above all, service to his fellow man. The Sigma Phi Epsilon Fellow is one of the Fraternity's highest undergraduate honors. This award is self-nominated through Headquarters.

ULYSSES GRANT DUBACH SCROLL: Awarded to the Brother in each chapter showing the greatest academic improvement between quarters/semesters. The award is in memory of Order of the Golden Heart recipient Dr. U.G. Dubach, Oregon State '16, who served as National Scholarship Chairman in the 1950s and 1960s. Nominations are made by the undergraduate chapter through Headquarters.

Individual Awards–Alumni

Given by the National Fraternity & the Sigma Phi Epsilon Educational Foundation

DISTINGUISHED ALUMNUS AWARD: Presented annually at Carlson Leadership Academies to alumni who have given outstanding service to a chapter, district, or on the national level for at least five years. Chapters, Chapter Counselors, Alumni and Volunteer Corporations, and District Governors submit nominations to the National Board of Directors.

ORDER OF THE GOLDEN HEART: The Fraternity's highest honor, awarded to alumni who, with great personal sacrifice, have given exceptional service to Sigma Phi Epsilon. The award is a medallion accompanied by a scroll. This award is presented at Conclave.

SIGMA PHI EPSILON CITATION: The Fraternity's recognition of a Brother who has excelled in his career field. The Citation, an embossed scroll, is awarded to a select few alumni at Conclave.

Individual Awards–Alumni

Given by Each Chapter through Headquarters Provided by the Sigma Phi Epsilon Educational Foundation

CAREER ACHIEVEMENT AWARD: Awarded annually to alumni who have excelled in their careers. The award consists of a framed and matted certificate presented by the chapter.

VOLUNTEER EXCELLENCE AWARD: Awarded annually to alumni who have given outstanding service to a chapter. The award consists of a framed and matted certificate presented by the chapter.

Chapter Awards

Given by the National Fraternity & the Sigma Phi Epsilon Educational Foundation

BENJAMIN HOBSON FRAYSER AWARD: A framed certificate presented at Conclave to chapters with outstanding alumni newsletters. The award was established by the mother of the late Benjamin Hobson Frayser, Tennessee '31.

BUCHANAN CUP: Every two years, at the Grand Chapter Conclave, the Fraternity recognizes its outstanding chapters with the Buchanan Cup. This Revere bowl mounted on a base is given in honor of Edwin Buchanan, Ohio State '11, who served as Sigma Phi Epsilon's Grand Treasurer for 34 years. The award is given to chapters displaying excellence in all areas of operation over a two-year period.

CHAPTER HOME OF THE YEAR: Selected by the Regional Director, this award recognizes one chapter per region that best maintains and cares for its chapter living environment. It is presented at the Carlson Leadership Academies.

DONALD C. MCCLEARY EXCELLENCE IN MEMBERSHIP DEVELOPMENT AWARD: Named in honor of Past Grand President and Order of the Golden Heart recipient Donald C. McCleary, Texas '71, this award recognizes a chapter's development program that emphasizes Sound Mind, Sound Body programming and continuous four-year development.

EXCELSIOR AWARD: Chapters showing significant improvement in chapter operations receive the Excelsior Award. This Revere bowl is presented at Carlson Leadership Academies each year. The award may be presented for overall chapter improvement or for improvement in one specific area of chapter operations in accord with the strategic plan. The award bears the name Excelsior—"Ever Onward—Ever Upward."

GRAND CHAPTER SCHOLARSHIP CUP: Presented by the Sigma Phi Epsilon Educational Foundation to chapters ranking first in academics among fraternities on their campuses. This award is presented at Carlson Leadership Academies.

HONOR OF PHILIAS: Established in 1989 by Past Grand President and Order of the Golden Heart recipient Jack Wheeler, North Texas '61. Chapters and/or individuals may receive the Honor of Philias as recognition of their special expression of the Fraternity's Cardinal Principle of Brotherly Love. The recognition presented at the Grand Chapter Conclave to the recipient(s) is a replica of the Honor of Philias permanently displayed at Sigma Phi Epsilon Headquarters. Selection is made jointly by the Trustees of the Sigma Phi Epsilon Educational Foundation and the Fraternity's National Board of Directors. A grant in support of the recipient's special expression is available from the Educational Foundation.

MANPOWER EXCELLENCE AWARD: An engraved plaque awarded to chapters whose manpower is number one on campus. This award is presented at Carlson Leadership Academies.

WILLIAM A. MACDONOUGH BROADENING THE BROTHERHOOD AWARD: Chapters which have helped form a new SigEp chapter or provided considerable support to an existing Sigma Epsilon Chapter (a new chapter working toward obtaining a charter) are recognized by the Broadening the Brotherhood Award. The award is named in honor of Past Grand President and Order of the Golden Heart recipient William MacDonough, Washington & Lee '29. The award consists of a certificate presented at the Grand Chapter Conclave.

UNDERGRADUATE CHAPTERS

As of August 25, 2005
Italics indicate chapter is currently dormant
SEC indicates a Sigma Epsilon Chapter striving for its charter
RLC indicates a Residential Learning Community

Chapter Roll #	Chapter	College/University	Date Chartered	Charter Dormant
1	Virginia Alpha RLC	University of Richmond	11/01/1901	1996-2001
2	Virginia Beta	Virginia Commonwealth University	10/30/1902	1905-71, 1993
3	Pennsylvania Alpha	Washington & Jefferson College	11/28/1902	1906
4	Virginia Gamma	Roanoke College	02/20/1903	1905
5	West Virginia Alpha	Bethany College	03/23/1903	1905
6	West Virginia Beta	West Virginia University	03/25/1903	**/**/****
7	Pennsylvania Beta	Jefferson Medical College	09/23/1903	1912
8	Pennsylvania Gamma	University of Pittsburgh	12/12/1903	1912-49, 1963-90
9	Illinois Alpha RLC	University of Illinois	12/18/1903	1913-17, 1996-2001
10 SEC	Colorado Alpha	University of Colorado	02/19/1904	1994
11	Pennsylvania Delta	University of Pennsylvania	03/24/1904	**/**/****
12	South Carolina Alpha	University of South Carolina	05/02/1904	1906-29
13	*Virginia Delta*	*College of William & Mary*	*06/11/1904*	*1938-61, 2004*
14	Ohio Alpha	Ohio Northern University	02/18/1905	**/**/****
15	*North Carolina Beta*	*North Carolina State University*	*03/04/1905*	*2004*
16	Ohio Beta	Wittenberg University	03/21/1905	1906
17	Indiana Alpha	Purdue University	03/24/1905	**/**/****
18	New York Alpha RLC	Syracuse University	12/21/1905	1995-2005
19	Virginia Epsilon	Washington & Lee University	03/30/1906	1940-60, 2003
20 SEC	Virginia Zeta	Randolph-Macon College	12/26/1906	1990
21	Georgia Alpha RLC	Georgia Institute of Technology	04/01/1907	**/**/****
22	Virginia Eta	University of Virginia	04/27/1907	**/**/****
23	Delaware Alpha	University of Delaware	04/29/1907	1981-85,2002-2005
24	Arkansas Alpha RLC	University of Arkansas	09/16/1907	1938-48, 1995-1999
25	Pennsylvania Epsilon	Lehigh University	09/17/1907	1991-96
26	Virginia Theta	Virginia Military Institute	01/25/1908	1912
27	Ohio Gamma RLC	Ohio State University	01/30/1908	2000-02
28	Vermont Alpha	Norwich University	03/18/1908	1960
29	Pennsylvania Zeta	Allegheny College	10/17/1908	1909
30	Alabama Alpha	Auburn University	11/07/1908	**/**/****
31	North Carolina Gamma	Duke University	03/27/1909	1960-68, 1994-2001
32	New Hampshire Alpha	Dartmouth College	04/24/1909	1970-81
33	D.C. Alpha	George Washington University	10/09/1909	1993-2001
34	Kansas Alpha RLC	Baker University	04/02/1910	**/**/****
35 SEC	California Alpha	University of California-Berkeley	11/10/1910	1972-84, 2002
36	Nebraska Alpha RLC	University of Nebraska	04/15/1911	**/**/****
37	*Washington Alpha*	*Washington State University*	*03/02/1912*	*2003*
38	Massachusetts Alpha	University of Massachusetts	04/27/1912	**/**/****
39	Ohio Delta	College of Wooster	06/01/1912	1914
40	New York Beta	Cornell University	09/24/1912	**/**/****
41	Rhode Island Alpha	Brown University	11/27/1912	1919
42	Michigan Alpha	University of Michigan	12/14/1912	1994-1999
43	Iowa Alpha	Iowa Wesleyan College	02/01/1913	1976
44	Colorado Beta	University of Denver	05/21/1913	1973-91, 1994
45	Tennessee Alpha	University of Tennessee	05/29/1913	**/**/****
46	Missouri Alpha	University of Missouri-Columbia	04/10/1914	**/**/****
47	Wisconsin Alpha	Lawrence University	02/27/1915	1976-80

Chapter Roll #	Chapter	College/University	Date Chartered	Charter Dormant
48	Pennsylvania Eta	Pennsylvania State University	05/08/1915	**/**/****
49	Ohio Epsilon	Ohio Wesleyan University	11/20/1915	**/**/****
50	Colorado Gamma RLC	Colorado State University	11/27/1915	**/**/****
51	Minnesota Alpha RLC	University of Minnesota	04/15/1916	1941-49, 1958-78
52	Iowa Beta RLC	Iowa State University	04/20/1916	**/**/****
53	Iowa Gamma	University of Iowa	04/28/1917	**/**/****
54	Montana Alpha RLC	University of Montana	02/02/1918	**/**/****
55	Oregon Alpha	Oregon State University	02/09/1918	**/**/****
56	Kansas Beta	Kansas State University	02/23/1918	**/**/****
57 SEC	Oklahoma Alpha	Oklahoma State University	04/03/1920	2005
58	Wisconsin Beta RLC	University of Wisconsin	11/13/1920	**/**/****
59	North Carolina Delta	University of North Carolina	02/26/1921	1939-47
60	Washington Beta	University of Washington	01/14/1922	**/**/****
61	Colorado Delta	Colorado School of Mines	04/21/1923	**/**/****
62	Kansas Gamma	University of Kansas	04/28/1923	**/**/****
63	Florida Alpha RLC	University of Florida	03/28/1925	**/**/****
64	Vermont Beta	Middlebury College	05/16/1925	1941-49, 1971-83, 1990
65	Pennsylvania Theta RLC	Carnegie Mellon University	10/10/1925	1937-1998
66	Oregon Beta	University of Oregon	05/20/1926	**/**/****
67	Alabama Beta	University of Alabama	12/14/1927	**/**/****
68	Mississippi Alpha	University of Mississippi	06/02/1928	1976-89
69	California Beta	University of Southern California	06/09/1928	**/**/****
70	Missouri Beta	Washington University in St. Louis	04/06/1929	1941-49, 1971-83
71	New Mexico Alpha	University of New Mexico	04/13/1929	**/**/****
72	Louisiana Alpha	Tulane University	04/20/1929	1941-90
73	Maryland Alpha	Johns Hopkins University	06/15/1929	**/**/****
74	North Carolina Epsilon	Davidson College	04/15/1930	**/**/****
75	Alabama Gamma	Samford University	05/16/1930	1935-97
76	Texas Alpha	University of Texas-Austin	05/24/1930	**/**/****
77	New York Gamma	New York University	06/07/1930	1970-80
78	*Indiana Beta*	*Indiana University*	*06/06/1931*	*1938-47, 2002*
79	Kentucky Alpha	University of Kentucky	03/04/1933	1989-94
80 SEC	Utah Alpha	Utah State University	03/21/1936	1998
81	Massachusetts Beta	Worcester Polytechnic Institute	04/03/1938	**/**/****
82	Pennsylvania Iota	Muhlenberg College	04/10/1938	**/**/****
83	New York Delta	Rensselaer Polytechnic Institute	04/23/1938	**/**/****
84	Mississippi Beta	Mississippi State University	04/30/1938	**/**/****
85	Pennsylvania Kappa	Bucknell University	04/30/1938	1993-2000
86	Pennsylvania Lambda	Westminster College	04/30/1938	**/**/****
87	*Pennsylvania Mu*	*Temple University*	*05/07/1938*	*1972-90, 2005*
88 SEC	New Jersey Alpha	Stevens Institute of Technology	05/07/1938	2003
89	*North Carolina Zeta*	*Wake Forest University*	*04/19/1940*	*2002*
90	Wisconsin Gamma	Carroll College	12/01/1940	1983
91	Wyoming Alpha	University of Wyoming	05/01/1943	1963-95
92	New Jersey Beta	Rutgers University	01/15/1944	**/**/****
93	Oklahoma Gamma	University of Tulsa	05/26/1946	1959
94	Oklahoma Beta	University of Oklahoma	06/01/1946	**/**/****
95	Missouri Gamma	University of Missouri-Rolla	05/10/1947	**/**/****
96	Kentucky Beta	University of Louisville	05/17/1947	1958-78
97	California Gamma	University of California-Santa Barbara	06/15/1947	1972-78
98	California Delta	San Diego State University	11/16/1947	1996-2004
99	West Virginia Gamma	Marshall University	12/06/1947	**/**/****
100	*Ohio Zeta*	*Baldwin-Wallace College*	*03/13/1948*	*2005*
101	Illinois Beta	Illinois Institute of Technology	04/24/1948	**/**/****
102	Iowa Delta RLC	Drake University	05/09/1948	1996-2002
103	Illinois Gamma RLC	Monmouth College	05/22/1948	**/**/****

Chapter Roll #	Chapter	College/University	Date Chartered	Charter Dormant
104	Maine Alpha RLC	University of Maine	05/30/1948	1994-2002
105	Pennsylvania Nu	Thiel College	11/12/1948	**/**/****
106	Ohio Eta RLC	Miami University	12/04/1948	2001-2004
107	Illinois Delta	Bradley University	01/09/1949	**/**/****
108	Florida Beta RLC	Stetson University	02/12/1949	**/**/****
109	West Virginia Delta	Davis & Elkins College	03/19/1949	**/**/****
110	Tennessee Beta RLC	University of Memphis	04/02/1949	1993-99
111	Maryland Beta	University of Maryland-College Park	05/07/1949	1947-85, 1998-2003
112	Missouri Delta	Drury College	05/14/1949	1988
113	Florida Gamma	University of Miami	05/21/1949	1976-83, 1993-2000
114	Florida Delta	Florida Southern College	05/28/1949	1991
115	Ohio Theta RLC	University of Cincinnati	07/30/1949	**/**/****
116	Utah Beta	University of Utah	02/25/1950	**/**/****
117	Florida Epsilon	Florida State University	05/06/1950	**/**/****
118	Vermont Gamma	University of Vermont	05/27/1950	1993-2002
119	Ohio Iota RLC	University of Toledo	09/30/1950	**/**/****
120	*Massachusetts Gamma*	*Boston University*	*11/11/1950*	*1970-89, 1998*
121	Ohio Kappa	Bowling Green State University	12/09/1950	**/**/****
122	Kansas Delta RLC	Washburn University	02/03/1951	**/**/****
123	Kansas Epsilon	Emporia State University	02/10/1951	**/**/****
124	Nebraska Beta	University of Nebraska-Omaha	02/17/1951	**/**/****
125	*Pennsylvania Xi*	*Indiana University of Pennsylvania*	*01/05/1952*	*1974-92, 2004*
126 SEC	Arizona Alpha	Arizona State University	02/16/1952	2002
127	*Massachusetts Delta*	*Massachusetts Institute of Technology*	*02/22/1952*	*2005*
128	Missouri Epsilon	Culver Stockton College	03/15/1952	1986-88, 1993
129	Oklahoma Delta	Oklahoma City University	05/031952	1961
130	Texas Beta	University of North Texas	05/10/1952	**/**/****
131	Wisconsin Delta	University of Wisconsin—Stevens Point	12/06/1952	1983
132	Colorado Epsilon	University of Northern Colorado	12/13/1952	1980-92, 1996
133	Indiana Gamma	Ball State University	02/21/1953	**/**/****
134	North Carolina Eta	High Point College	03/21/1953	1965
135	Ohio Lambda	Kent State University	04/25/1953	1983-91
136	North Carolina Theta	Lenoir Rhyne College	05/09/1953	1984
137	Mississippi Gamma	University of Southern Mississippi	05/16/1953	**/**/****
138 SEC	Florida Zeta	University of Tampa	05/23/1953	1976-85, 2000
139	Missouri Zeta	Southeast Missouri State University	12/05/1953	1989-99
140	New York Epsilon	State University of New York-Buffalo	04/10/1954	1971-79, 1989-92
141	Tennessee Gamma	East Tennessee State University	04/10/1954	**/**/****
142	Arizona Beta	University of Arizona	05/08/1954	**/**/****
143	Arkansas Beta	Henderson State University	05/15/1954	**/**/****
144	Indiana Delta	Indiana State University	05/15/1954	**/**/****
145	*Ohio Mu*	*Youngstown State University*	*05/22/1954*	*2002*
146	Iowa Epsilon	Morningside College	05/22/1954	1985
147	Texas Gamma	Texas Christian University	02/05/1955	1976-2000
148	*Arkansas Gamma*	*Arkansas State University*	*02/26/1955*	*2002*
149	Indiana Epsilon	University of Evansville	03/12/1955	**/**/****
150	Georgia Beta	Georgia State University	05/21/1955	1991-93, 2000
151	Michigan Beta	Western Michigan University	11/19/1955	**/**/****
152	Texas Delta	University of Houston	02/04/1956	1971-84
153	*Michigan Gamma*	*Central Michigan University*	*03/17/1956*	*2000*
154	Michigan Delta	University of Detroit	04/21/1956	**/**/****
155	Indiana Zeta RLC	Valparaiso University	05/05/1956	**/**/****
156	Iowa Zeta	Parsons College	05/05/1956	1973
157	Connecticut Alpha	University of Connecticut	12/08/1956	1973-80
158	Texas Epsilon	Lamar University	03/02/1957	**/**/****
159	Missouri Eta RLC	Missouri State University	04/27/1957	1996-2002

Chapter Roll #	Chapter	College/University	Date Chartered	Charter Dormant
160	Oregon Gamma	Lewis & Clark College	06/01/1957	1993
161	California Epsilon	San Jose State University	03/08/1958	1973
162	Idaho Alpha	Idaho State University	04/19/1958	1972
163	North Carolina Iota	Barton College	04/26/1958	**/**/****
164	*Kansas Zeta*	*Fort Hays State University*	*05/03/1958*	*2000*
165	Kansas Eta	Wichita State University	04/04/1959	**/**/****
166	Kentucky Gamma	Kentucky Wesleyan College	04/11/1959	**/**/****
167	Tennessee Delta	Tennessee Wesleyan College	03/26/1960	1982
168	Georgia Gamma	Valdosta State College	04/02/1960	1974
169	*West Virginia Epsilon*	*West Virginia Institute of Technology*	*04/09/1960*	*2004*
170	Michigan Epsilon	Michigan State University	05/07/1960	1974-80
171	Texas Zeta	East Texas State University	03/04/1961	1988
172	Louisiana Beta RLC	Louisiana State University	04/08/1961	1979-92
173	North Carolina Kappa	East Carolina University	04/15/1961	**/**/****
174 SEC	Montana Beta	Montana State University	04/22/1961	1987-
175	Michigan Zeta	Ferris State University	02/10/1962	**/**/****
176	Nevada Alpha	University of Nevada-Reno	03/10/1962	1963-97
177	Texas Eta	Sam Houston State University	05/12/1962	**/**/****
178	Georgia Delta RLC	University of Georgia	03/30/1963	1994-2000
179	*California Zeta*	*California State University-Long Beach*	*05/04/1963*	*1973-89, 2004*
180	California Eta	University of California-Davis	05/11/1963	1993-1999
181	Indiana Eta	Indiana Institute of Technology	11/02/1963	**/**/****
182	California Theta	California State University-Sacramento	09/01/1963	**/**/****
183	*Pennsylvania Omicron*	*Philadelphia College of Textiles & Science*	*11/14/1964*	*2000*
184	Ohio Nu	Cleveland State University	11/21/1964	1990
185	Michigan Eta	Michigan Technological University	05/08/1965	**/**/****
186	Nebraska Gamma	University of Nebraska-Kearney	05/15/1965	**/**/****
187	North Carolina Lambda	Belmont Abbey College	10/29/1965	1993
188 SEC	Rhode Island Beta	University of Rhode Island	11/20/1965	1998
189	Kentucky Delta	Western Kentucky University	03/18/1967	**/**/****
190	*Florida Eta*	*Rollins College*	*04/29/1967*	*2000*
191	Wisconsin Epsilon	University of Wisconsin—Oshkosh	05/13/1967	1976
192	Ohio Xi	Ohio University	11/18/1967	1980-88
193	Florida Theta	Jacksonville University	02/03/1968	**/**/****
194	California Iota	California State University-Chico	02/10/1968	1987
195	Missouri Theta	Central Missouri State University	03/30/1968	**/**/****
196	Indiana Theta	Tri-State University	05/04/1968	**/**/****
197	Florida Iota	University of South Florida	05/25/1968	1992-97
198	Georgia Epsilon	Georgia Southern University	02/01/1969	1988-93
199	Kentucky Epsilon	Murray State University	05/17/1969	**/**/****
200	Tennessee Epsilon	Tennessee Technological University	09/26/1969	1988-2000
201	West Virginia Zeta	University of Charleston	01/10/1970	1987
202	*Texas Theta*	*St. Mary's University*	*01/31/1970*	*2003*
203	Ohio Omicron	Defiance College	04/04/1970	1993
204	South Carolina Beta	Clemson University	04/04/1970	**/**/****
205	Virginia Iota	James Madison University	04/11/1970	**/**/****
206	Virginia Kappa	Virginia Polytechnic Institute & State University	04/25/1970	**/**/****
207	Wisconsin Zeta	Marquette University	04/25/1970	1985-90
208	Kentucky Zeta	Morehead State University	04/25/1970	**/**/****
209	Texas Iota	Texas Tech University	11/21/1970	1996-2003
210	New Jersey Gamma	Seton Hall University	12/05/1970	1985-90
211	Illinois Epsilon	Northern Illinois University	10/02/1971	**/**/****
212	Wisconsin Eta	University of Wisconsin—Stout	10/09/1971	1979
213	Tennessee Zeta RLC	Lambuth University	10/16/1971	**/**/****
214	Michigan Theta	Lawrence Technological University	10/23/1971	**/**/****

Chapter Roll #	Chapter	College/University	Date Chartered	Charter Dormant
215	Illinois Zeta	Illinois State University	11/13/1971	**/**/****
216	Indiana Iota	Vincennes University	02/26/1972	1992
217	Pennsylvania Pi	Duquesne University	04/22/1972	1976
218	Texas Kappa	University of Texas-Arlington	04/29/1972	**/**/****
219	Florida Kappa	Miami-Dade Community College	05/06/1972	1991
220	Georgia Zeta	North Georgia College	05/20/1972	1990
221	California Kappa	Northrop University	12/02/1972	1976
222	Texas Lambda	Tyler Junior College	12/09/1972	1988
223	Tennessee Eta	Austin Peay State University	01/27/1973	1976-96
224	Illinois Eta	Southern Illinois University-Edwardsville	02/10/1973	**/**/****
225	Texas Mu	Texas A&M University	03/31/1973	**/**/****
226	Texas Nu	Texas Wesleyan University	03/31/1973	1995
227	*North Carolina Mu*	*Elon College*	*04/28/1973*	*1998*
228	Texas Xi	West Texas State University	04/28/1973	1984
229	Missouri Iota	Missouri Western State College	11/17/1973	1982
230 SEC	North Carolina Nu	University of North Carolina-Charlotte	12/01/1973	1998
231	Kansas Theta	Pittsburg State University	12/08/1973	**/**/****
232 SEC	Arizona Gamma	Northern Arizona University	02/16/1974	1996
233	Ohio Pi	Wright State University	02/16/1974	**/**/****
234	*Iowa Eta*	*Loras College*	*11/09/1974*	*2002*
235	Arkansas Delta	University of Arkansas-Little Rock	12/07/1974	1991
236	New Jersey Delta	Fairleigh Dickinson University	12/07/1974	1976
237	Texas Omicron	Angelo State University	12/07/1974	**/**/****
238	California Lambda	Santa Clara University	05/24/1975	1990
239	North Carolina Xi	Appalachian State University	11/01/1975	**/**/****
240	Alabama Delta	University of Alabama-Birmingham	11/01/1975	1989-92, 1997
241	*Texas Pi*	*Stephen F. Austin State University*	*01/17/1976*	*1983-89, 1997*
242	Illinois Theta	Western Illinois University	02/21/1976	1994
243	Illinois Iota	Lewis University	04/10/1976	1984
244	*Texas Rho*	*Baylor University*	*12/04/1976*	*2005*
245	Tennessee Theta	Middle Tennessee State University	03/12/1977	**/**/****
246	*Pennsylvania Rho*	*Villanova University*	*03/19/1977*	*2000*
247	Indiana Kappa	Indiana University-Purdue University-Fort Wayne	03/19/1977	**/**/****
248	Arkansas Epsilon	Arkansas Tech University	04/02/1977	**/**/****
249	Missouri Kappa	University of Missouri-Kansas City	04/16/1977	**/**/****
250	Alabama Epsilon	Auburn University-Montgomery	10/22/1977	1991
251	Virginia Lambda	Longwood College	03/11/1978	**/**/****
252	Alabama Zeta	Huntingdon College	03/25/1978	**/**/****
253	Michigan Iota	Northwood University	04/01/1978	**/**/****
254	Massachusetts Epsilon	Bentley College	04/08/1978	1997
255	Idaho Beta	Boise State University	04/22/1978	1990
256	*New York Zeta*	*Marist College*	*03/03/1979*	*1997*
257	South Carolina Gamma	Francis Marion College	03/31/1979	1992
258	South Carolina Delta	Winthrop University	03/31/1979	1995
259	Texas Sigma	University of Texas-San Antonio	03/03/1979	**/**/****
260	New York Eta	Buffalo State College	04/07/1979	**/**/****
261	*Illinois Kappa*	*Southern Illinois University-Carbondale*	*04/14/1979*	*2000*
262	Pennsylvania Sigma	York College	04/21/1979	1993
263	Maryland Gamma	Towson State University	04/28/1979	1985-89, 1991
264	South Carolina Epsilon	Coastal Carolina University	11/10/1979	**/**/****
265	Pennsylvania Tau	West Chester University	12/01/1979	**/**/****
266	Missouri Lambda	Northwest Missouri State University	04/19/1980	**/**/****
267	New York Theta	State University of New York-Geneseo	04/26/1980	1991
268	California Mu	California State Polytechnic University-Pomona	04/26/1980	**/**/****

Chapter Roll #	Chapter	College/University	Date Chartered	Charter Dormant
269	Tennessee Iota	Lincoln Memorial University	10/25/1980	1984
270	New York Iota	State University of New York-Fredonia	11/01/1980	**/**/****
271	New Jersey Epsilon	Rowan College	11/15/1980	1994
272	Virginia Mu	George Mason University	11/22/1980	**/**/****
273	Georgia Eta	Southern College of Technology	02/14/1981	1992
274	California Nu	Chapman University	03/07/1981	1996
275	*Texas Tau*	*Texas State University-San Marcos*	*03/07/1981*	*1997*
276	Virginia Nu	Radford University	03/21/1981	1992
277	Florida Lambda	St. Leo College	03/28/1981	1993
278	Missouri Mu	Truman State University	03/28/1981	**/**/****
279	New York Kappa	Daemen College	04/11/1981	1995
280	*California Xi*	*San Francisco State University*	*12/05/1981*	*1997*
281	Pennsylvania Upsilon	Clarion University of Pennsylvania	01/23/1982	1994
282	North Carolina Omicron	University of North Carolina-Greensboro	03/20/1982	**/**/****
283	New York Lambda	Canisius College	04/24/1982	**/**/****
284	New York Mu	State University of New York-Cortland	04/24/1982	1989
285 SEC	Kentucky Eta	Northern Kentucky University	10/30/1982	1992-
286	New Hampshire Beta	New England College	03/12/1983	1993
287	Michigan Kappa	Grand Valley State University	04/23/1983	**/**/****
288	Maryland Delta	McDaniel College	04/30/1983	**/**/****
289	North Carolina Pi	Western Carolina University	11/05/1983	**/**/****
290	Louisiana Gamma	Loyola University	11/19/1983	**/**/****
291	New Hampshire Gamma	University of New Hampshire	04/28/1984	**/**/****
292	Pennsylvania Phi	Susquehanna University	05/05/1984	**/**/****
293	California Omicron	University of California-Los Angeles	11/03/1984	**/**/****
294	Massachusetts Zeta	Tufts University	03/09/1985	**/**/****
295	Florida Mu	University of Central Florida	04/13/1985	**/**/****
296	Texas Upsilon RLC	Southern Methodist University	04/13/1985	2002-2004
297	Virginia Xi	Old Dominion University	04/20/1985	**/**/****
298	California Pi	Stanford University	05/18/1985	**/**/****
299	*New York Nu*	*State University of New York-Binghamton*	*03/01/1986*	*2002*
300	New York Xi	University of Rochester	04/19/1986	**/**/****
301	Nebraska Delta	Creighton University	12/06/1986	**/**/****
302	Florida Nu	Florida International University	01/17/1987	**/**/****
303	Alabama Eta	University of South Alabama	02/28/1987	1991
304	New York Omicron	State University of New York-Albany	03/21/1987	1991-97, 1998
305	*Pennsylvania Chi*	*Albright College*	*04/04/1987*	*2001*
306	Nevada Beta	University of Nevada-Las Vegas	11/14/1987	1995
307	California Rho	University of California-San Diego	02/06/1988	**/**/****
308	Arkansas Zeta	University of Central Arkansas	03/19/1988	**/**/****
309	*New York Pi*	*State University of New York-Oswego*	*04/09/1988*	*2004*
310	Pennsylvania Psi	St. Joseph's University	11/12/1988	**/**/****
311	Missouri Nu	St. Louis University	03/25/1989	**/**/****
312	Connecticut Beta	University of Hartford	04/15/1989	1996
313	*Michigan Lambda*	*Eastern Michigan University*	*11/04/1989*	*2005*
314	California Sigma	California State University-Northridge	01/13/1990	**/**/****
315	New York Rho	St. John's University	03/10/1990	**/**/****
316	California Tau	California Polytechnic State University-San Luis Obispo	04/07/1990	**/**/****
317	Alabama Theta	Jacksonville State University	04/14/1990	**/**/****
318	Rhode Island Gamma	Bryant College	05/05/1990	1994
319	Illinois Lambda RLC	Northwestern University	05/12/1990	**/**/****
320	*North Carolina Rho*	*University of North Carolina-Wilmington*	*03/16/1991*	*2005*
321	Pennsylvania Omega	LaSalle University	04/06/1991	**/**/****
322	Washington Gamma RLC	Eastern Washington University	06/01/1991	**/**/****
323	Illinois Mu	University of Chicago	10/19/1991	**/**/****

Chapter Roll #	Chapter	College/University	Date Chartered	Charter Dormant
324	*New York Sigma*	*Ithaca College*	*11/23/1991*	*1998*
325	New Hampshire Delta	Plymouth State College	03/07/1992	**/**/****
326	Ohio Rho	University of Dayton	03/28/1992	**/**/****
327	South Carolina Zeta	College of Charleston	04/11/1992	**/**/****
328	Massachusetts Eta	Northeastern University	02/29/1992	**/**/****
329	Illinois Nu	Eastern Illinois University	11/21/1992	**/**/****
330	Iowa Theta RLC	University of Northern Iowa	01/30/1993	**/**/****
331	*Maryland Epsilon*	*University of Maryland-Baltimore County*	*01/30/1993*	*2002*
332	*New Mexico Beta*	*New Mexico State University*	*04/17/1993*	*2000*
333	D.C. Beta	Gallaudet University	05/01/1993	1996
334	*Hawaii Alpha*	*University of Hawaii*	*04/09/1994*	*2000*
335	California Upsilon	California State University-San Bernardino	04/23/1994	**/**/****
336	North Dakota Alpha RLC	University of North Dakota	02/04/1995	**/**/****
337	Tennessee Kappa	University of Tennessee-Martin	03/25/1995	**/**/****
338	California Phi	California State University-Fresno	05/13/1995	**/**/****
339	Ohio Sigma RLC	Case Western Reserve University	10/21/1995	**/**/****
340	Massachusetts Theta	Babson College	04/23/1996	**/**/****
341	Florida Xi	Florida Atlantic University	04/27/1996	**/**/****
342	Virginia Omicron	Lynchburg College	09/21/1996	**/**/****
343	*New York Tau*	*Hofstra University*	*10/12/1996*	*1999*
344 SEC	Maryland Zeta	Salisbury University	11/02/1996	**/**/****
345	*New York Upsilon*	*Adelphi University*	*10/26/1996*	*1998*
346	South Dakota Alpha	South Dakota State University	02/15/1997	**/**/****
347	California Chi	Loyola Marymount University	03/01/1997	**/**/****
348	Alaska Alpha	University of Alaksa-Fairbanks	03/01/1997	**/**/****
349	California Psi	Pepperdine University	04/11/1997	**/**/****
350	*Connecticut Gamma*	*Eastern Connecticut State University*	*04/12/1997*	*2001*
351	California Omega	California State University-Fullerton	04/12/1997	**/**/****
352	*Louisiana Delta*	*University of Louisiana-Monroe*	*05/03/1997*	*2004*
353	*Texas Phi*	*University of Texas-El Paso*	*09/06/1997*	*2004*
354	California Beta Alpha	University of California-Irvine	11/16/1997	**/**/****
355	Ohio Tau	Denison University	03/09/1998	**/**/****
356	New York Phi	Columbia University	03/27/1999	**/**/****
357	Wisconsin Theta RLC	University of Wisconsin-Platteville	10/14/2000	**/**/****
358	Pennsylvania Beta Alpha	Moravian College	10/15/2000	**/**/****
359	California Beta Beta	University of San Diego	05/05/2001	**/**/****
360	Texas Chi	Texas A&M University-Corpus Christi	10/15/2002	**/**/****
361	New Jersey Zeta	Rider University	02/02/2002	**/**/****
362	New York Chi	Clarkson University	04/07/2002	**/**/****
363	Pennsylvania Beta Beta	Drexel University	10/19/2002	**/**/****
364	Illinois Xi	DePaul University	06/28/2003	**/**/****
365	Virginia Pi	Christopher Newport University	10/31/2004	**/**/****
366	Connecticut Delta	Yale University	04/09/2005	**/**/****
367	Ohio Upsilon	John Carroll University	04/09/2005	**/**/****
SEC	Alaska	Universiy of Alaska-Anchorage		
SEC	California	California-Riverside		
SEC	Connecticut	Quinnipiac University		
SEC	D.C.	American University		
SEC	D.C.	Georgetown University		
SEC	*Florida*	*Florida Gulf Coast University*		*2004*
SEC	Idaho	University of Idaho		
SEC	Tennessee	Vanderbilt University		

CITATION RECIPIENTS

Recipient, Year Presented, Chapter, School, Year of Graduation, Position. * Indicates deceased.

JAMES E. ALDERMAN (1983)
Florida Alpha, University of Florida, '58; Chief Justice, Florida Supreme Court.

WILLIAM A. ALEXANDER (1969)
Colorado Alpha, University of Colorado, '20; Chairman, Denver Tramway Corporation.

THOMAS G. ALLARDYCE (1997)
Texas Epsilon, Lamar University, '70; President, Hendrix/Allardyce.

CHARLES S. ANDERSON (1985)
Kansas Gamma, University of Kansas, '62; City Manager, Dallas, Texas.

WARREN M. ANGELL (1973)
New York Alpha, Syracuse University, '33; composer of religious anthems; Dean of Fine Arts, Oklahoma Baptist University; author, Improvisation on Piano.

ARMAND ARABIAN (1991)
Massachusetts Gamma, Boston University, '56; Associate Justice, Supreme Court of California.

* **CRAIG S. ATKINS** (1965)
D.C. Alpha, George Washington University, '24; Judge, U.S. Tax Court.

JOHN P. BAIRD, JR. (1973)
Illinois Alpha, University of Illinois, '50; Director of Labor Relations, Ralston Purina Co.

TOM H. BARRETT (1979)
Kansas Beta, Kansas State University, '53; Executive Vice President, The Goodyear Tire & Rubber Co.

SCOTT A. BAXTER (1997)
New York Eta, Buffalo State University, '84; President, ICON CMT Corporation.

* **J. WARREN BECK** (1965)
Wisconsin Alpha, Lawrence University, '21; professor of English, Lawrence University.

* **WILLIAM O. BEERS** (1971)
Wisconsin Beta, University of Wisconsin, '37; Chairman, Kraft, Inc.

CLARENCE B. BELL (1973)
Colorado Alpha, University of Colorado, '30; real estate investor.

RICHARD W. BENNET, III (2001)
Missouri Theta, Central Missouri State University, '74; Vice Chairman, The May Department Stores Company.

* **GEORGE N. BENSCHEIDT** (1973)
Kansas Gamma, University of Kansas, '51; Chairman, Western Food Products, Inc.

SCOTT H. BICE (1983)
California Beta, University of Southern California, '65; Dean, University of Southern California Law School.

* **ROBERT W. BIGGS** (1971)
Ohio Alpha, Ohio Northern University, '29; Chairman, Brush Wellman, Inc.

* **BEDFORD W. BLACK** (1971)
North Carolina Zeta, Wake Forest University, '40; attorney; North Carolina State Legislator.

BRUCE N. BLACKBURN (1977)
Ohio Theta, University of Cincinnati, '61; Partner, Danne & Blackburn; designer, official U.S. Bicentennial Commission symbol.

* **HERBERT C. BLUNCK** (1967)
California Alpha, University of California, '25; Senior Vice President, Hilton Hotels Corp.

GERALD E. BOLTZ (1977)
Ohio Alpha, Ohio Northern University, '55; Regional Administrator, U.S. Securities & Exchange Commission.

DAVID E. BOND (1983)
New Hampshire Alpha, Dartmouth College, '60; Federal Economic Development Coordinator, Providence of British Columbia.

PARKER W. BORG (1991)
New Hampshire Alpha, Dartmouth College, '61; Ambassador to Burma.

* **HAROLD V. "HAL" BOYLE** (1967)
Missouri Alpha, University of Missouri, '32; Pulitzer Prize-winning Associated Press Correspondent.

RUDOLF BREDENBECK (1977)
Ohio Theta, University of Cincinnati, '54; President, Teledyne Efficient Industries, Inc.

GENE C. BREWER (1983)
Oregon Beta, University of Oregon, '34; President, National Institute of Building Sciences.

* **ELLIS O. BRIGGS** (1965)
New Hampshire Alpha, Dartmouth College, '21; U.S. Ambassador to the Dominican Republic, Uruguay, Czechoslovakia, Korea, Brazil, Greece, and Spain.

* **ROBERT W. BROEG** (1989)
Missouri Alpha, University of Missouri, '41; Sports Editor, "St. Louis Post-Dispatch," J.G. Taylor Spink Award for meritorious service to baseball writing, Baseball Hall of Fame in Cooperstown, New York (1980).

* **RONALD H. BROWN** (1991)
Vermont Beta, Middlebury College, '62; Chairman, Democratic National Committee.

MARVIN K. BRUMMETT (1969)
Oklahoma Alpha, Oklahoma State University, '34; Chairman, Life Insurance Company of Southwest Dallas.

* **DANIEL P. BRYANT** (1969)
Oregon Alpha, Oregon State University, '30; Chairman, Bekins Van Lines, Inc.

* **EDWIN BUCHANAN** (1967)
Ohio Gamma, Ohio State University, '11; Vice President, The First Wisconsin National Bank.

* **HOWARD E. BUHSE** (1965)
Minnesota Alpha, University of Minnesota, '29; Chairman, Hornblower & Weeks-Hemphill, Noyes, Inc.

* **WILLIAM L. BUNTEN** (1971)
Kansas Alpha, Baker University, '53; banker.

ALLAN B. BURDICK (1973)
Iowa Beta, Iowa State University, '45; professor & Chairman, Department of Genetics, University of Missouri.

ROBERT A. BURGIN (1983)
Tennessee Alpha, University of Tennessee, '49; Chairman, Leaseway Transportation Corp.

DONALD C. BURNHAM (1975)
Indiana Alpha, Purdue University, '36; Chairman & Chief Executive Officer, The Westinghouse Electric Corp.

* **WILLIAM J. BURRUD** (1991-Posthumous)
California Beta, University of Southern California, '47; film producer, Bill Burrud Productions.

HAROLD E. BURRY (1971)
Pennsylvania Lambda, Westminster College, '35; Head Football Coach, Westminster College; Small College Coach of the Year, 1967.

* **HARRY C. BUTCHER** (1967)
Iowa Beta, Iowa State University, '24; President, Cable T.V. & Radio Broadcasting Company; Vice President, CBS; Aide to General Dwight D. Eisenhower, 1942-1945.

* **HARRY F. BYRD, SR.** (1965)
Virginia Alpha, University of Richmond, '27; U.S. Senator from Virginia.

CURTIS L. CARLSON (1969)
Minnesota Alpha, University of Minnesota, '37; Chairman, The Carlson Companies; founder, Gold Bond Stamps.

* EMMETT B. CARMICHAEL (1967)
Colorado Alpha, University of Colorado, '18; professor of Chemistry, University of Alabama Medical Center.

RONALD E. CARRIER (1973)
Tennessee Gamma, East Tennessee State University, '55; President, James Madison University.

DAVID L. CHALK (1975)
Texas Alpha, University of Texas, '72; shortstop, Kansas City Royals.

* JOHN A. CHAPMAN (1965)
Colorado Alpha, University of Colorado, '21; Columnist & Drama Critic, "The New York Daily News."

ROGER C. CHAPMAN (1985)
Texas Alpha, University of Texas, '49; Chairman, Chapman Oil Company.

J. STEVEN CLARK (1979)
Arkansas Gamma, Arkansas State University, '69; Attorney General, State of Arkansas.

W. H. CLARK (1991)
North Carolina Beta, North Carolina State University, '56; Chairman and CEO, Nalco Chemical.

CALVIN M. CLASS (1973)
Maryland Alpha, Johns Hopkins University, '44; professor of Nuclear Physics, The Johns Hopkins University.

JAMES L. CLAYTON (1987)
Tennessee Alpha, University of Tennessee, '56; Chairman, Clayton Homes.

* JOHN P. COLEMAN (1971)
Virginia Eta, University of Virginia, '26; President, First National Bank, Richmond, Virginia.

THOMAS E. COLLINS (1991)
Mississippi Beta, Mississippi State University, '59; Assistant Secretary of Labor.

* THAD L. COLLUM (1965)
New York Beta, Cornell University, '21; Treasurer, Henderson-Johnson Company.

LEROY J. CONTIE, JR. (1979)
Michigan Alpha, University of Michigan, '41; 28th District Judge, Northern District of Ohio.

* JAMES A. CRABTREE (1965)
Tennessee Alpha, University of Tennessee, '21; Dean, Graduate School of Public Health, University of Pennsylvania.

GORDON L. CRENSHAW (1991)
Virginia Eta, University of Virginia, '43; Chairman, Universal Corporation.

PAUL M. DEAN, JR. (1965)
Colorado Alpha, University of Colorado, '43; Senior Engineer, Mechanical Techniques, Inc.

* DONALD G. DECKER (1973)
Colorado Epsilon, University of Northern Colorado, '35; Provost, University of Northern Colorado.

CORWIN D. DENNEY (1981)
Michigan Alpha, University of Michigan, '43; Chairman, Venus Oil Company; founder, Automation Industries; philanthropist.

KENNETH T. DERR (1989)
New York Beta, Cornell University, '59; Chairman and Chief Executive Officer, Chevron Corporation.

* ANTHONY DONATO (1969)
Nebraska Alpha, University of Nebraska, '31; composer; violinist; professor of Musical Composition & Conductor of Symphonies, Drake and Northwestern Universities.

* ROY M. DORCUS (1973)
Maryland Alpha, Johns Hopkins University, '22; university official.

WALLACE C. DOUD (1971)
Wisconsin Beta, University of Wisconsin, '48; Vice President, IBM Corp.

JOHN E. DOUGLAS (1999)
Montana Beta, Montana State University, '67,; Profiling Pioneer for the FBI/Best Selling Author.

* **J. ROSCOE DRUMMOND** (1965)
New York Alpha, Syracuse University, '24; nationally syndicated columnist.

* **ULYSSES G. DUBACH** (1971)
Oregon Alpha, Oregon State University, '31; Dean of Students, Oregon State University; professor of Political Science, Lewis & Clark College.

ROBERT G. DUNLOP (1967)
Pennsylvania Delta, University of Pennsylvania, '31; Chairman, Sun Oil Corp.

BARNEY A. EBSWORTH (1989)
Missouri Beta, Washington University-St. Louis, '57; Founder, Chairman, Intrav, international travel company.

* **NILS O. EKLUND, JR.** (1973)
Oregon Beta, University of Oregon, '32; Vice President, Kaiser-Frazier Corp.

* **JOSEPH C. ELGIN** (1969)
Virginia Eta, University of Virginia, '24; Dean, School of Engineering & Applied Science, Princeton University.

WILLIAM K. EMERSON (1987)
California Delta, San Diego State University, '48; Curator, American Museum of Natural History.

DOUGLAS C. ENGELBART (1989)
Oregon Alpha, Oregon State University, '48; Stanford Research Institute, inventor of the computer mouse, 25 patents.

ROLAND R. EPPLEY, JR. (1977)
Maryland Alpha, Johns Hopkins University, '53; President, Eastern States Bank Card Association.

* **JAMES S. EVANS** (1987)
Indiana Alpha, Purdue University, '42; President and CEO, Media General, Inc.

JOHN R. EVANS (1969)
Oklahoma Beta, University of Oklahoma, '55; Director, Pan American Petroleum Corp.

* **TOM EWELL** (1965)
Wisconsin Beta, University of Wisconsin, '37; television & motion picture actor.

* **WILLIAM C. FINE** (1979)
Kansas Eta, Wichita State University, '38; Chairman of the Board, The Sherwin-Williams Co.

ROBERT M. FREEMAN (1981)
Virginia Eta, University of Virginia, '63; President, Signet Bank.

* **JASPER J. FRENCH** (1973)
Colorado Gamma, Colorado State University, '39; Executive Director, Colorado State University Foundation.

EARLE W. FROST (1967)
Kansas Beta, Kansas State University, '20; Judge, Municipal Court, Kansas City, Missouri.

* **THEODORE R. GAMBLE** (1969)
Indiana Alpha, Purdue University, '46; President, the Pet Milk Corp.

* **THEODOR SEUSS GEISEL** (1973)
New Hampshire Alpha, Dartmouth College, '25; author & cartoonist; creator of Dr. Seuss books.

* **DOUGLAS G. GEMEROY** (1967)
New Jersey Beta, Rutgers University, '48; professor of Zoology, Rutgers University.

* **CHRISTOPHER J. GEORGE** (1975)
Florida Gamma, University of Miami, '56; television & motion picture actor.

* **ATTICUS J. GILL** (1965)
North Carolina Gamma, Duke University, '35; Dean, Southwestern Medical School, Dallas, Texas.

* **X.R. GILL** (1969)
Texas Alpha, University of Texas, '15;
banking & insurance executive; oil
producer.

WILLIAM Z. GOSSETT (1971)
Texas Alpha, University of Texas, '42;
President, Bank of Austin, Texas.

* **REUBEN G. GUSTAVSON** (1965)
Colorado Beta, University of Denver, '16;
chemist.

* **ALBERT C. "WHITEY" GWYNNE**
(1967)
West Virginia Beta, West Virginia University,
'33; Associate professor and Head Athletic
Trainer, West Virginia University; Trainer,
U.S. Olympic Team, 1968.

* **FELIX S. HALES** (1965)
North Carolina Beta, North Carolina State
University, '13; President, Nickel Plate
Railroad.

DR. EDWARD H. HAMMOND (2001)
Kansas Epsilon, Emporia State University,
'66; President, Fort Hays State University.

ROBERT E. HAMPTON (1975)
Tennessee Alpha, University of Tennessee,
'48; Chairman, U.S. Civil Service
Commission.

JAY K. HARNESS (2003)
Arizona Beta, University of Arizona, '65;
Medical Director, St. Joseph's Hospital
Comprehensive Breast Center Clinical
Professor of Surgery, University of
California-Irvine, International Lecturer-
Surgical Techniques.

ROBERT E. HARPER (1965)
New York Delta, Rensselaer Polytechnic
Institute, '54; aerospace engineer, designer.

GEORGE T. HARRELL, JR. (1967)
North Carolina Gamma, Duke University,
'32; Dean, College of Medicine,
Pennsylvania State University.

HUGH A. HARTER, PH.D. (1999)
Ohio Epsilon, Ohio Wesleyan University,
'41; Educator/Author/Internationalist.

KENNETH W. HARTER (1971)
Kansas Beta, Kansas State University, '34;
journalist & editor.

* **CARL T. HAYDEN** (1969)
Arizona Alpha, Arizona State University,
'64; U.S. Senator from Arizona.

JEFFREY O. HENLEY (2005)
California Gamma, University of
California-Santa Barbara '66; chairman
of Oracle Corporation.

* **WOODROW C. "WOODY"
HERMAN** (1967)
Kansas Gamma, University of Kansas, '42;
musician and band leader.

OREL L. HERSHISER (1993)
Ohio Kappa, Bowling Green State
University, '80; Cy Young Award-winning
Los Angeles Dodgers pitcher.

* **BENJAMIN HIBBS** (1965)
Kansas Gamma, University of Kansas, '23;
Editor, "The Saturday Evening Post."

* **BOURKE B. HICKENLOOPER** (1965)
Iowa Beta, Iowa State University, '18; U.S.
Senator from Iowa.

R. STEVEN HICKS (1999)
Texas Alpha, University of Texas-Austin '72;
Radio Broadcasting Executive.

THOMAS O. HICKS (1987)
Texas Alpha, University of Texas, '68;
partner, Hicks & Haas Merchant Bankers.

HENRY C. "LADD" HITCH, JR. (1981)
Oklahoma Alpha, Oklahoma State
University, '39; head of Hitch Family
Agribusiness Companies; Trustee, National
Cowboy Hall of Fame.

A.E. DICK HOWARD (1971)
Virginia Alpha, University of Richmond, '54; White Burkett Miller professor of Law & Public Affairs, University of Virginia; Executive Director, Virginia Commission on Constitutional Revision.

DONALD W. HUDLER (1999)
Ohio Epsilon, Ohio Wesleyan University '56; Saturn Retail Enterprises Chairman.

BRIG. GEN. JOSEPH D. HUGHES (1967)
Alabama Alpha, Auburn University, '31; Administrative Trustee, Richard King Mellon Foundation; Vice President & Governor, T. Mellon & Sons; President, National Wildlife Federation Endowment; Director, Corporation for Public Broadcasting.

* JOHN A. HUNTER (1969)
North Carolina Epsilon, Davidson College, '34; President, Louisiana State University.

* EVERETT HUTCHINSON (1967)
Texas Alpha, University of Texas, '37; first Deputy Secretary, U.S. Department of Transportation; Chairman, U.S. Interstate Commerce Commission.

FREDERICK E. HUTCHINSON (1993)
Maine Alpha, University of Maine, '53; President, University of Maine.

ELTON M. HYDER, JR. (1975)
Texas Alpha, University of Texas, '43; Special Prosecutor of Japanese war criminals after World War II; Chairman, Western Savings & Loan Association.

* ALLEN JACKSON (1965)
Illinois Alpha, University of Illinois, '41; CBS Radio News commentator.

LEONARD E. JAMES (1965)
Virginia Delta, College of William & Mary, '34; National Commander, American Legion.

PAUL C. JENNINGS (1993)
Colorado Gamma, Colorado State University, '58; Vice President and Provost, California Institute of Technology.

* HERBERT L. JONES (1973)
Pennsylvania Iota, Muhlenberg College, '33; authority on electrical engineering.

* ROGER W. JONES (1965)
New York Beta, Cornell University, '28; Chairman, U.S. Civil Service Commission.

* WILLIAM E. JONES (1967)
Tennessee Alpha, University of Tennessee, '31; President, Southern Greyhound Lines.

* ELMER L. KAYSER (1965)
D.C. Alpha, George Washington University, '17; Dean, George Washington University.

* JAMES W. KETTLE (1969)
Indiana Alpha, Purdue University, '37; Director, Stauffer Chemical Corp.

GARRY C. KIEF (2005)
California Beta, University of Southern California, '70; founder, Stiletto Entertainment.

* IVEN C. KINCHELOE (1987 posthumous)
Indiana Alpha, Purdue University, '49; United States Air Force test pilot.

RICHARD B. KING (1973)
Michigan Alpha, University of Michigan, '48; Executive Vice President-Services & Director, Merrill Lynch, Pierce, Fenner & Smith, Inc.

ROBERT L. KING (1973)
Virginia Epsilon, Washington & Lee University, '24; professor of Medicine, University of Virginia.

NEAL W. KLAUSNER (1973)
Wisconsin Alpha, Lawrence University, '31; professor & Chairman, Department of Philosophy, University of Redlands.

* **FRANCIS J. KNAUSS** (1965)
Colorado Alpha, University of Colorado, '08; Justice, Colorado Supreme Court.

* **FREDERICK H. KORTH** (1965)
Texas Alpha, University of Texas, '32; U.S. Secretary of the Navy.

* **WALTER C. KURZ** (1971)
Illinois Alpha, University of Illinois, '29; President, The Chicago Tribune Co.

JAMES D. LATHAM (1995)
Kansas Beta, Kansas State University, '69; U.S. Air Force General; Commander, Shaw Air Force Base, South Carolina.

* **MAX A. LEAGUE** (1973)
Kansas Beta, Kansas State University, '52; Executive Vice President, Arthur Young & Co.

ROBERT L. LILLY (1975)
Texas Gamma, Texas Christian University, '59; professional football player, Dallas Cowboys.

ROBERT C. LONDERHOLM (1971)
Kansas Gamma, University of Kansas, '53; Attorney General of Kansas.

JOHN A. LOVE (1965)
Colorado Beta, University of Denver, '40; Governor, Colorado; President & Chief Executive Officer, Ideal Basic Industries.

* **CARTER O. LOWANCE** (1977)
Virginia Delta, College of William & Mary, '76; Executive Assistant to the Governors of the Commonwealth of Virginia, 1947-1977.

AUBREY K. LUCAS (1977)
Mississippi Gamma, University of Southern Mississippi, '55; President, University of Southern Mississippi.

TERRY J. LUNDGREN (1993)
Arizona Beta, University of Arizona, '74; Chairman and CEO, Neiman Marcus Group.

DANIEL M. LITYNSKI (2003)
New York Delta, Rensselaer Polytechnic '65; Immediate Past Interim President, Current Provost and Vice President for Academic Affairs, Western Michigan University Brigadier General, United States Army Retired.

ELLIS C. MACDOUGALL (1975)
West Virginia Delta, Davis & Elkins College, '50; Director, State of Arizona Department of Corrections.

* **TED MACK** (1965)
Colorado Beta, University of Denver, '24; creator of "The Original Amateur Hour."

KENNETH S. MADDOX (1997)
Oregon Alpha, Oregon State University, '75; Executive Director, Sigma Phi Epsilon Fraternity.

* **JOSEPH E. MARMON** (1965)
Ohio Alpha, Ohio Northern University, '38; Vice President, Eli Lilly, Inc.

* **J. FRANK MARTINO** (1969)
Illinois Alpha, University of Illinois, '21; Director, Butler Brothers.

* **ANTHONY C. "NUTS" MCAULIFFE** (1965)
West Virginia Beta, West Virginia University, '20; U.S. Army General at the Battle of the Bulge.

MARK B. MCCLELLAN (2005)
Texas Alpha, University of Texas '84; Administrator of Centers for Medicare and Medicaid Services.

SCOTT K. MCCLELLAN (2005)
Texas Alpha, University of Texas '90; President George W. Bush's White House Press Secretary.

* **THEODORE R. MCKELDIN** (1971)
Maryland Alpha, Johns Hopkins University, '36; Mayor of Baltimore; Governor of Maryland.

* GEORGE M. MCSHERRY (1977)
Ohio Gamma, Ohio State University, '33; Designer & Manager, Miami International Airport; Manager, Los Angeles & John F. Kennedy International Airports.

SAMUEL L. MEYER (1975)
Ohio Alpha, Ohio Northern University, '71; President, Ohio Northern University.

* LOUIS S. MIDDLEMIST (1973)
Colorado Beta, University of Denver, '32; Director, Division of State Purchasing, State of Colorado.

GARY L. MILLENBRUCH (1995)
Kansas Beta, Kansas State University, '59; Executive Vice President & Chief Financial Officer, Bethlehem Steel Corporation.

* THOMAS E. MILLSOP (1967)
West Virginia Beta, West Virginia University, '48; President, National Steel Corp.

KENNETH W. MONFORT (1973)
Colorado Gamma, Colorado State University, '51; President & Director, Monfort of Colorado, Inc.; member of Colorado House of Representatives.

HANK MOONJEAN (1993)
California Beta, University of Southern California, '52; Hollywood film producer.

ROBERT K. MUELLER (1985)
Missouri Beta, Washington University at St. Louis, '55; Chairman, Arthur D. Little.

KENT C. NELSON (1995)
Indiana Gamma, Ball State University, '59; Chairman & CEO, United Parcel Service.

LEONARD C. NELSON (1971)
Missouri Gamma, University of Missouri-Rolla, '43; President, West Virginia Institute of Technology.

EDWARD E. NOBLE (1983)
Oklahoma Beta, University of Oklahoma, '51; Chairman, United States Synthetic Fuels Corporation.

* BASIL J. O'CONNOR (1965)
New Hampshire Alpha, Dartmouth College, '12; founder of the March of Dimes.

CARROLL J. O'CONNOR (1973)
Montana Alpha, University of Montana, '52; motion picture & television actor; winner of 1973 Emmy Award for the role of Archie Bunker in "All in the Family."

* FLOYD B. ODLUM (1965)
Colorado Alpha, University of Colorado, '09; Chairman & Chief Executive Officer, The Atlas Corp.; Chairman, RKO Radio Pictures; Director, U.S. Office of Production Management.

DUFFY S. OYSTER (2003)
Texas Beta, University of North Texas, '69; Chairman and Owner Poncho's Mexican Buffet Restaurants Oyster Investment Corporation.

GARLAND G. PARKER (1975)
Ohio Theta, University of Cincinnati, '37; Registrar, Vice Provost for Admissions & Records, University of Cincinnati; principal national statistician of higher education in America.

RICHARD E. PECK (1997)
Wisconsin Gamma, Carroll College, '61; President, University of New Mexico.

ARTHUR L. PETERSON (1979)
Wisconsin Alpha, Lawrence University, '44; professor & Chairman, Department of Politics & Government, Ohio Wesleyan University; Executive Director, Republican Party Platform Committee; member, National Council on the Humanities.

ARTHUR B. POINIER (1967)
Ohio Epsilon, Ohio Wesleyan University, '55; nationally syndicated political cartoonist.

HAROLD A. POLING (1999)
Illinois Gamma, Monmouth College, '48; Ford Motor Company Chairman.

SAMUEL L. POOLE (2005)
Pennsylvania Nu, Thiel College, '69;
former President and CEO of Maxis, Inc.;
Founder, Poole Investment Ventures.

PHILIP W. PORTER (1967)
Ohio Gamma, Ohio State University,
'22; Executive Editor & Columnist, "The
Cleveland Plain Dealer."

DONALD L. PORTH (1983)
Iowa Beta, Iowa State University, '38;
Chairman, Culligan International.

DR. BARRY Z. POSNER (2001)
California Gamma, University of
California, Santa Barbara '70; Dean, Leavey
School of Business, Santa Clara University.

RALPH PRATOR (1973)
Colorado Alpha, University of Colorado,
'29; President, Bakersfield College, San
Fernando Valley State College, Fresno
State College.

* CYRIL R. PORTHOUSE (1967)
Ohio Gamma, Ohio State University, '32;
President, Dunhill International, Inc.

* EVERETT H. QUALLS (1965)
Tennessee Alpha, University of Tennessee,
'25; Director, Bureau of Motor Carriers,
Interstate Commerce Commission.

ROBERT L. QUALLS (1977)
Mississippi Beta, Mississippi State University,
'54; President, College of the Ozarks.

* JOHN D. RANDALL (1965)
Iowa Gamma, University of Iowa, '23;
President, American Bar Association.

B.M. "MACK" RANKIN, JR. (1981)
Texas Alpha, University of Texas, '50;
founder, McMoran Oil Company;
independent oil operator; owner, Texas
Rangers baseball club.

* HARRY E. REDMAN (1979)
Indiana Alpha, Purdue University, '49;
President, E.F. MacDonald Travel Company.

MERVIN W. RETTENMUND (1975)
Indiana Gamma, Ball State University, '65;
Coach, California Angels.

* CHARLES G. RIDL (1973)
Pennsylvania Lambda, Westminster
College, '42; Director of Athletics,
Westminster College.

PAUL O. RITCHER (1973)
Illinois Alpha, University of Illinois, '31;
Chairman, Department of Entomology,
Oregon State University.

C. DONALD ROBERTSON (1971)
West Virginia Beta, West Virginia
University, '49; Attorney General of
West Virginia.

* JOHN ROBSON (1975)
Wisconsin Alpha, Lawrence University, '28;
Editor, Baird's Manual of American
College Fraternities.

CHARLES S. RUSSELL (1985)
Virginia Eta, University of Virginia, '46;
Associate Justice, Virginia Supreme Court.

WALTER E. ROGERS (1969)
Texas Alpha, University of Texas, '35;
Member of Congress from Texas;
President, Interstate Natural Gas
Association.

DONALD B. RUTHENBERG (1977)
Ohio Zeta, Baldwin-Wallace College, '53;
President, Southwestern College.

GABE K. SACHS (2003)
California Nu, Chapman University, '83;
Partner, Sachs-Judah Production Television
Production Companies.

* R. NEVITT SANFORD (1973)
Virginia Alpha, University of Richmond,
'29; Director, The Wright Institute;
professor of Psychology, University of
California at Berkeley, Vassar College,
Stanford University.

* ALBERT W. SCHLECHTEN (1973)
Missouri Gamma, University of Missouri-Rolla, '40; professor & head, Department of Metallurgical Engineering, Colorado School of Mines.

WILLIAM A. SCHREYER (1979)
Pennsylvania Eta, Pennsylvania State University, '48; President, Merrill Lynch, Pierce, Fenner & Smith, Inc.

ADRIAN J. SCRIBANTE (1995)
Kansas Beta, Kansas State University, '54; Chairman & CEO, Vital Learning Corporation.

BOBBY S. SHACKOULS (2003)
Mississippi Beta, Mississippi State University, '72; Chairman, President and Chief Executive Officer Burlington Resources.

STEWART A. SHAFER (1973)
Colorado Alpha, University of Colorado, '36; Judge of the Probate Court, City & County of Denver, Colorado.

* EDWIN M. SHAWN (1967)
Colorado Beta, University of Denver, '21; professional dancer.

GARY SHEPARD (1989)
Massachusetts Gamma, Boston University, '61; ABC News West Coast national correspondent.

RT. REV. RICHARD L. SHIMPFKY (1993)
Colorado Alpha, University of Colorado, '63; Bishop, Episcopal Diocese of El Camino Real, Monterey, California.

* ALBERT P. SHIRKEY (1967)
Virginia Zeta, Randolph-Macon College, '29; Methodist clergyman; President, Washington, D.C., Council of Churches.

HUBERT O. SHUPTRINE (1983)
Tennessee Alpha, University of Tennessee '55; artist; book, *Jericho: The South Beheld.*

* STEWART W. SMITH (1973)
Wisconsin Beta, University of Wisconsin, '30; modernizer of the American library cataloging system.

LELAND K. SMULL (1969)
Michigan Alpha, University of Michigan, '37; Special Assistant to the Administrator, U.S. National Aeronautics & Space Administration.

ROBERT C. STEMPEL (1989)
Massachusetts Beta, Worcester Polytechnic Institute, '55; President, General Motors Corporation.

* WILLIAM P. STEVEN (1967)
Wisconsin Beta, University of Wisconsin, '30; Editorial Vice President, "The Chicago Daily News & Sun Times."

* ARTHUR E. STODDARD (1967)
Kansas Gamma, University of Kansas, '51; President, The Union Pacific Railroad.

* RALPH W. STOODY (1969)
Ohio Epsilon, Ohio Wesleyan University, '17; Methodist clergyman.

* CHARLES W. STREIT, JR. (1971)
Virginia Epsilon, Washington & Lee University, '10; President, Southern Cement Company; Chairman, U.S. Olympic Wrestling Committee; President, Southeastern Amateur Athletic Union.

DANIEL B. STUART (1993)
Texas Alpha, University of Texas, '49; President, Stuart & Co., investments.

ALBERT A. THORNBROUGH (1967)
Kansas Beta, Kansas State University, '36; President, Farm Equipment Institute; President & Director, Massey Ferguson, Ltd.

WILLIAM G. TRAGOS (1973)
Missouri Beta, Washington University at St. Louis, '56; Chairman, TBWA Advertising, Inc.

* BEVERLY A. TRAVIS (1973)
Washington Beta, University of Washington, '22; electrical engineering consultant.

* RICHARD A. TRIPPEER (1969)
Ohio Epsilon, Ohio Wesleyan University, '27; President R.A. Trippeer, Inc.

* WILLIAM M. TUCK (1967)
Virginia Zeta, Randolph-Macon College, '17; Governor of the Commonwealth of Virginia; member of Congress from Virginia.

RALPH D. TURLINGTON (1981)
Florida Alpha, University of Florida, '42; Commissioner of Education, State of Florida.

C. MAYNARD TURNER (1971)
Washington Beta, University of Washington, '22; Vice President, Cincinnati Gas & Electric Co.

CECIL H. UNDERWOOD (1969)
West Virginia Gamma, Marshall University, '65; Governor of West Virginia.

THOMAS W. UTTERBACK (1971)
Oklahoma Beta, University of Oklahoma, '31; Chairman, Oklahoma National Bank.

DEAN VANLYDEGRAF (1975)
Oregon Beta, University of Oregon, '42; Major General, U.S. Army.

* WILLARD D. VOIT (1969)
California Beta, University of Southern California, '31; Chairman, AMF Voit Rubber Corporation.

WALTER S. WALLA (1973)
Colorado Beta, University of Denver, '40; Executive Vice President, Ford Motor Co.

JAMES H. WARSAW (2001)
Oregon Beta, University of Oregon, '69; Founder of the Warsaw Center for Sports Marketing; Mentor, Parkinson's Cure Advocate.

HARRISON R. WELLMAN (1969)
Oregon Alpha, Oregon State University, '21; Vice President, Acting President, University of California.

CHARLES N. WHITE, JR. (1981)
Michigan Beta, Western Michigan University, '62; Executive Director, Sigma Phi Epsilon Fraternity.

* JUNIUS P. WHITEHURST (1969) Illinois Alpha, University of Illinois, '38; President, Miami Margarine Co.

KENNETH R. WILLIAMS (1967)
Florida Alpha, University of Florida, '29; President, Winston-Salem State University.

G. DUNCAN WIMPRESS (1973)
Oregon Beta, University of Oregon, '50; President, Monmouth College, Trinity University.

ROBERT J. WOOD (1967)
Virginia Zeta, Randolph-Macon College, '29; Commanding General, U.S. Army Air Defense Command; Director, Military Assistance Program, Office of the Secretary of Defense.

* BENJAMIN H. WOOTEN (1967)
Texas Beta, North Texas State University, '17; Chairman, North Texas State University Board of Regents; Chairman, Dallas Federal Savings & Loan Association.

JAMES L. WYATT (1973)
Kentucky Alpha, University of Kentucky, '47; Vice President, National Gypsum Co.; President, Wyatt & Co., Ambassador Industries, Inc.

J. EDWARD ZOLLINGER (1973)
Virginia Delta, College of William & Mary, '26; Special Assistant to the President, IBM Corp.

SONGS

The S.P.E. Marching Song

Hail Fraternity

The Blessing

Bamboo Bungalow

I met a girl one day, she stole my heart a-way, I grew to love her and gave her my pin.

She said she'd mar-ry me, now she's my S. P. E. Say, boys, that's how the chap-ter grows!

I'll build a bam-boo bun-ga-low __ for you, big e-nough for one but room e-nough for two.

Then we'll be mar-ried, hap-py as __ can be down in our bam - boo __ bun-ga-low __ for

one, or two, or three or four, or may-be more; let your con-science be your guide! Be-

tween your chair and my chair, we'll build a lit-tle high chair and we'll call him Sig Ep Sam!

Anthem

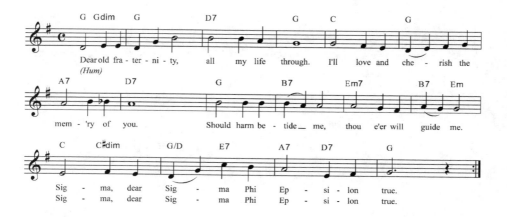

Dear old fra - ter - ni - ty, all my life through. I'll love and che - rish the
(Hum)
mem - 'ry of you. Should harm be - tide— me, thou e'er will guide me.

Sig - ma, dear Sig - ma Phi Ep - si - lon true.
Sig - ma, dear Sig - ma Phi Ep - si - lon true.

I Want To Be A College Man

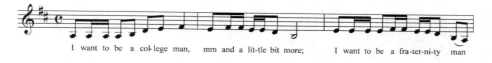

I want to be a col-lege man, mm and a lit-tle bit more; I want to be a fra-ter-ni-ty man

mm, and a lit-tle bit more; I want to be a Sig Ep man,— who could ask— for more? Then

I'll have all that's com-in' to me and mm and a lit-tle bit mm and a lit-tle bit mm and a lit-tle bit more!

2. I want to date a college girl, mm and a little bit more;
   I want to date a sorority girl, mm and a little bit more;
   I want to date a _____ girl, who could ask for more? (etc.)
3. I want to be a friend of yours, mm and a little bit more;
   I want to be a pal of yours, mm and a little bit more;
   I want to be a clinging vine, climbing up your wall...we'll have a ball.
4. Repeat verse 1.

Rum Rum

To the tune of
Scotland, The Brave

Rum rum rum rum Rum rum the foot-steps com-ing,
We march the road to - ge - ther

beat like the sound of drum-ming, beat for the voi-ces hum-ming Sig Eps are we!
and we will sing for - e - ver, this bond will ne - ver se - ver

Sig Eps are we! Migh-ty we'll al-ways be, a bro-ther-hood of u-ni-ty. Glo-ry to the gol-den heart of

our fra-ter-ni-ty! To Sig - ma our hearts are cling-ing, Phi through the air goes ring-ing,

Ep - si-lon we'll keep on sing-ing, Sig Eps are we! Sig Eps are we!

Wonderful SigEp Girl

Of all the girls of col-lege years, there's one that I've loved long.____ For
me she wears the gol-den heart, for her I sing this song.____ My
Sig - ma Phi Ep - si - lon Sweet - heart, won-der-ful Sig Ep girl.____
True as the heart that you're wear - ing you set my heart in a whirl.____
Vio - lets and ro - ses, my heart dis - clo - ses, say that you love me, too;____ My
Sig - ma Phi Ep - si - lon Sweet - heart, won-der-ful Sig Ep girl!____

The SigEp Call

A great old bunch of bro-thers are the Sig Eps, none fi-ner in this land will e'er be found. We

use the slo-gan al-ways stick to - ge-ther, and — help a bro-ther when he's down. No mat-ter if in business or in

plea-sure, we ral-ly to the Sig Ep call; a whis-tle that is known by ev - 'ry mem-ber and —

means so much to one and all: — We whis-tle it with all our might, and

oft you hear it day or night. — The whis-tle of Sig Ep Fra-ter-ni - ty!

GREEK ALPHABET

English Spelling	Greek Upper Case Letters	Greek Lower Case Letters	Greek Spelling	Corresponding English Letter	Corresponding English Sound	English Pronunciation
Alpha	A	α	Αλφα	A	ä	'al-f ä
Beta	B	β	Βητα	B	b	'bât-ä
Gamma	Γ	γ	Γαμμα	G	g	'gam-ä
Delta	Δ	δ	Δελτα	D	d	'del-tä
Epsilon	E	ε	Εψιλον	E	ë	'ep-se-län
Zeta	Z	ζ	Ζητα	Z	z	'zât-ä
Eta	H	η	Ητα	E	â	'ât-ä
Theta	Θ	θ	Θητα	Th	th	'thât-ä
Iota	I	ι	Ιοτα	I	î	î-'ôt-ä
Kappa	K	κ	Καππα	K	k	'kap-ä
Lambda	Λ	λ	Λαμβδα	L	l	'lam-dä
Mu	M	μ	Μυ	M	m	'myü, 'mü
Nu	N	ν	Νυ	N	n	'nyü, 'nü
Xi	Ξ	ξ	Ξι	X	z	'zî, 'ksî
Omicron	O	o	Ομικρον	O	ô	'äm-e-krän
Pi	Π	π	Πι	P	p	'pî
Rho	P	ρ	Ρω	R	r	'rô
Sigma	Σ	σ	Σιγμα	S	s	'sig-mä
Tau	T	τ	Ταυ	T	t	'tau, 'tô
Upsilon	Y	υ	Υψιλον	U	û	'yüp-se-län
Phi	Φ	φ	Φι	Ph	f	'fî
Chi	X	χ	Χι	Ch	k	'kî
Psi	Ψ	ψ	Ψι	Ps	s, ps	'sî
Omega	Ω	ω	Ωμεγα	O	ô	ô-'meg-ä

EPILOGUE

"Know Thyself."

"All Things in Moderation."

~ TWO GUIDING PRINCIPLES
ENGRAVED ON THE TEMPLE
AT DELPHI IN GREECE.